Leadership Triumphs & Failures

ISBN 978-9963-599-06-6

Arion Publishing
P.O.Box 25385
CY-1309
Nicosia
Cyprus

LEADERSHIP TRIUMPHS & FAILURES

ARIS PETASIS

Arion Publishing
Nicosia, Cyprus

Contents

Dedicated to my eldest grandchild, Pausanias.

Note

Unless the context otherwise requires, a reference to one gender shall include a reference to the other genders.

Unless the context otherwise requires, words in the singular include the plural and in the plural include the singular.

Acknowledgements

My interest in the subject of leadership will have to be credited first to my father, a former school teacher until forced by the British Colonial government of Cyprus to resign in the 1930s after first being exiled. He initiated me in the subject of leadership very early in life through his teachings, but also through his own actions and the positions he took on important matters, his unwavering belief in true independence and unfettered freedom for all peoples. Here I ought to give full credit to the powerful influence on me of my spiritual father, teacher, mentor and friend, the late Robert L. Whitt, formerly professor at Drake University, USA.

As regards the support I received to write this book I unreservedly single out my friend and former British diplomat, professor William D. Mallinson who supported me throughout this project and also invested much precious time reading the draft of this treatise and providing me with very valuable ideas and comments. Most importantly William provided me with the confidence of knowing that someone of William's stature and knowledge was present to support and advise me. My thanks go to former Upper Tribunal Judge Andrew Lloyd-Davies who read parts of this treatise and offered me invaluable advice. More importantly Andrew set for me the high standards that learned people of high professional status and intelligence are able to set for others.

I am also indebted to British educators Mark Steven Bedford and Damian James Ettinger and equally to American Professor Van

Koufoudakis for reading parts of this treatise and for making valuable comments.

Church Father Thomas Costi from Nicosia was always ready and willing to help me with several matters and as such I am indebted to him. His thoroughness has been most valuable. Special thanks go to Russell Phillips of Author Help in the UK for assisting me through all the hurdles authors have to clear after they complete writing their work and until the work goes to printing press.

As always my wife Sophie was a great inspiration through her deep insight into human behaviour. She provided me unfailingly with encouragement to continue with my pursuit telling me that she believed strongly in what I was trying to do and that this treatise would be beneficial to readers. She approved the distinct approach this treatise takes to the subject of leadership.

My appreciation also goes to the welcoming and peaceful Stadtbibliothek, Winterthur Switzerland where I spent a considerable number of hours working on this treatise.

Examples of leadership behaviour(s) using real-life people

In this publication I try to give examples of leaders that engaged in specific behaviours that this treatise considers to be good or bad in terms of leadership. To prepare the reader for what he can expect to see in this publication the list below notes specific behaviours that are mentioned in this treatise preceded by the name of an actual real-life leader that displayed the specific behaviour.

The specific behaviours mentioned below clearly do not provide the full profile of the leader whose name appears in the text. For example, if a leader has the weakness of falling for greediness that does not necessarily mean that he is not a good leader when all his behaviours (good and bad) are taken into account. This treatise is not about presenting a complete profile of leaders mentioned in this publication. Rather, it is more about presenting specific leadership behaviours which, when taken into account in their totality, help us add to our knowledge of leadership. A leader that has a love for money can in the end prove to be a skilful planner and an excellent manager of the country's economy, for example. In fact, when all is taken into account he could in the end earn a high overall ranking as leader despite a specific weakness. For example, former president Nixon had his character flaws that led to his resignation from the position of President of the USA. But, when all things are considered I believe that he did great things for America through legislation on social issues and wise decisions on foreign affairs and peace. It is my belief that his ranking as president will improve with the passage of time and in the end he will probably take his position as one of the greatest American presidents on account of his record of achievements.

Good and/or bad leadership behaviours as displayed by real-life individuals

Adams, John (US President). Example of: Overcoming adversity, little love for money or hoarding

Adonis, Andrew. Example of: Overcoming severe personal adversity, achievement

Alexander the Great. Example of: Piety, brilliant strategy, oratory, charisma, good and bad management of succession, hubristic behaviour at times and feeling of being the "one and only", ability to make amends when first misjudging a situation, single-minded focus, mistreatment of most precious fellow-officers, jealousy

Alexandros, Ypsilantis. Example of: Self-sacrifice, opening new pathways for freedom, no concern for wealth or money, driven by the great legacy of his forefathers, going head-on against massive political and military powers

Attlee, Clement. Example of: Uncharismatic winner, all-substance-and-no-frills leader

Blair, Tony. Example of: Greed for money after leaving office

Cassander (of Macedon). Example of: Viciousness against own people and benefactors, lust for power

Castro, Fidel. Example of: Charisma and tenacity and fearlessness under immense threat from a power neighbour

Churchill, Winston. Example of: Tenacity, charisma, reading (correctly and wrongly) a situation/misjudgement, good and bad politics

Cimon of Athens. Example of: All that is good in a leader, charisma, oratory, selflessness, strategy, boldness, sharing, aristocratic behaviour

Clinton, Bill and Hillary. Example of: Greed for money after leaving office

Cyrus the Great. Example of: Model of kingly behaviour, piousness, problematic succession, great leadership, single-minded focus, vision

Demetrius, Ypsilantis. Example of: Personification of all that is decent in a man, self-sacrifice, no concern for wealth and money, model of decency and ethical behaviour, princely behaviour, fearlessness

Ferguson, Alex (of UK). Example of: Practicality and high achievement, borrowing from the past and building on the present, unmatched achievements in his field of expertise

Jefferson, Thomas (US President). Example of: Little love for money though enjoyed being surrounded by good things, leader dying insolvent (he could have turned his fortunes had he wished to exploit his position), overcoming adversity, sound judgement about a country's international role, leader with a philosophical grounding, giving democracy the needed boost

Kennedy, John. Example of: Charisma, bad luck, providing the world a breath of fresh air, optimism

Kissinger, Henry. Example of: Peddling influence, greed, concentration of excessive power, misuse of power

Lincoln, Abraham. Example of: Honesty, fairness, little love for money and hoarding, overcoming setbacks, forgiveness, great leadership

Lula (Luiz Inacio Lula da Silva of Brazil). Example of: Man of the people with great desire to improve people's lot, falling victim to materialism and small-scale corruption

Mobutu Sese Seko. Example of: A man full of lust for power falling victim to the attendant perils of absolute power

Monroe, James (US President). Example of: Leader not attracted to money and not greedy

Mubarak, Hosni (of Egypt). Example of: Former national military hero who with time turned hubristic with his behaviour and as such antagonised his followers and others, suffering humiliation

Mugabe, Robert. Example of: Correct reading of the situation to enable the leader to rise to power, violence against his people, possessed by hatred towards people of different colour, totally inept in government

Mujica, Jose (of Uruguay). Example of: Demureness, modesty and love for his people, personification of a president that sees himself as a mere humble civil servant, example of a leader rarely seen in our times

Napoleon. Example of: Charisma, easily discouraged when things do not go well

Nixon, Richard. Example of: Competence, smartness, managing adversity, victim of hubris, introversion, political scheming

Obama, Barack. Example of: Poor-rich, making money deservedly and in measure

Obote, Milton (of Uganda). Example of: Amorality, lust for power, violence, leader out of his depth

Papandreou, Yiorgos (of Greece). Example of: Failed leadership, incompetence, exploitation of family name, weird and bizarre view of internationalism that harmed his country

Pausanias (of Sparta). Example of: Leader par excellence in times of great peril, boldness against all odds, hubris, victim of his successes at a young age, victim of others' envy

Pericles (of Athens). Example of: Charisma, oratory, selflessness, strategy, boldness, rationality, aristocratic behaviour, failure to read correctly certain situations

Putin, Vladimir. Example of: Reading situation correctly, competent leadership, ability to arrest a frighteningly bad situation, putting the country on a path of greatness

Sadat, Anwar (of Egypt). Example of: Former national military hero who with time turned hubristic with his behaviour and as such antagonised his followers and others, worked unsuccessfully for reconciliation

Stalin, Joseph. Example of: Controversial figure, charismatic, severe trampling on human rights to achieve his objective, little concern for human life, paragon of iron feast efficiency, overcoming adversity

Themistocles (of Athens). Example of: Leader par excellence, high achiever who would not shy away from using unorthodox means to achieve the objective of saving his country, cunning, fighter against all odds

Tupolev, Andreyi. Example of: Genius that would not allow severe hardship to stop him in his scientific endeavours for the benefit of his country

Wilson, Harold. Example of: Decency, intelligence, little or no love for money and hoarding

Xenophon (of Athens). Example of: Willingness to lead, charisma, morality, efficiency, great strategist, saviour of his people

Yeltsin, Boris. Example of: Incompetence, falling prey to personal weaknesses, chaos, getting it right as regards giving the country a competent successor

Zedong, Mao. Example of: Charisma, little concern for human life if seen as a barrier to reforms, efficiency, unifier of country, putting country on the path of greatness

Zemin, Jiang. Example of: How dynamic homeostasis works in national politics at a time of great turmoil in the neighbourhood, knew how much change to allow and when, sound decision-making, level headedness

Zhukov, Georgi. Example of: Everything a military leader would wish to have, results-orientation, luck, single-minded focus, fighter against all odds.

Below, the reader is provided with a list of names in alphabetical order of other leaders that are briefly mentioned in this book in reference to specific displayed behaviours.

Leaders whose names appears briefly in this publication

Abakumov, Victor
Aoun, Michel
Aristides (of Athens)
Aristotle
Assad, Bashar
Aurelius, Marcus
Beethoven, Ludwig

Belisarius, Flavius
Beria, Lavrentiy
Brusilov, Aleksei
Buber, Martin
Busby, Mat
Bush, George W
Callicles (of Athens)
Callisthenes (Greek historian)
Carter, Jimmy
Chirisophus (Spartan general)
Chuikov, Vasili
Cleitus (Alexander's general)
de Gaulle, Charles
Dulles, Allen
Dulles, John Foster
Einstein, Albert
Eisenhower, Dwight
Elizabeth II (of UK)
Erdogan, Tayyib
Ghandhi, Mahatma
Hippias (of Athens)
Hitler, Adolph
Hyphaestion (Alexander's general
Johnson, Andrew (US President)
Jordan, Michael (sportsman)
Justinian (emperor)
Kapodistrias, Ioannis
Kennedy, Robert
Khameini, Ali (Iranian Supreme Leader)
Lee, Robert
Lenin, Vladimir
Mardonius (Persian leader)
McCain, John

Book 1

Introduction

The subject of leadership should be of concern to each and every one of us, given that as social animals we all belong to one or another group. Even anarchic groups have leaders and followers.

What made me write this treatise

As a student of leadership I obviously came across countless books and article on the subject, some written by great and inspiring authors. What I could not find though was a book that was somewhere between a reference book and handbook with a discursive series of comments on leadership. So, I set about writing this treatise to bridge the gap between the many books that offer analytical critiques of leadership (whatever 'leadership' might mean in our days!) and the many others that offer a generalised approach to leadership and come in the form of "here is what great leaders do" or "great leaders have this or that trait." Simply, I did not wish to write another analysis of leadership seeing that some great books on this theme have already been written. Equally, I did not wish to reduce leadership to generalizations around traits because I believe that leadership is a complex matter that defies a generalised definition and clearly cannot be explained through a list of traits.

As such I set out to write this book using examples of real people hoping to make it easy for the reader to a) understand the main issues that lay behind leadership besides traits and b) make the point that leadership defies a universal definition. When reading the real life examples I use in this book the reader will, I hope, quickly realise that a multitude of forces and factors lay behind leader emergence and leader performance. Some of the books already in the market concentrate heavily on traits to explain leadership. Whilst this treatise does not underestimate the value of traits it goes a step further and explains that a list of traits is not sufficient to define leadership. Traits can be helpful in explaining leadership but can also confuse and mislead the reader. A multitude of other factors, besides traits, unavoidably play a role in leader emergence and leader effectiveness.

Take, for example, the factor (trait) of "lust for power" that has been the driving force behind so many [often] failed leaders in history. Is lust for power an isolated trait that some aspiring leaders possess and which pushes them to gain leadership positions for the good of the group or is "lust for power" a manifestation of character flaws that push some people to aspire to securing as much power as they can, not as a means to better leadership but as a means of compensating for the character deficiency they have? A leader that throws his weight around or uses power as a means of making money and accumulating wealth, for example, is not a true leader even if he is a power-wielder. He is more of a shenanigan using power mischievously. Yet, "lust for power" makes the list in many books as a unique and even positive leadership trait.

Willingness to lead is one thing and lust for power is clearly another. Some of the most corrupt power-wielders in history had a lust for power which they used to carry out their corrupt practices paying little or no heed to leading their people to better things. Here is the example of Mobutu:

Mobutu Sese Seko. Former President of Zaire (now Democratic Republic of the Congo). Approaches the complete personification of greed and lust for power. He served the West well that in exchange helped him stay in power. He was later jettisoned when he had little to offer them. A great example of what leadership ought not to be.

Mobutu Sese Seko of Zaire (full name: Mobutu Sese Seko Kuku Ngbendu Wa Za Banga) rose to power when some Western countries noticed his lust for power and helped him ascend to power to serve their interests, while allowing him to serve his lust for money and authority over others. In the process Mobutu amassed untold wealth, while bankrupting his country and setting the scene for a civil war. He kept his position, never intending to step down willingly in the future, considering that he served Western interests well and the West obliged by turning a blind eye to his dishonest and deceitful practices, not to say that some in the West assisted him in money laundering. In the end, after he was of no use to the West, he was even refused a visa to visit America.

So, was Mobutu's lust for power a leader trait or a cheat's trait? Some would put lust for power as a positive trait that drives leaders but others, like the author of this treatise, would say that this "trait" is more of a disastrous passion that consumes the power wielder and plays havoc with the led. After May 1997 Mobutu was expelled and exiled by forces loyal to Laurent-Desire Kabila. Subsequent investigations (after he had left Zaire) threw ample light on his corrupt and nepotistic practices. He is reckoned to have embezzled between US$4 billion and 15 billion; a staggering amount of money to satisfy his lust for power and money.

What I have done in this book is highlight the complexity of leadership and the difficulty of defining it. I tried to demonstrate through examples that leadership traits have two sides and that the same trait can define a leader both as a success and as a failure. As an example I use "charisma," that is billed by many as a great and positive leadership trait, to demonstrate the fallacy of relying on traits to explain effective leadership seeing that charisma has two sides to it. When used properly charisma can be a very positive leadership trait but when used wrongly it can be a potent instrument in the hands of the unscrupulous. Is charisma in the end an effective leadership trait? "Yes" and "no" says this book. Take Hitler as an example, who through his great charisma managed to galvanise the Nazi army and turn it into a ferocious fighting machine. But, where did charisma lead him and the Nazis in the end? Well, Hitler's charisma was instrumental in the killing of millions of fighting men and millions of innocent people including the horrendous killings of the holocaust that shocked the civilized world. With his charisma Hitler laid several countries waste and brought so much misery; more so to the Jews, the Poles, the Greeks and of course the people of the Soviet Union that experienced the brunt of his bloodletting. Ghandi, who Churchill once described as fakir-looking, was charismatic even if he didn't have the outward looks of a charismatic person. Ghandi generally lacked the common description of persons with charisma which include: being attractive and handsome, well groomed, youthful and the like. So, not only are we unsure whether charisma fosters good leadership, we are also unsure as to what a charismatic person is and how charismatic persons look.

To add to the confusion around what leadership is one could legitimately ask this: was Churchill the great leader he was made out to be? Did outside events beyond his control help him look a better leader than he actually was? Would Churchill have looked so good if in the end his side, the Allies, were defeated by the Nazis? By how much did the Soviet victory over the Nazis enhance Churchill's image though Churchill had little to do with this great Soviet victory? No doubt Churchill displayed great leadership during the Battle of Britain but the reality is that he was absent from the central war theatre of WWII which was in Ukraine, Belorussia and of course Russia in which the Soviets suffered tens of millions of dead before emerging victorious and thus settling the outcome of the war once the battles of Stalingrad and Kursk were won. Did this Soviet victory that crushed Hitler allow all the rest of the Allied leaders, such as Churchill, to look better than they actually were just because they were on the winning side? What would have happened to Churchill's legacy as leader had the Soviets lost against the Germans?

This book is full of examples that are intended to give the reader multiple lenses through which to view leadership. Simply, the author of this book believes, that there are no well-delineated lines to help us arrive at one universal definition of what leadership is. In fact, this book puts forward the view that leadership is more of an abstract construct rather than a term that is amenable to a clear definition using "leader traits" and other similar approaches.

This book provides a tripod on which the reader can place the three building blocks of leadership, namely: a) the "will to manage" which if absent will not allow one to come forward and lead no matter how much potential he might have, b) "leader performance" which if absent will render a leader worthless and of no value to the group and c) "leader morality" which if absent will render the leader of no true value to society and the group and worse, will make him a bad example for others.

My interest in the subject of leadership

Certain powerful images, words and events captured my imagination at an early age. These were embedded in my subconscious and to a large extent defined my value system. My absorption with the subject of leadership goes back decades, starting when I was in the first classes of primary school. My enthralment with leadership gradually turned into a passion for the subject. It all started with my father, a former school teacher, who introduced me to leadership when I was about six. As a little Greek boy, I naturally started my journey into leadership with ancient Greek history. I then branched out into Russian, American, British, Egyptian and Southern African history. Most people get fascinated by one or the other thing, one would think. A friend of mine has a fascination with cars, spends his free time visiting car exhibitions, reads books about cars and discusses the subject endlessly. Others are fascinated by art, not for its economic value per se, but for the pleasure and happiness that this 'hobby' gives them. I am not at all interested in cars, but I love art and music and have a life-long fascination with the subject of leadership.

Though as a young boy I was restless and even with the attention span of my age, I still managed to sit for long periods listening to my father talk about Miltiades of Marathon, his illustrious son Cimon, Themistocles and his miraculous defence of Athens, and his courage and phenomenal insistence on preparedness. I listened to stories about Leonidas and his last stand at Thermopylae, and how he became a world symbol of resistance and love for freedom, and thus capturing the imagination of the world for more than 2,500 years. The relatively recent movie '300' is a reminder of Leonidas and his fallen 300 comrades at Thermopylae. Most of all, I was fascinated with the military genius of disciplinarian General Pausanias, son of Leonidas' brother Cleombrotus, and his exploits at Plataea in the summer of 479BC. I have a soft spot for Pausanias, largely because of the ill-treatment this great strategist received at the hands of the Spartan Ephors. The Ephors were the bureaucrats and politicians of those times who sat out the wars and then passed judgement on those who risked their lives for Sparta and Greece. These holier-than-thou megalomaniacs put Pausanias to death by starvation.

Admittedly, Pausanias grew arrogant after his momentous feat at Plataea, given that he was only in his mid-twenties when he achieved unthinkable fame. Typically, young people find it difficult to manage sudden and unprecedented success. This explains why some young millionaire artists end up in trouble, unable to handle fame and wealth. Pausanias led the Greeks at the battle of Plataea after the successive deaths of his uncle King Leonidas at Thermopylae and his own father Cleombrotus, who had succeeded his twin brother, Leonidas. The two deaths occurred within a space of less than twelve months. And, suddenly, it was Pausanias' turn to lead the mighty army of Sparta, but also of the allies. Leonidas' son Pleistarchus was a minor, and as such Pausanias took over as regent and guardian of Pleistarchus (his first cousin), on prior instructions from Leonidas. At Plataea, the fortunes of the Greeks rested on young Pausanias as Commander of the Hellenic Army and his fellow officers from Sparta and Athens, not to mention officers from other cities that had joined the coalition. Against the Greeks were arrayed the Persians, outnumbering the Greeks many times, with massive reserves standing by. A loss for the Greeks would have meant death or at best slavery. These were the only two options that lay before Pausanias as he led the Greeks to an epic victory that in many ways saved western civilisation.

In my quest to understand leadership, I unavoidably suffered many shocks as I began to realise that leadership can be a mixed bag, and that most leaders have great vices as well as great virtues. Alexander the Great was one such leader of virtues and vices but so were King David before him and President Kennedy in more recent times.

Looking for leaders to admire

I made a point of searching for leaders who would impress me with their virtues, while bearing in mind that such leaders would probably also shock me with their vices. John Kennedy is such an example, as we shall see later. My search concentrated largely on leaders from America, Europe, Russia, Africa and to a large extent from the Eastern Mediterranean and the Middle East.

I hold the view that there is no such phenomenon as a complete, wholesome, ideal or perfect leader, although some like Cimon of Ancient Greece may have approached the ideal. Simply, the human brain and man's facilities do not have the capacity to make optimal and fully beneficial decisions. In the end, leadership is largely a matter of ability to make sound decisions. Humans have passions, and as such their rationality is bounded. Their innate limitations are also a hindrance. Fame and wealth can be great corruptors of a leader's character (March and Herbert 1958); as is the lust for power for its own sake.

Cimon—Mandela—Lee—Wilson

The princely Cimon was a model of fairness, generosity and courage. Princely Mandela was a model of magnanimity and justice for all; though not exactly a paragon of competence. Cimon and Mandela were both of aristocratic stock, bred in different eras and in different cultures who lived under different conditions and different times. But both were aristocrats in terms of the meaning the Ancient Greeks ascribed to the word aristocrat (αριστοκράτης); 'rule of the best-born'. Both were also exceedingly popular. It seems that in the end followers are able to appreciate the difference between gold and gold-plated, true and false leaders. This pair of leaders goes to prove that model leadership is not confined to eras, countries or races. Both had the advantage of high breeding and most importantly both were aware of how their background obliged them to behave. Both did what they believed was right. All these things made them immensely popular.

The Cimon — Mandela pair stands out as a beacon of moral leadership. Through morality and goodness these two leaders connect the ancient and the modern (2,500 years apart) worlds of leadership. Though appointed rather than elected, General Robert E. Lee provides us with yet another leader with aristocratic breeding (but financially challenged at some point in his life). It is nowadays fashionable for some to berate this great general of the 19th century. But, deep and sober reading of this great man's life clears up everything for the objective reader and leads him to see in Lee an example of princely and moral leadership. The fact that Lee behaved in an exemplary manner, even under civil war conditions that are typically characterised by viciousness, extreme violence and blood-letting, places him amongst the great and exemplary leaders of the last three centuries.

Woodrow Wilson, the 28th President of the USA and son of a preacher, was another leader with an immense record of achievement. Just as the other three (Cimon, Mandela and Lee), Wilson was widely read, a scholar and a high-minded idealist, something unfortunately not often seen in modern day leaders! His many legislative accomplishments are held in high esteem to this day. He led the USA into WWI and felt the sufferings of war. His war experiences were instrumental in shaping his views about what the world needed, which was a League of Nations, as conceived by Wilson. He achieved that, and in the process earned a Nobel Prize. The creation of the League of Nations was a predominantly British and American affair after both warmed to the idea when Jan Christian Smuts of South Africa presented his blueprint. But in the end Woodrow Wilson was unable to convince the Americans to commit to membership of the new organisation. It was in his time as President that American women were given the right to vote. And, following a long "tradition" that sees many great leaders visited by calamity, he suffered a stroke while campaigning in favour of the Treaty of Versailles which bedevilled the remainder of his term in office. Other good leaders of gentle disposition, well-meaning and idealistic suffered bad luck as well. Cimon was ostracised, Lee had to suffer the humiliation of surrendering his great army and Mandela suffered long imprisonment and hard labour. FDR was sick whilst in office, suffering from seizure-like black-outs. Ronald Reagan suffered from Alzheimer's disease and it is not yet clear whether he had signs of Alzheimer's while still in office.

Leadership is not limited to business, politics or the military

Just to complete the influences of my childhood on my understanding of leadership, I will now take the reader to my village, Pano Arodes in the district of Paphos in Cyprus. At the time the village had about 600 residents, nearly all of them with less than six years' schooling. Some were very poor almost to the point of destitution. For many generations (certainly for more than two centuries) my family played a central role in the affairs of this small farming community. My father, Polydoros, was a teacher but I never remember him in this role as I explain below. He had graduated from the Ierodidaskalion (Seminary-cum-Teacher Training College). This tertiary education institution was in essence a seminary that trained youngsters to be teachers and/or priests. On completion of their studies most graduates became teachers but others moved into the priesthood. He was born in the Cypriot village of Kythrea, now occupied by the Turkish army, which lies some 250 kilometres away from where I was born. Soon after graduation and for punitive reasons he was sent to far-away Pano Arodes as a teacher. In reality he was there on unannounced banishment to punish him for using his mesmerising rhetorical skills to encourage people to raise their voice against colonialism and in favour of freedom. He advocated peaceful means (passive resistance), patience and dogged determination. Funnily enough, he liked the British people and had a high regard for British traditions and most certainly for British education. He knew the English language as well. But these are another matter, considering that our country was then under British colonial rule and people wanted freedom from colonialism.

My father had as his role model his grandfather (my great-grandfather), father Zacharias, who as a young teenager (and before entering the priesthood) in the early 19th century fled Cyprus to volunteer for service in the nascent Greek navy. Greece had just earned its fettered independence, but was continuously threatened with a return of Turkish occupation. He stayed in the navy as a volunteer for more than twelve years, defending Greek independence against the threat of the Ottomans. At the time Cyprus was under Ottoman occupation, as was much of present-day Greece, and so he had to brave not only the waves, but also the marauding Ottoman navy, no matter how shambolic this was after its reduction and humiliation at the hands of a joint Russian, British and French naval expeditionary force at Navarino in 1827. Another of his role models was his spirited father (my grandfather) Christos. Anecdotal evidence has it that when the colonial authorities visited his village of Kythrea in the late 19th century to convince people to pay increased taxes he challenged them verbally. He told them that it was grossly unfair to tax penniless Cypriots to finance an Empire and the British Crown. He was briefly arrested for remonstrance and dissent.

Father in internal exile

Upon arriving in our village as a teacher, and long before I was born, my father started giving public speeches about freedom. A local agent of the colonial authorities was in the church one day when my father was giving a speech to the congregation about liberty. This was swiftly reported to the authorities in the nearby village. In no time the colonial police descended on the church to arrest him — inside the actual church building. After considerable tribulations he was sentenced to internal banishment. This meant internal exile, but with the right to continue teaching in the school of the place of his exile; under surveillance, of course. He was banished to a place some 250 kilometres away at a time most transport was via mules, horses and donkeys. This in effect meant the start of considerable problems for his young wife and infant daughter (my mother and sister). He held out for a number of years until, on the death of my maternal grandfather and after considerable pressure from the colonial authorities, he had to submit his resignation as a teacher. This is called constructive dismissal in our times. At the time, a teaching post in poor agrarian Cyprus put one on a pedestal and was a dream job for most young men. After his enforced resignation he took over our family's farm from my grandfather, who had died a few months earlier.

Most interestingly, many years later and after my father had died, I discovered a letter from the commander of a British naval unit that had visited Cyprus, thanking my father for offering dinner to the whole unit at our ancestral home in the village, which he had to leave not many years before to start his term of internal exile. I found it fascinating and spiritually uplifting to see a man forgetting and forgiving what the authorities had done to him, and viewing a group of young visiting British sailors and naval cadets as guests who had to be offered Greek hospitality. After all, these innocent young men had done no harm to anyone and where just visiting. I consider it a blessing to have discovered this letter. No trace of vengefulness (noblesse oblige!). No sign of bitterness. Great stuff, I thought! My father's speeches were not against people, but against actions that took people's freedom away from them. Here is what others in Athens had to say about him: "Mr Polydoros Petasis did honour to his name and could not have taken any other name [incidentally the name Polydoros in Greek means a person of many gifts]. A gentleman he was, and all the gifts were bestowed on him by God…his brown eyes were full of sweetness and humaneness/ ανθρωπιά." (Papademetriou, 2011) (The above passage was freely translated from Greek to English by me.)

(for more the reader can visit http://archive.churchofcyprus.org.cy/documents/)

An indoctrinated "communist" with leadership qualities

There was a near-landless person in the village with a few years of schooling who I respected very much and even tried to emulate some of his behaviours. Kyriakos had volunteered to join the British army as a mule driver during WWII, and came back after the war as a fully indoctrinated communist. I am still at a loss as to why Cypriots in the British army during WWII came back, almost in their entirety, as indoctrinated communists and Stalin admirers. The only explanation I can give is that the British colonial government wanted to create a buffer against the power of the church hierarchy that represented Greek consciousness. But this did not go according to plan, because in spite of the indoctrination, many found it hard to understand internationalism. Though I tried very hard, I never managed to understand what communism meant to him. He had probably not read a book in his life and lived in an inward-looking and closed environment. Though near-destitute he had influence on people, and many looked up to him because of his kindness and the virtue of never talking against anyone in the village. Small Greek villages are notorious for employing gossip as a pastime; not that British villages are any better!

The village blacksmith as leader.

The other person in the village that I looked up to became a great friend of mine in later life. Petros (known as Petris) was the blacksmith of the village, who later left to work in town owing to the meagre opportunities the village offered him. He had more than half a dozen children and a poor wife, just as he was absolutely poor. He was also perennially afflicted by one or the other sickness, maybe the result of poor lifestyle and bad nutrition. Tuberculosis troubled him all his life. But nothing put him down and he never let penury affect his legendary respectfulness towards others. He was indomitable, without a trace of pride. I find it difficult to find many equals to Petros' good character. If anyone in the village offered him coffee he would immediately find the next opportunity to reciprocate twofold, though nearly penniless.

Some years back, the village was visited by a devastating earthquake that forced most of the residents to leave their homes and to seek shelter in makeshift tents under wintry conditions and bitter westerly winds. I was in Nicosia when I first heard about the earthquake, and immediately drove some three hours to the village to see if I could help in any way and to see the extent of the suffering. By the time I arrived, the Red Cross had visited the village and provided literally everything people needed under the prevailing conditions: tents, heaters, blankets, ample food and clean water. I took some extra cash with me, knowing a few things about the conditions in the village. The first person I visited was my ageing uncle, who was in a tent, and then my friend Petros the village blacksmith, who was still living in the village. As I was about to depart, I left one hundred pounds for him, telling him that this could come in handy, given the circumstances he lived in. Despite his destitution and our friendship, he absolutely refused to accept even one pound, telling me: "The Red Cross provided us with all we need. In fact, I have food to spare. It would be greedy of me to accept more help than I need." I said to myself, here is another lesson in self-respect coming from my friend the village blacksmith. He remained optimistic, even though the village had been visited by an earthquake, was living in a tent and suffering from tuberculosis. This poor, sick and uneducated — in the formal sense — man left an indelible mark on my soul, with his frugal lifestyle and indomitable courage. He died of illness a few years later, just after reaching seventy. I had lost a great friend and was deprived of a great role model.

A high-IQ leader with a few years of education

And now one last example of a role model in the village who had only a few years of education. I refer to Xenophon, a part-time farmer, who for many years regularly assisted my father in his post-teacher tasks. We later grew to become great friends. What made him stand out was his raw IQ and competence that impressed anyone who met him. What he lacked in formal education he more than made up through his formidable brain and talent. He could retain in his head masses of data and information, process data almost like a computer, carry out farming work to perfection, fix water pumps and ploughs, and ride horses, even acted as the village "vet" by helping in the delivery of young animals. He was very unpretentious and did not take himself seriously. He would help anyone (literally everyone) who asked for his help, particularly in his role as amateur 'vet'. When he died of old age not long ago I was asked by his family to give the funeral oration. What a great honour that was!

Leadership and legacy

It is not my objective to write a book on leadership focusing on my life's experiences. Through the above examples, I simply wished to demonstrate that leadership can be exercised in more than one way and by all sorts of people, even by the self-effacing. Leadership, in many ways has to do with leaving a positive legacy. Thus the village blacksmith was a leader in his own right, and left a legacy in his small community by being unselfish, living frugally, being optimistic and above all having philotimo (the Greek word which former President Obama defined as, 'what decent people are expected to do'). He had forsaken greed, which is an all-consuming human weakness that most of us carry to our death. And, by his behaviour, he made his contemporaries and others at the village aware of the beauty of being free from the shackles of greed. Though sick and destitute, he never moaned or complained about his situation and thus in his own way taught his co-villagers resoluteness and steadfastness. He was humility incarnate.

"It was pride that changed angels into devils; it is humility that makes men angels." Saint Augustine

Philosopher vs village blacksmith

A few years back, I was invited to give the keynote speech at a college graduation ceremony. I told the students that they were fortunate to have had the opportunity to earn a degree. I then warned them against the danger of pride that often accompanies young men who demonstrate an aptitude for academic work and are successful in passing exams. I told them: "At times you will feel superior to those that were less fortunate than you in terms of opportunities to study. So, you must guard against the temptation of looking down on people, because first of all it is a sin and second, you will in the end hurt both yourselves and the persons you look down upon." Little did I know that I had hit the raw nerve of an atheist professor of mathematics who was in the audience. He took offence at my reference to 'sin' because, he told me, this word had a religious connotation. I told him that all I was trying to do was transfer to students some of the lessons on morality that I had learned from my friend the humble village blacksmith. On hearing the word 'blacksmith' he snapped, "Students are supposed to learn from philosophers and not from blacksmiths"! What could I say after that?

All I tried to do in the above few paragraphs was demonstrate that the potential for leadership is in all of us. As long as our behaviour is good enough to be emulated by others then we are exercising some form of leadership. The humble and semi-literate villagers Kyriakos, Petros and Xenophon serve as good examples of inconspicuous leadership through good behaviour.

From my readings and field experiences I am now more likely than before to accept that leadership is not only about influencing the masses, or opening of new paths or even expressing vision or possessing the "right" leadership traits that we often read about in the literature or in the press. Leadership seems to have a lot to do with leaving a positive legacy. So, the blacksmith in our example above was a leader in his own way because he left a legacy amongst the small community he lived in about how to live a frugal life with self-respect even if penniless and sick. His greatest achievement was that he was able to forsake greed, that horrible human weakness that in the extreme engulfs and destroys any speck of humanity in the person suffering from this terrible disease. The village blacksmith's character and behaviour gave me comfort and made me aware at a very young age of the Manichean conflict between light and darkness and how the most unlikely people manage to stay on the right side of the divide. He had won the struggle between the good of the spiritual world of light and the evil of the extreme materialistic world. In his poverty and sickness he taught me a lot about leadership which I now share with the reader.

The way this book attempts to explain leadership

This treatise is comprised of: a) essays that cover specific aspects of leadership, b) real-life examples of leadership in action, intended to put each essay into context. I felt that the script can be understood better when tied together with concrete examples and real people. These examples come from countries that have always interested me and which I studied extensively and researched their leaders' practices. I provide numerous examples from Russia, to counter the fact that most books on leadership are restricted to Western figures and practices. But I also use material from America, which has plenty of examples to offer through its otherwise short history. The Eastern Mediterranean and the Middle East (where I live) and the turbulent history of the region are a treasure trove for anyone wishing to write about leadership.

The subject of leadership is inexhaustible. All I am doing here is adding examples to help the reader understand better some of the issues surrounding leadership that have been discussed for hundreds of years. Equally, I am hoping to convince the reader that leadership is not amenable to simple definitions nor can it be explained through lists of traits that successful leaders are supposed to have. Luck and circumstances, as determinants of leadership successes and failures, are often neglected in most debates on the subject and so I try in this book to bring these issues to the fore for the benefit of the reader.

More than anything, great leaders leave behind great legacies that have the power to propel others to greatness.

Conclusions

My conclusions about leadership are these:

- Leadership is not amenable to a single universal definition
- Leadership is a complex construct that cannot be reduced to, "here is what leaders do" or "here are the ten commandments of leadership" and so on.
- Leadership in its most fundamental form rests on:
  - The will to lead
  - Competence
  - Morality

These three broad headings could be a good starting point for the examination of leadership:

The will to lead: Not all of us wish to take positions of leadership or to exercise power over others even if we have the wherewithal to do so. Some of us need to be pushed hard to accept a leadership position. Apparently when Moses was called by God to lead the Israelites, he gave an array of reasons why he was the wrong person for the job. He suggested that his brother Aaron take the lead rather than he. Equally, some very bad leaders found themselves leading not because they had the qualities to lead effectively but because they had an overwhelming need for power and pushed themselves forward using various methods.

Competence: When a leader fails to produce results he is typically viewed as disappointing. Those in leadership positions need to achieve results otherwise they will not be tolerated for long. Yet we see that somehow many incompetent leaders manage to hang on to their position, with disastrous consequences. This we see more and more in politics where populism and propaganda can do great things for incompetent leaders.

Morality: Morality is probably the most difficult of the three to explain its necessity, seeing that under some circumstances many would view morality as just a "nice to have" rather than a "must have" leader quality. It is unlikely that many of the survivors of the siege of Stalingrad cared much about Stalin's morality after he had helped save them from disaster.

In summary:

1) No single quality or trait on its own can even come near to fully explaining leadership. There is a place for charismatic leaders, just as there is a place for dour ones. The same holds for extroverts and introverts and so on.

2) There is no 'one size fits all' leader. We have all seen time and time again how previously successful leaders in one context can fail in another. "Usain Bolt: Sprinter-turned-footballer declares his 'sports life over'" read one headline at the time of writing (BBC Sport, 2019).

3) Some great leaders owe their success to their virtues, and others to their vices turned virtues. King David was a great sinner before repenting and then turning out to be a beacon of great leadership and a unifier of his people and country. The Psalms of David and their splendour can be most beneficial to any leader of our day.

4) There is no such a thing as an "ideal" leader, because the ideal is impossible to achieve in practice. Additionally, human frailty, weaknesses and passions preclude the achievement of the "ideal".

5) As social animals we are either leaders or followers, depending on context, and as such we all have a chance to lead in our own way. The village blacksmith with the ability to make a mark on others with his behaviour and

indomitability serves as a good example of leadership that is limited in scope, since his influence was confined to a small village. He would not qualify to be included in a book on corporate, political or military leadership, where the requirements of profit, market share, domination of the opponent and expansion hold centre stage.

6) The ubiquitous question of whether leaders are born or made is still unresolved, considering the complexity of the subject of leadership. Dogmatic answers have not solved the impasse.

7) Some of the smartest leaders can make ruinous decisions when carried away by the atmosphere of the times or by their emotions. The debilitating Korean and Vietnam Wars serve as a good example. An unwinnable war in Vietnam managed to sack five US presidents in this order: Truman, Eisenhower, Kennedy, Johnson and Nixon. In the end America suffered a humiliating withdrawal and horrific loses on both sides. The Korean conflict is open to this day and is a source of potential conflagration.

8) Hubris (extreme pride) and greed have been the downfall of many a formerly great leader. "Hubris causes many heroic figures to fall even in our time and no better example can be found than the Yankee slugger Alex Rodriguez", read one headline (Vincent, 2014).

References

BBC Sport. (2019). Usain Bolt: Sprinter-turned-footballer declares his 'sports life over'. [online] Available at: https://www.bbc.com/sport/athletics/46966279 [Accessed 25 Jan. 2019].

March J. G. and Herbert S. (1958). Organisations. Hoboken, NJ: John Wiley.

Papademetriou, A. [Παπαδημητρίου Α.] (2011). Παράλληλοι δρόμοι: Αφήγημα. Αθήναι: Εκδόσεις Κασταניώτη.

Vincent, F. (2014). Alex Rodriguez — a victim of hubris in a modern-day Greek tragedy. [online] Fox News. Available at: https://www.foxnews.com/opinion/alex-rodriguez-a-victim-of-hubris-in-a-modern-day-greek-tragedy [Accessed 25 Jan. 2019].

Book 2

Making leadership meaningful

"There are no great men without virtue..." (Tocqueville and Heffner, 1956: 105)

In this book I attempt to clarify a number of critical issues that impact on our understanding of leadership considering the multitude of meanings that have been ascribed to leadership at different times. Undoubtedly leadership has received more than its fair share of attention considering that nearly half a million books have been written on the subject and more are probably in the pipeline. In view of this I have not tried to give my own definition of leadership but rather I attempted to put the subject in context, thus allowing the reader to draw his own conclusions and assign his own meaning to leadership. In this regard I discuss the following:

Identifying leadership potential

Undoubtedly each one of us has a modicum of leadership in him except that not all of us have the opportunity to express this in the traditional way (leading others formally). But, unbeknown to us, maybe, we exercise leadership in other 'non-traditional' ways such as when we act decently and ultimately become a model for others to follow. I put forward the position that the identification of leadership potential, especially in young people, is not an easy matter. In this regard I give the example of the celebrated Marshal of the Soviet Union (Маршал Советского Союза) Georgi Zhukov When he was conscripted into the Soviet Army hardly anyone noticed his potential. As such, he was relegated to the rank of private rather than being enlisted in the army's leadership program from the start. Had someone in authority detected his leadership potential Zhukov would have had a totally different treatment to the one he received at the beginning of his career.

In search of a universal definition of leadership

Attempting to define leadership in terms of specific traits, such as charisma and oratory skill for example, is likely to prove futile because leadership is too complex a meaning and as such it cannot be confined in defined boxes. Leadership can only be explained holistically, considering the diverse and often contradictory factors surrounding it. No single factor or individual group of factors can explain the multidimensional nature of leadership.

Nature vs nurture

The debate over whether leaders are born or made has been raging for centuries with no end in sight. I cannot see a winner in this debate because neither nature nor nurture alone can explain leadership. Let alone that we are still unclear as to what nurture and nature are all about. But, when all is considered one can say with some certainly that nature as well as nurture impact on leadership. I will try to explain the need for both through a debate I had with my former professor when he visited me in Cyprus from the United States.

Intellectual and moral leadership

Here I will employ Socrates and Plato to explain two "soft" but exceedingly powerful ingredients of leadership which we do not often encounter in debates over the subject. An examination of intellectual and moral leadership can help us understand the role played by the mind and the soul in the process of decision-making. Understanding intellectually the nature of man helps us better comprehend why some leader decisions and behaviours are what they are. Realpolitik in foreign policy matters, for example, is nothing more than the adoption of an intellectual decision-making model which allows the leader to use raw power and employ primitive instincts to decide outcome. As regards morality the employment of torture champers, for example, is nothing more than the adoption by leaders of amorality in war.

Leadership and circumstances

Here I will try to explain how leadership style varies (and in fact ought to vary) with circumstances. Copying a successful leadership style of the past and blindly applying to the present will not work because each set of circumstances brings with it its own set of leadership requirements.

Ideal leader

Here I will attempt to explain that ideal leadership falls outside the realm of reality and as such it is futile to search for the ideal leader.

Leader succession

Here I will try to explain that all the work of a great leader can be undone literally overnight if the leader fails to take care of the issue of leader succession. I will give the example of Alexander the Great, a singular icon of leadership, who failed to deal with succession and as a result got his brothers-in-arms to fight amongst themselves for more than ten years over who was to succeed him. In the end (though it took many years) the empire collapsed, leading ultimately to the weakening of the Greeks and their occupation by the Romans.

Change and leadership

As nothing remains static the future cannot be a photocopy of the past. As such, new challenges require new approaches and new leadership formats. In the age of tanks the great marshal of the Soviet Union Semyon Mikkailovich Budyonny was more interested in cavalry than in tanks. As such, and though he was a great marshal in his own right, Budyonny contributed below his capabilities in WWII.

Leaders seem to come in clusters

Historically certain eras seem to have been more conducive to the growth of leaders than others. Seemingly undistinguished personalities that would have never shone under normal conditions suddenly surface in times of war taking the country by storm. Within a span of roughly 100–200 years the world saw the largest concentration of seminal leaders probably in history. This period was the 5th and 4th Centuries BC and the place was Greece. These great leaders together gave the world philosophy, politics, democracy, history, the sciences, art, liberty, generalship, respect, patriotism, and a host of other great works of intrinsic value. And this was not all, considering that much of their work was destroyed and as such we are unable to access it. This period saw the likes of Solon, Miltiades, Themistocles, Pausanias, Cimon, Aristides, Herodotus, Pericles, Socrates, Plato, Aristotle, Philip II, Alexander the Great, Parmenion, Seleucus, Ptolemy and a long string of other giants. Greece probably had more true leaders in this brief period than in all of its later history.

The Age of Reason (pursuit of knowledge and use of the critical approach) and Enlightenment (the application of reason) gave us a host of leaders in philosophy, science and rationality. All these greats came together within a short span of time and mostly in the period covering the 18th century. They revolutionised thinking in that they brought science into the equation and reduced the power and centrality the church had in life and politics. Liberalism and republicanism (as opposed to monarchism) and modern political ideologies were the products of the Age of Reason. Importantly the thinking of this period lit the fuse that ultimately drove two major revolutions in the west: the American and the French revolutions.

The Romans gave us many great thinkers such as Marcus Aurelius (121–180 AD) the stoic philosopher; even if Bertrand Russell had said that none of the Roman philosophers were original (considering the impact of the Greek philosophical schools). Later, Rome gave us Constantine the Great (272–337 AD) and others. But why did it take roughly 2,000 years after the Greek giants such as Socrates, Plato and Aristotle for the English philosopher and statesman Francis Bacon (1561–1626) to seriously revisit Aristotle's ideas on the scientific method and rationality? Why did it take more than 2,000 years for the great French philosopher Rene Descartes (1629–1649 AD) to appear after Pythagoras to give mathematics another great boost? Interestingly this same period saw the Jewish-Dutch philosopher Baruch Spinoza (1632–1677 AD) and his criticism of religious scriptures to open up a debate on subjects that had been closed to debate. Emanuel Kant was another great philosopher of this age as was John Locke. The man behind the Law of Gravity and the Laws of Motion, Isaac Newton, also lived in this period, as did Voltaire (real name François-Marie Arouet). Voltaire gave us Candide and a criticism of social convention. His criticism of the monarchy ended up inciting the French Revolution. Jan Jacques Rousseau and his Social Contract that promoted an egalitarian form of government was the product of this age as well. The great innovator, politician and philosopher, Benjamin Franklin, lived in this era. The great, perhaps the greatest, economist and philosopher Adam Smith lived in this period and gave us the "Wealth of Nations". Thomas Jefferson, the towering giant of democracy, the writer of the Declaration of Independence, the revolutionary and US President lived in this period as well. (Pettinger, 2018)

> *A great leader can be an enormous stimulus for others to rise to the top. When this happens a spiral of greats is sometimes created. Sadly this spiral soon comes to an end forcing society to brace itself for a long wait until the next gift can arrive.*

Are certain times in history more fertile for the nurturing of clusters of great leaders? Is that likely that DNA changes over time giving some eras an advantage over others? Probably not! Does the existence of a great leader, such as Socrates, play a pivotal role in encouraging others to emulate and become great as well (Plato followed Socrates and Aristotle followed Plato)? Does true competition play a role? Why do we have periods of great leadership activity and periods where a dearth of good leaders is the rule? These are some of the questions that spring to mind when analyzing leader concentrations and leader densities over periods of time. The 4th Century AD gave us not only John Chrysostom (349–407) but also Basil the Great (330–379) and Gregory the Theologian (329–389). These three were born in the space of twenty years and all three were instrumental in shaping Christian theology particularly Eastern Christianity (Byzantium). They are known as the "Three Great Hierarchs and Ecumenical Teachers" and as "Doctors of the Church" and are venerated as saints in Eastern Orthodoxy, Catholicism, Anglicanism and elsewhere. The three most recent saints of Eastern Orthodoxy, Paisios, Porfirios and Iacovos are also contemporaries.

Contemporaries Belisarius and Justinian formed a formidable partnership that made Rome great. Belisarius (c.505–565 AD) was probably one of the world's greatest generals. Justinian (527–565 AD) is known for having defeated the Vandals and other attackers on Constantinople. Belisarius started as Justinian's bodyguard and, as is the case with people of promise, at the age of twenty-five he was appointed to a position of command. Then [inevitably perhaps] jealousy entered into the relationship and Justinian tried to humble the great Belisarius only to be forced to eat humble pie whenever Constantinople was threatened and Justinian needed Belisarius to take command.

Belisarius' great success and popularity attracted the attention of people who envied him, starting with Justinian himself who proved to be ungrateful towards his great and humble servant. Whilst Belisarius served his emperor loyally Justinian kept thirsting for worldly fame and did not wish to see Belisarius as equal in fame. This is what Leo Tolstoy had to say about worldly fame. In the introduction, and in reference to Leo Tolstoy's "Father Sergius", Paul Foote quotes a letter from Tolstoy to Chertkov in 1881 in which he says that the struggle with lust is, "...only stage; the main struggle is with worldly fame." (Tolstoy, 1977: 8). Belisarius is still considered to this day to have been a man of virtue who embodied all that was good in a Roman general. The results of his partnership with Justinian were impressive. These gave Justinian the freedom to bring about great improvements in law, the economy, etc in the thirty years of his reign. Belisarius died shortly before his [pursuer of worldly fame] emperor, Justinian. (Brownworth, 2009: 113).

Other famous, but more recent, pairs were: a) Chairman Mao Zedong and Zhou Enlai, first Premier of the Communist Republic of China and b) Stalin and Zhukov, a formidable pair during WWII. Just as Justinian envied Belisarius, Stalin envied Zhukov for his success and popularity. Alexander must have envied Parmenion and his family.

The problem with great pairs is that both members of the pair grow old at the same time and die more or less in the same period. On the death of the pair society rushes off to find the next pair; but alas, disappointment typically follows, for great pairs do not come often. Most societies are forced to spend long years in prayer waiting patiently for the next tranche of leaders to arrive. And, in this waiting period all sorts of bad things can happen. When the great and heroic Greek pair of Ioannis Capodistrias and Demetrius Ypsilantis died some two hundred years ago within a year of each other, Greece was orphaned and more or less remains so to this day; save perhaps for a short flash of light during the (controversial) Venizelos era. As a result, Greece is today relegated to the second division of EU countries, is laden with crippling debt and squabbling politicians and in many ways is a client state, particularly of the USA. The following comment summarizes well what can happen as society waits for its new greats, "To maintain such an expanded empire with diminished [Byzantium] resources would have required the ability and energy of both a Justinian and a Belisarius—two luxuries Byzantium would never have again." (Brownworth, 2009: 113). Will Africa, and the world for that matter, see another pair like Nelson Mandela and Walter Sisulu?

The Scottish Enlightenment provides us with ample evidence that certain times bring to the surface groups of great men. Roughly the second half of the 18th century in Scotland is a case in point. Edinburgh then was the "hotbed of genius." Voltaire had written in 1762 in that it was from Scotland that all rules of taste, poetry, art, etc came; perhaps reminding one vaguely of Athens of the 5th century (the Golden Age of Athens). Here are some names of contemporaries in that Scottish period: a) the philosophers: David Hume, Thomas Reid and Dugald Steward and Adam Smith, b) the architecture geniuses: Robert and James Adam, William Playfair, c) the literature and poetry greats: Hugh Blair, James Thomson, Allen Ramsay, Robert Burns, the playwright John Home, d) the portrait artists: Allan Ramsay and Henry Raeburn and the miniature wax and paste portraitists: James Tassie and his nephew William Tassie and John Henning, and e) the lasting contributors to science and mathematics: Colin Maclaurin, William Cullen,

Joseph Black, James Watt (engineering) and Thomas Telford, and in geology James Hutton just to name a few. (Sutherland, n.d.)

The following giants in literature and poetry: Percy Shelley (born 1792, drowned 1822), John Keats (1795–1821), George Gordon (Lord) Byron (born1788, died of illness in Greece in 1824) lived in the same era. And the great writers: William Wordsworth (1770–1850), Jane Austen (1775–1817) and Charles Dickens (1812–1870) were all contemporaries.

The 19th century AD gave us three Russian literature geniuses: Ivan Turgenev, Leo Tolstoy and Theodore Dostoyevsky were contemporaries. All three lived in an era full of vicious debates between Slavophiles, that had strong nationalist feelings, and the admirers of the West. All three lived through the conflicts between liberals and conservatives, radicals and moderates, dreamers and realists, young and old, crooks and honest people. The charismatic social leaders François Mitterrand and Olof Palmer were contemporaries. Forbes of 5 August, 2016 in an article under the title, "The Nine Most Influential Technology Leaders Of Our Time" gives a list of towering technology giants that changed our world including Tim Berners-Lee that invented the World Wide Web, Mark Zuckerberg that gave us Facebook, Steve Jobs of Apple fame, Mark Benioff, the master of cloud computing and the unknown to date that gave us Blockchain. All are products of the same era. (Forbes Technology Council, 2016).

> *It seems that certain historical periods are infectious when it comes to nurturing great leaders.*

Essay 1: Recognizing leadership potential

This treatise on leadership you are about to read starts with the celebrated marshal of the Soviet Union Georgi Konstantinovich Zhukov (Chaney, 1996). He was one of the most renowned and efficient leader-strategists and clearly one of the greatest military leaders of all time. As a life-long student of history (but not a historian) and leadership in particular I am constantly baffled by this question: Who first identified Zhukov's immense military talent and leadership potential and at which point in his career? Georgi Konstantinovich Zhukov was conscripted into the Russian Imperial Army as a teenager at the start of World War One (WWI). He was, at the time of his conscription, working with his uncle in central Moscow as a young apprentice hat-maker.

Knowing how Zhukov started his career in the Imperial Russian Army and the heights he ultimately reached on merit in the Soviet Army one is legitimately tempted to ask: First. When Zhukov was asked to join the Imperial Russian Army as a conscript did someone from the Russian Officer Corps that had contact with him at the time notice or realize that in young Zhukov they were maybe conscripting a future leader of monumental proportions? Second. Did someone amongst these officers see in this young Russian peasant boy any special and rare qualities? Third. During Zhukov's basic training, did someone from amongst the Russian officers detect anything special in Zhukov's character and demeanour considering that physically he had little to differentiate him from other soldiers? Fourth. Did someone suspect that young Zhukov had luck on his side that would prove a life-saver for his physical existence and his career? Luck followed him in revolution, in civil war, in the time of Stalin's brutal purges of the 1930s and in the vagaries of WWII. Competence and luck allowed him in the end to join the ranks of Alexander the Great (Cartledge, 2005) and Genghis Khan (McLynn, 2016).

Before emerging as a great leader Zhukov first had to escape certain death at the hands of the near-manic Beria and other secret agents of the Stalin era, "The decapitation [in the 1930s] of the Red Army—90 percent of all generals and 80 percent of all colonels suffered in Stalin's manic drive—not only had the overall effect of destroying so many trained officers, but had specific results which badly hurt the armed forces. By wiping out [the gifted] Tukhachevsky and the 'modern warfare' enthusiasts, by eliminating those who studied German methods and British theories, the purges left the army in the hands of such politically safe but intellectually retarded figures as Voroshilov and Kulik." (Kennedy, 1987: 325).

I am sure the reader suspects that at conscription time hardly anyone (most probably no one) took any notice of peasant-boy Zhukov as he moved inconspicuously amongst the troops. So, when does one begin to show his leadership potential and skills and when do officers and managers begin to notice leadership and leadership potential in young men and women?

> *The detection of leadership potential is sometimes a matter of luck though undoubtedly systematic analysis helps.*

In the olden days leaders were groomed from the ranks of the aristocracy. Society knew almost from day one who the next ruler would be and from whose ranks he would emerge. Things are different now and as the Zhukov example amplifies for us, leaders can come from anywhere provided the right circumstances exist to allow their brilliance to shine.

The right circumstances for leadership emergence include above all a system of meritocracy. In this case at least, Stalin the autocrat seems to have allowed a considerable degree of meritocracy to flourish; otherwise one cannot see how the war could have been won by the Soviets. It is indicative that besides Zhukov other great Soviet officers made it to the ranks on merit including marshals: Aleksandr Vasilevsky, Ivan Bagramyan (the first non-Slav-origin marshal), Konstantin Rokossovski (of Polish descent) and the highly determined and courageous General Vasily Chuikov who led the 62nd army in the epic Battle of Stalingrad. Apparently less than competent, but admittedly brave, officers such as Kliment Voroshilov also made it through the ranks. But, superbly competent officers such as Mikhail Tukhachevsky and Vasily Blyukher were not as lucky. They were both purged by Stalin and executed in 1937 and 1938 respectively; both aged 44 at the time of their execution. Apparently, people like Beria had done their work perfectly. Of course, Stalin appreciated that WWII was about life or death and capitulation or victory and as such, he had to think twice before stopping the progress of all able officers, including Zhukov. Without them the war would have certainly been lost.

> *Meritocracy is central to the emergence of a leader but so are the right circumstances.*

Essay 2: Searching in vain for a universal definition of leadership

"The only thing you can say about a leader is that a leader is somebody who has followers." Peter Drucker. (Karlgaard, 2019)

The American Management Association reports that, "If you google the word leader, you get more than 300 million hits. On Amazon, there are 480,881 books today whose topics have to do with leaders. It doesn't help to go to Wikipedia to get a clearer definition because, right off the bat, 11 different types of leaders are named, from bureaucratic through transformational, to laissez-faire. In the field of leadership, there are as many opinions as there are writers, and there is also a lack of common language and tools." (Ulrich, 2019)

> *No matter how widely the subject of leadership has been studied, a common definition of the term remains elusive.*

There is also the perennial question of whether leaders are born or made. And here again we run into problems because the answer to this question also remains elusive. Jean Jacques Rousseau (1712–1778), the non-academic bohemian philosopher from the age of the enlightenment, had this to say on the question of whether leaders are born (nature) or developed (nurture), "I conceive that there are two kinds of inequality among the human species; one, which I call natural or physical, because it is established by nature, and consists in a difference of age, health, bodily strength, and the qualities of the mind or of the soul; and another, which may be called moral or political inequality, because it depends on a kind of convention, and is established, or at least authorised by the consent of men. This latter consists of the different privileges, which some men enjoy to the prejudice of others; such as that of being more rich, more honoured, more powerful or even in a position to exact obedience." (Rousseau, 1991: 163)

And Rousseau continued, "It is useless to ask what is the source of natural inequality among human species: one, which I call natural or physical, because that question is answered by the simple definition of the word. Again, it is still more useless to inquire whether there is any essential connection between the two inequalities; for this would be only asking, in other words, whether those who command are necessarily better than those who obey, and if strength of body or of mind, wisdom or virtue are always found in particular individuals, in proportion to their power or wealth; a question fit perhaps to be discussed by slaves in the hearing of their masters, but highly unbecoming to reasonable and free men in search of the truth." (Rousseau, 1991: 163)

Leadership and all attendant issues have always fascinated humans and captured their imagination. Scholars and researchers on the subject of leadership abound whilst the subject never ceases to be in vogue; nowadays largely on account of the emphasis business schools put on leadership and the general fascination with the subject people have. Bookstores in major airports around the world sell books on leadership as standard items these days. This has in many ways helped to popularise the subject. Attractive titles in the following format proved beneficial to the selling process: "Twelve steps to Leadership...", "Twenty-three things leaders do..." and, "Fifteen dos and don'ts of leadership...". People's thirst for books on leadership does not seem to be quenching any time soon.

Current philosophers and leadership

It is not that the subject is new considering that philosophers began to show an interest in leadership thousands of years ago; even if their interest lay mostly in political leadership, societal affairs, and leadership-ethics-idealism. Plato was one of the first to talk about leadership just as was his student Aristotle. And in our time we see current philosophers talk about leadership with the same vigour as before. Here are examples of current philosophers with an interest in leadership issues: Chomsky, one of the most cited philosophers of the modern age wrote about politics, history, religion, and other subjects. Aleksandr Dugin is also keen on the subject. Martha Nussbaum, whose interests range from ancient Greek philosophy to political philosophy and to ethics, enjoys the subject. Alasdair Macintyre covers leadership through his treatises in ethics, politics, and morality. Apparently modern philosophers are as concerned about leadership as Plato was a few millennia ago.

Questions on leadership that do not seem to go away

Amongst the many questions on leadership, three seem not to go out of fashion and largely remain unanswered. These are: First: "What is the best path to a leadership position"? Second: "Are leaders born or made"? This second question is a popular one as any university leadership student will testify and, Third: "Are there any specific universally accepted traits that leaders need to have if they are to be successful in their role as leaders"? I will touch on all of these issue in several places below.

> *The debate over the question of whether leaders are born or made continues unabated.*

Essay 3: Leaders—born or made

"Which contributes more to the area of a rectangle, its length or its width?"
psychologist Donald Hebb, when asked which contributes more to
personality, nature of nurture. (Hannay, 2014)

Leader emergence

The search for an answer to the question of whether leaders are born or made was the subject of an article by Connson Chou Locke in the Harvard Business Review (14 March, 2014). The author of this article made the point that the question of whether leaders are born or made is actually not relevant, "Whether Leaders Are Born or Made Is the Wrong Question". He noted that invariably the vast majority of responses to the question of whether leaders are born or made favour that leaders are made. I do not agree fully with the above position because political correctness often weighs heavily on respondents' minds when answering the nature vs nurture question. 'Leaders are made' is a more convenient position for most people to take (and more socially acceptable) than 'leaders are born' which basically means that nature largely determines who we become.

Extraversion and intelligence

Connson Chou Locke went on and said that some researchers found two traits that correlate with leadership potential: "... extraversion and intelligence, differentiate leaders from others," he wrote. But, he then warned the reader to be careful not to draw the wrong conclusions from the above findings. He noted that people with potential for leadership (leadership emergence) are also endowed with the traits of extraversion and intelligence though this does not guarantee that once these people are in a position of leadership they would be better leaders than others with less extraversion and intelligence. The former are not necessarily more effective than the latter. The gist of the matter is that in the end, extraversion and intelligence offer no guarantee of successful leadership. Simply, extraversion and intelligence are likely to make one more influential in the group and to put him in a favourable position to emerge as leader. This, however, does not mean superior leadership. (Chou Locke, 2014)

"Though many psychologists argue that extroversion and introversion exist on a sliding scale, and that very few people can be 'pure' extroverts, someone's degree of extroversion is a core factor of their personality and is generally difficult to modify." (Psychology Today, 2019a)

One of my favourite leaders, Thomas Jefferson, was not exactly the epitome of an extravert and yet he went down in history as one of the most outstanding leaders of America and the world, in fact. Amongst others he was: First. Author of the Declaration of Independence, Second. President of the United States, Third. Linguist, inventor, architect and Fourth. Founder of the University of Virginia. He avoided and in fact shunned public speaking; he was shy to speak but could be intense in conversations and even emotional at times. Jefferson was clearly no extravert and few could have claimed to know Jefferson well because he largely kept to himself. Jefferson's 'protégé, 'father' of the US Constitution and former President, James Madison was not an extrovert either. Yet he gave so much to making America a great country. "In his personal life, Madison was extremely introverted and a voracious reader" wrote the Business Insider quoting from "James Madison: A Biography". (Cain, 2018)

Had Zhukov been a 'pure' extrovert would he have been identified early in his life as a potential leader? Had he possessed extraversion would this have been apparent during his basic army training and his early years as a soldier? Zhukov was not an extrovert. As for intelligence, the army would have probably detected at conscription time that he was a brilliant man. All they needed to do was use some of the primitive assessment techniques of the time; but this probably did not happen and consequently he ended up as private in the cavalry rather than as an officer cadet.

"Any person from any walk of life can be highly intelligent, and the trait, in the abstract, is typically considered desirable, but how, and how much, it impacts one's chances of career or relationship success have yet to be fully determined." (Psychology Today, 2019b)

How about Richard Nixon who was probably one of the world's most enigmatic and controversial introverts? He was highly efficient and produced considerable and great legislative work. Most importantly he succeeded at putting an end to the Vietnam War, met with Khrushchev and eased relations with the Soviet Union and opened up China through his "ping-pong diplomacy". As regards intelligence, Nixon was clearly and undoubtedly exceptionally smart. But unfortunately for him many loved to hate him and wanted to bring him down. Many of these "Nixon haters" belonged to the powerful "Eastern Establishment" of the United States. Not of course that Nixon was an angel!

We will see that even if extraversion and intelligence are important for leadership there is no guarantee that two leaders with the same level of extraversion and intelligence will behave and act in the same way. Nor does the fact that they differ in extraversion and intelligence mean the they will take divergent positions on important issues. Nixon was an introvert whilst Reagan was an extrovert. Nixon was highly intelligent and probably better performer academically than Reagan. Yet both took the same line when it came to the truth. Both were the 'cynical version of the truth'. Jill Leporte tells us. (Lepore, 2018) Equally both were not concerned about evidence and fact that were so important to the founder fathers of America. Equally, Nixon employed vengefulness and Reagan used his charisma to his advantage, Jill Leporte tells us.

> *If extraversion and intelligence can predict leadership emergence so can many other factors. Clearly no single factor can guarantee leader success.*

Essay 4: A debate with Bob Whitt on whether leaders are born or made

"Had you stayed in your village you would probably have been a clever donkey rider"

The above observation is credited to the late Robert (Bob) L. Whitt, former Professor at Drake University, Iowa, USA. Bob was my professor, mentor, and friend who taught me in practical terms what it means to 'owe life to one's parents and good life to one's teacher'. He was undoubtedly a powerful influence on me. As my doctoral advisor Bob kept challenging me over the question of whether leadership, intelligence, etc are genetically defined (nature) or are learned (nurture); or maybe a combination of nature and nurture but not necessarily of equal impact. At the time, I had strong views in favour of nature and argued that people largely bring with them the traits of leadership, intelligence, charisma, extraversion, etc and that nurture and further development played a much lesser role than nature. I was strongly influenced by the views of some of the ancient Greeks and Plato in particular, who to a large extent favoured nature. I was also influenced by later philosophers such as Emanuel Kant for example. After all what the ancient Greeks called 'character' (Greek: χαρακτήρας) is not easy to change. In Greek, character literally means something innate (that which is engraved) and which therefore does not change easily. So, I thought at the time, if innate traits (character) do not change then intelligence and leadership should follow the same rules. The Merriam Webster dictionary definition of 'character': '[character is] the complex of mental and ethical traits marking and often individualizing a person, group, or nation.' (Character, n.d.). Notice the words 'marking' and 'individualising'.

In our debates, Bob took the position that nature and nurture play an equally significant role in the development of intelligence and leadership (in fact, I often sensed that Bob supported nurture more than nature). He placed great importance on education and training in shaping people's character and abilities. After all he was a great educator and nurturer of people himself. Years after I had graduated, and after Bob retired, we had occasion to work together briefly in Cyprus on a project involving teacher job grading and pay (job evaluation and reward for public sector primary school teachers). At some point during Bob's visit we went for a trip to my small and remote village in Paphos to visit my parents who lived there. I was born in this village. On arrival I saw a man, my age then, coming towards Bob riding on a donkey and going to work in the fields. On seeing him I told Bob, 'the man riding the donkey is a friend of mine since childhood and from the days I used to live in the village'. Bob knew that I had left the village as a child to study at an American-founded missionary school in another town.

More than a hundred and ten years ago the American Academy was founded and run by generally selfless and devoted American Protestant missionaries who had chosen this as the school's motto, 'to grow and to serve'. In my time at the school these American missionaries offered us a heavy dose of religious instruction and plenty of courses on ethics which I thoroughly enjoyed. But no attempt was made to convert us from Greek Orthodoxy to Protestantism. The school was very strict on matters of behaviour and teachers tried their best to build in us moral fortitude. In addition to religion and ethics, the school's standard curriculum included, of course, maths, language, history, sciences, sport, music, and all the rest. My friend riding the donkey received primary school education at the village and then went on to work as a farmer. He rarely, if ever, left the village and worked mostly within a radius of four to five kilometres (if that) from the centre of the village. On hearing this little story of mine and the contrasting lives of my village friend and myself, Bob was quick to commend (and to catch me out perhaps). 'Do you remember our debates on nature versus nurture back at Drake University in Iowa? he asked me. 'Of course I do' I said. Well, Bob continued with a 'mischievous' smile on his face, 'Had you stayed at the village you too would have been a donkey rider and most likely a clever donkey rider at that. But, you would have not had the benefit of education, languages, travel and opportunity to mix with people of diverse backgrounds. Your whole world would have been the small village'. I am sure that Bob felt he had scored a knock-out as regards our debate over 'nature versus nurture'.

> *Living in a socially and educationally confined environment inevitably constricts one's vista and diminishes the ability to take a spherical view of things.*

The two of us then discussed the importance of prime years on development and the influence these have on later behaviour, seeing both my village friend and I spent our prime years at the village. So, did these prime years form our respective characters? Bob and I agreed that there is a plurality of opinion supporting that the first, say, six years of life are critical to the development of character. But, do these first years determine definitively how we behave in later years as members of society, as followers and/or leaders? Of course, two people that are raised in the same small village for the same period of time do not necessarily have the exact same environmental influences, nor is the influence of the family necessarily similar. This gave us a good opportunity to revisit Dewey, which was part of my university studies under Bob's tutelage. In Dewey's view a person's character and abilities are formed by the time he reaches three. So, does this mean that as regards character, nurture has just three short years to work on what nature gives us? (further reading: MacDermott, 1981)

> *If character is formed at a very early age then nurture has a very narrow window to change what nature bestows on us.*

Inherited propensities

William McDougall separates motives from other human characteristics and argues that certain behavioural tendencies (that is, particular 'propensities') are inherited, instinctive, and 'common to men of every race and age.' This in practice would mean that one can find people with an inherited need for power, for example, in every historical era, everywhere in the world and amongst every diverse group. So, here again, we cannot escape the power of nature and inheritance. (McDougall, 1912)

Of course, the theory of inherited traits turns on its head when one begins to compare the lives of Emperor Marcus Aurelius and his autocratic son Commodus. The former was one of history's kindest and noblest leaders, whilst the latter was a master of intrigue and a conspirator who behaved in a most authoritarian manner that allowed him to achieve a god-like personality cult. But, here again we are talking about a single father and son pair, which prohibits us from generalising. (For a short glimpse into the lives of the two, read Norris, 2016).

Essay 5: Intellectual & moral foundations

Takala reminds us that when it comes to the topic of leadership, Plato towers above most others and justifiably is considered by a plurality of scholars as perhaps the most influential thinker of all time. Some in fact believe that all philosophy after Plato is just notes addressed to Plato. Takala then warns us about the difficulties of defining leadership considering that the word leadership came from the common vocabulary and was then given a technical form without ever having been defined; hence the confusion over the definition of the term and over our general understanding of the concept. I would fully agree that leadership carries no common and precise meaning in the heads of the multiplicity of users of the term. (Takala, 1998)

If we were to go into the realm of definitions (even at the level of a working definition) to give the term "leadership" a more precise meaning we will, most likely, fall into a trap. Many have fallen into similar traps before, particularly when they have plunged into the jungle of definitions in haste. The present treatise avoids this temptation and stays free of descriptions that can constrain the debate. As we have already seen, to be a leader one does not have to lead an army or run a country. Nor does the fact that someone was appointed (or voted) into a position of leadership make him automatically a leader of substance. Clearly an elected representative does not automatically turn into a leader of men. Nor does one have to run a multi-national corporation to be a leader. Socrates of ancient Greece (died 399 BC) led no army, ran no country and in agrarian ancient Greece certainly ran no multinational organisations. Yet, he led through his ideas and actions and provided the world with a legacy whose brilliance never seems to fade.

> *One does not have to lead an army, run a country, or manage a multinational to be a leader.*

Leadership can come from the most amazing places. I am greatly impressed with the work a church bishop has done in his diocese silently and behind the scenes in the short time span of about thirty years; and without any fanfair or trumpets. Out of nothing he set up afternoon learning centres for children who had nowhere to go in the afternoon because both of their parents worked until late in the evening. He set up a restaurant for the destitute, kids' play areas, a library, and other functional and helpful services. Most importantly he got people to attend services (which ought to be a major objective of every bishop) and improved immensely the intake of young men into the priesthood; he built many churches and literally set the place alight. Most importantly he set up a highly successful centre for freeing drug addicts from their terrible affliction. Many consider this to be the number one centre of its kind in the area. Equally, I have seen peasants with no education at all doing great things and getting followers to help their cause, other people and/or their country. We already saw three minor examples in the preface of this treatise.

> *The fact that someone is appointed to (or is voted into) a position of leadership does not automatically make him a leader of substance.*

Intellectual and moral leadership are at the higher end of the leadership debate. Socrates is an example of both these types of leadership. Though he died some two-and-a-half thousand years ago his intellectual and moral leadership continue to amaze the world. He was probably the world's first documented conscientious objector; a subject now in vogue in many countries. Socrates demonstrated in practice and in truth what it means to be a conscientious objector for no personal gain. He was condemned to death for his ideas and did not shy away from punishment even if the verdict was totally unjust. He did what he had to do and took the consequential punishment. Socrates kept his belief in the law of the land even if he disagreed with it and continued to teach about matters he valued and which were suspect in the eyes of his detractors. With his posture Socrates stands to this day as a beacon of moral fortitude and a shining model of intellectual and moral leadership. Crito encouraged and advised Socrates to escape from prison, through a plan he devised, and in this way avoid an unjustifiable death sentence on account of his ideas. Socrates refused to do so and opted to suffer the fate of death by drinking hemlock (poison). More impressively he took the hemlock and then walked around so that death could come speedily and, in this way, not make the project unduly awkward for his executioners (Plato's Crito, Phaedo and Gorgias).

Conscientious objection can lead people to extreme action and defiance in certain cases. Yet, we see Socrates being a model of how one should go about putting forward one's views no matter how controversial these might be, and then patiently taking the consequences no matter how unfair these were. Simply, the law had to be enforced. As such, Socrates sacrificed himself for his ideas and in the process made him a martyr-model for others, including people in the 21st century AD. He did not opt for, "When I refuse to obey an unjust law, I do not contest the right of the majority to command, but I simply appeal from the sovereignty of the people to the sovereignty of mankind." (de Tocqueville, 1954: 114).

Pragmatism vs idealism in leadership

In Plato's Gorgias we see Socrates supporting moral values once again and setting a precedent for others to follow. We see Callicles (Καλλικλῆς) in debate with Socrates supporting what is now referred to as realpolitik. The Merriam-Webster dictionary defines realpolitik as, "politics based on practical and material factors rather than on theoretical and ethical objectives" (Realpolitik, n.d.). The laws of nature, contends Callicles, favour the strong and as such the strong are entitled to exercise their will over the weak without qualms or restraints. Convention and laws are not of Callicles' concern. What nature allows has precedence over what the law allows. The strong have the right to claim exceptionalism. Nature, claims Callicles, also gives us gifted people with superior abilities who are more determined, more focused, and more courageous than the less gifted. The gifted and strong, therefore, should rule over others and impose their will on them (Plato's Crito, Phaedo and Gorgias). It seems that Callicles was the forerunner of Metternich in some ways!

What Callicles' position meant in practice is this: First. Nature predetermines who is to lead and as such nurture has no place and Second. Once the person nature favours takes the helm there should be nothing wrong in him exercising his power at will. This means leading without any controls and barriers to the leader's will. In such a case idealism goes out of the window just as law and morality disappear from the scene. Leadership is then turned into an exercise of self-interest unless the leader shows compassion towards the led and allows them to have minimal rights. Of course, when the leader's self-interest becomes the focal point almost inevitably disaster for the led and the weak is likely to follow. It is all about how the strong (individuals or countries) use their strength. Michael Burleigh helps us put Callicles' views in the context of modern times and modern strong countries. Writing in

The Times of 18 September, 2018 he suggests, "We must not alienate Turkey's strongman" adding, "President Erdogan may be a nationalist but the West cannot let him fall into Russia's orbit." (Burleigh, 2018). In other words, let the West put self-interest first and forget all about the law and probity. Do not worry about the consequences of a strongman's actions on the weak. As such there should be no place for idealism, justice and fairness that are the declared pillars of the constitutions of western countries.

> *Blind pursuit of self-interest does not serve the cause of moral leadership.*

Socrates opposes Callicles' position and takes the side of the rule of law and convention. To Socrates, the combined will of the demos (of the people) ought to outweigh that of a strong individual whom nature imposes on society. For Socrates the laws of morality should therefore be the source of power. Socratic morality goes counter to the notion of "might is right" that typically prevails in international affairs throughout most of history. This parallel (Callicles vs Socrates) can easily be applied to today's international politics and the power-play of strong nations and the plight of weaker ones. Callicles would have certainly been very comfortable in the world of modern realpolitik, at-will meddling by strong powers in the affairs of weaker countries, regime change and support for internal revolution; not to mention support for outright military interventions and bombings. The Americans use their global power in half of the world under the guise of wanting to bring about democracy to countries that disagree with their policies. Other powerful nations are not any better in this regard, except that their global reach is limited and nowhere near that of America's. At the time of writing Turkey keeps bullying Greece, Cyprus, Syria, Iraq, the Kurds and a host of other weak targets. Strong countries make sure that weak countries know that the former have the will to use their power as necessary "to protect their interests".

> *Though in our day few remember Callicles and all praise Socrates, it is Callicles' legacy of realpolitik and not Socrates' moral code that guides the actions of most powerful countries.*

For some, Socrates' position may even sound idealistic, naive and impractical because it rests on principles and virtues which may sound strange! The good thing is that there will always be voices of reason and people of justice that will somehow contain the latter-day Callicles'. In the main, however, the practical is likely to take precedence over the ideal in today's world politics just as it has always done in history; unless, of course, there is a sea-change in the orientation of politics as we know them today (for an interesting analysis of pragmatism and idealism read Melakopides, 2016).

> *Moral leadership will continue to stand out as the most resplendent of all forms of leadership, even if mocked by some.*

Essay 6: Leadership defined by circumstances

"...a clone would have its own personality, character, intelligence, and talents exactly as identical twins do (who are natural clones stemming from the same egg). You cannot clone a person's brain or mind, and chance factors, the environment, and a person's experiences..." (InfoPlease, n.d.)

History provides us with plenty of examples of people in power that attempted to copy leadership practices of the past but under new circumstances, only to realise the difficulty of doing so considering the situational nature of leadership. The example of Sir Alex Ferguson can help us understand how current and past can blend into effective leadership..

Sir Alex Ferguson: Sir Alex Ferguson, a towering giant in sports, may have had in mind Sir Mud Busby's successful [older] model of leadership when he first took the helm at Manchester United. He was smart enough not to apply it in toto. He was smart enough not to copy exactly a successful model of the past, realising that times had changed. Sir Alex probably first read the new circumstances he was facing and documented the demands these created. He then studied Sir Mud Busby's successful model, adopted some of his practices, dropped some and added many of his own. He then came up with what I call the 'Ferguson model'. Had he tried to copy word for word a successful model of the past he would have certainly failed, no matter how great a leader he later proved to be (Ferguson and Moritz, 2016). One can learn leadership principles and read about leadership practices but one cannot, and in fact should not, try to emulate someone else's style considering that each era brings with it its own particular demands. At any rate, no system can be copied correctly in its entirety. It is said that the biggest insult one can heap on a singer is to tell him that his voice sounds exactly like X's or Y's voice. Firstly, this cannot be and secondly every singer loves his own distinctive voice, wishes to be recognized as such and does not want to sound exactly like someone else.

Educational programmes that aim to help managers, educators, politicians and others to acquire specific leadership skill-sets that were found to be beneficial in the past under varying settings are developed all the time. The internet is full of leadership models that aim to help teach aspiring leaders how to lead. Leadership schools are now found in most universities and other institutions and these also teach students and businessmen how to lead and how to apply specific leadership models and practices. The success of many such programmes has been mixed, because when it comes to implementing practices of the past in defined work settings, one invariably realises that what has been learned in class does not exactly match reality. Experience tells us that there is always a serious transfer-of-learning problem to overcome when it comes to the teaching of leadership. So, there is no one single leadership style that can be taken off the shelf and applied in its entirety. Each leader ought to apply the style that suits him best under the circumstances that prevail at the time he is called to lead.

In Phaedo, Plato warned that we cannot copy the ideal or any perfect form, even if we can visualise how this would look. In the same way we cannot copy exactly an original picture or an original painting (Plato, trans. 2009). This applies to leadership as well. It is simply impossible to define the ideal leader and record precisely his traits and features using a past successful model. Even if we can create a perfect image in our mind of what an ideal leader looks like or should look like we cannot hope to define the ideal leader in words and in 'practical' forms. Was Zhukov the ideal leader? No, Plato would say because no matter how effective and powerful he was as a leader, it would be folly to think of him as an ideal leader in Plato terms. It was impossible for Zhukov to have been perfect and to have met the ideal model characteristics, simply because humans err at times. Was Jefferson the ideal leader? No, Plato would rightly tell us. In fact there is no ideal leader for us to copy fully.

In the same way, we cannot describe fully the exquisite painting "round my house" (вокруг моего дома) in the Pushkin museum in Moscow (not far from where Zhukov's statue now stands) and which fascinates many art lovers. Nor can we draw exactly the Kremlin or the White House, or the Parthenon for that matter, calling the end result an original. We simply cannot describe Zhukov fully and correctly and certainly we cannot describe fully his internal world and emotions. If in doubt the reader can ask people in the street to describe the perfect leader and then compare Zhukov to that description and see how this works out!

> *There is no such thing as an ideal leader considering that the ideal cannot be defined precisely by any man or group of men.*

In the same manner it is almost impossible for any one person to provide the perfect English translation of the Greek word "λόγος». Does the Greek original, "Εν ἀρχῇ ἦν ὁ λόγος, καὶ ὁ λόγος ἦν πρὸς τὸν θεόν, καὶ θεὸς ἦν ο λόγος" translate perfectly and precisely into English as, "In the beginning was the Word, and the Word was with God, and the Word was God." (John 1:1 King James Version)? It would be interesting to ask this question to several learned theologians at the University of Oxford and see what they say. I am sure they will disagree amongst themselves as to the correct (exact) translation. But even if they are to agree that would not mean they managed to get an exact translation from Greek into English. Now try translating the Russian word тоска (toska—pronounced as tahs-kah) into English and you will be faced with this, "toska translates as yearning or ennui. Except that it doesn't, because no English word can accurately reflect all the shades of the word." (the Guardian, 2018). What can toska mean? "Spiritual anguish, a deep pain, perhaps the product of nostalgia or love-sickness, toska is depression plus longing, an unbearable feeling that you need to escape but lack the hope or energy to do so." (The Guardian, 2018).

Essay 7: Leader succession

"Après moi, le déluge" ("after me let the flood come" or "I don't care what happens after I go", King Louis XV of France

One of the most amazing things about leadership is the fact that leaders often get intoxicated with their position and forget that sooner or later they will vacate it for certain: end-of-term, resignation, impeachment and death to mention a few ways. Equally, and just as well, no one knows the time of his death. Consequently, far too many leaders never prepare for their succession, often with catastrophic results. The outstanding work of great leaders can be undone fast by bad succession. Without proper succession it becomes a matter of luck whether or not the work of a great leader survives into the future. Some leaders can take downright irresponsible postures on succession ("Après moi, le déluge"); or perhaps out of haughtiness, overconfidence and a feeling of superiority some do not wish to have a competent person as second in command. Others are threatened by the presence of competent line managers. But proper succession is critical to the long-term survival of the organisation and the state. By tradition ancient Sparta had in place two kings and that guaranteed the smooth running of the country when one of the two had to leave Sparta on a military expedition.

With royalty, succession was more or less guaranteed, though performance was not. Oligarchy provided some guarantee of succession considering that the closed oligarchic circle was often rich in talent. In democracy, succession is guaranteed via the ballot box but this does not always ensure good results. In fact democracy often times produces mediocre leadership, particularly in countries with poor democratic polity and politically immature voters.

The colonial powers of the 19th and 20th centuries, as if by design, left a bad legacy in the area of succession in the countries they ruled. This explains why some post-colonial leaders, who ostensibly won democratic elections at the time of [often turbulent] transition from colonial rule, turned out to be tormentors of their own people. Simply, the structure for proper succession was not there. Here is the example of Milton Obote of Uganda.

Milton Obote: Take Uganda, for example, and what the official Statehouse site says, "It was also to Milton Obote that the very symbolically important National Flag was handed at Independence Day on October 9th, 1962. On the other hand, Obote is held responsible for much of the political and military turmoil, which characterized Uganda in the early years after independence." (Statehouse.go.ug, n.d.)

Here are more examples on the same theme:

Hosni Mubarak, Yorgos Papandreou: Some see succession as a family business. Mubarak was preparing his son to succeed him, but his scheme failed because the Arab Spring erupted at the wrong time for him and collapsed soon after his fall from power. And Mubarak is not alone in this respect. Even in democratic countries such as Greece we saw grand-father, son and grand-child ending up as Prime Ministers in a span of seventy years. And, I am not just referring to the Papandreou family and the disastrous last government of this dynasty. The first two of the Papandreou family to lead Greece were charming and connected well with the people. This helped them immensely to earn voter support. Regrettably, the consensus is that the third one (Yorgos Papandreou) had few if any leadership competencies. Yet, he managed to put the family name to good use to ascend to the Prime Minister's post; only to be overtaken, as was expected, by calamitous economic events he could not handle. He is now unloved and shunned politically, even by his former supporters, and vainly searching for a new political role through rebranding.

Here is what happened in the area of succession after the death of Cyrus the Great:

Cyrus the Great: Going back in history, Xenophon tells us that on the death of the brilliant Persian leader Cyrus the Great, "...no sooner was he [Cyrus] dead than his sons were at strife, cities and nations revolted, and all things began to decay...and first I shall speak of their impiety. In the earlier days, I am aware, the king and those beneath him never failed to keep the oaths they had sworn and fulfil the promises they had given, even to the worst of criminals." (Xenophon, trans. 2012: 191). And, "In other ways also the Persians have degenerated. Noble achievement in the old days was the avenue to fame: the man was honoured who risked his life for the king, or brought a city or nation beneath his way." (Xenophon, trans. 2012: 191)

Here is the tragic aftermath of Alexander's failure to grant succession:

Alexander the Great: Alexander's succession failures must put him on the top of the list of leaders that handed down catastrophe to their people after their own death. Of course he died young (just before reaching the age of thirty-three) and in many ways unexpectedly. But he knew full well the business he was in and the risks this entailed. He also knew full well the risk of dying young whilst in military campaigns in foreign countries that were infested by mosquitoes, sickness and so on. He also knew the dangers of assassination having seen his father Philip assassinated at the age of forty-four. He was fortunate enough to have with him some of the most brilliant generals of all time with the aristocratic general Parmenion leading the pack. Parmenion was the chief of staff of King Philip, Alexander's father. He also had general Cleitus (the Black) whom he 'inherited' again from his father. These and others such as Philotas, Parmenion's son, were leaders par excellence. It is said that Philip wondered aloud how come Athens needed ten generals to run her army whilst he only needed

Parmenion! On merit, Parmenion was maybe more of a general than dozens of other generals put together.

When Alexander left Macedon riding out of the town of Pella with his brothers-in-arms towards Asia, the array of generals must have struck fear in the hearts of their enemies. Many of these militarily brilliant men were his classmates at the Miaza under the stewardship of Aristotle the philosopher and were close childhood friends of Alexander. Nearly all were of aristocratic blood, which also meant military prowess, the result of special training. Quoting Justin (13.1.12), Waterfield notes, "'Never before that time did Macedon, or indeed any other nation, produce so rich a crop of brilliant men, men who had been picked out with such care, first by Philip and then by Alexander, that they seemed chosen less as comrades in arms than as successors to the throne.' Many of these men had known each other since childhood; all of them had bonded in the way soldiers do in the course of a long, hard campaign. But such sentiments could be crushed by personal ambitions." (Waterfield, 2011: 14–15)

In effect, Alexander was the man to sow the seeds of the bloodletting that followed his death by ignoring the important rule of leadership succession. But, what are some of the reasons for this terrible negligence that had catastrophic results and ultimately allowed the Roman armies to attack and dominate the weakened Greeks? Here again Waterfield provides us with some of the answers (Waterfield, 2011: 9–10):

First. There was no obvious heir. Alexander's half-brother Arrhidaeus was incapacitated and sometimes behaved embarrassingly in public. Plus the road to the throne was long and arduous and maybe in the end Arrhidaeus would not have made it even if he were appointed by Alexander because he would have had to meet the following criteria: birth into a royal house, nomination by his brother Alexander, acceptance by the Companions that acted as the inner council most of whom were aristocrats, and lastly acceptance by the army, assembly, and the citizens. Alexander's four-year-old boy Heracles had as mother Barsine, Alexander's mistress who was half Iranian. At any rate Alexander never acknowledged Heracles and never married his mother. So, he was out of the running. His Bactrian wife Rhoxane was pregnant and only months away from delivering. But, here again the child would not be fully Greek.

Second. Alexander never signed or left a will though at some point before his death he could have done so. Maybe he was just irresponsible or egotistical. The only thing he did was to pass the signet ring to Perdicas who was second in command in Babylon.

Third. Though the succession crisis started in Babylon, Babylon was only one of many centres of power. Macedonia was another and there Antipater ruled with an iron fist, if not viciously. So, there were many and varied interests to be taken into account when it came to succession (Waterfield, 2011: 14–15).

Fourth. I will add a fourth, and perhaps the most potent, reason for Alexander's succession failure. Parmenion was dead, victim of an assassin who was treacherously sent by Alexander himself to assassinate Parmenion after Alexander had first arranged for the inhumane torture and killing of General Philotas, Parmenion's brilliant son. Alexander was jealous of popular and competent Parmenion who not only was the most respected and oldest of his generals, his children were also generals and controlled vital military sectors. My view is that, had Parmenion been alive at the time Alexander died, the army in its entirety would have accepted his leadership without a whimper and would have been happy to see him control things until a final solution to the succession issue was found. Equally, Hyphaestion had died only months (324 BC) before Alexander and he too would probably have been acceptable to the army on account that he was second in command and greatly loved by Alexander. Maybe this was a case of posthumous nemesis on Alexander for ruthlessly, ungratefully, and wickedly assassinating Parmenion, his son Philotas, and generals Cletus and Callisthenes; and also a case of bad luck in the case of Hyphaestion's death from illness.

Just to show what happened in the violence that followed from the time Alexander died and which pitted brother against brother for a period of ten to fifteen years after Alexander's death I chose to show below what happened to some of the central players in Alexander's life. This can only be called a shocking catastrophe, especially for Alexander's family that paid a heavy price because of Alexander's thoughtlessness and the emergence of a rabid maniac killer by the name of Cassander (Antipater's son).

Cassander. To emphasise the work of this serial killer I have put his name in italics below.

Members of Alexander's family that were killed after Alexander's death

—Year 309 BC: Alexander IV (son of Alexander the Great): Killed by *Cassander*, to stop him from coming of age.

—Year 309 BC Barsine—Iranian noble and mistress of Alexander and mother to his son Heracles. Killed by *Cassander*.

—Year 309 BC Heracles, Alexander's illegitimate son. Killed by *Cassander*.

—Year 309 BC Rhoxane. Bactrian wife of Alexander. Killed by *Cassander*.

—Year 309 BC Alexander IV, son of Alexander with Rhoxane. Killed along with Rhoxane by *Cassander*.

—Year 309 BC Cleopatra, half sister of Alexander. Killed by Antigonus, Cassander's brother.

—Year 316 BC Olympias, Alexander's mother. Killed by *Cassander*.

—Year 316 BC Thessalonice. Alexander's half sister was captured, then wedded Cassander and later murdered by Antipater, Cassander's father.

—Year 317 BC Arrhidaeus (Philip III). Son of Philip II and half brother of Alexander: Killed on Olympias' (Alexander's mother) orders.

Close friends of Alexander family that were killed after Alexander's death

—Year 316 BC Perdicas, Alexander's second in command, assassinated by his staff officers during a failed river crossing in Egypt in revenge for his role in the assassination of Philotas.

—Year 316 BC Peithon, Alexander's bodyguard. Killed by Antigonus.

—Year 317 BC Eumenes of Cardia, secretary and archivist to Philip and Alexander. Killed by Antigonus.

—Year 320 BC Craterus, Alexander's most trusted marshal. Died in battle with Eumenes.

—Year 323 BC Meleager, Infantry Commander under Alexander. Killed by Perdicas.

—Year 281 BC Lysimachus, Alexander's bodyguard. Killed by Seleucus (Waterfield, 2011: 219–225).

The effects on Hellenism of this succession catastrophe were immense and incalculable even if the Hellenistic Period lasted for some 300 years after Alexander. The spilling of blood amongst Alexander's marshals weakened the Greeks and made them prey to the Romans. Had the Greeks been united, just as they were united during Alexander's life, they would not, in all probability, have allowed the Romans to expand outside their own terrain. "The Hellenistic World in the last thirty or so years of the third century BC has almost always...[been] a preparation for the arrival of the armies of an irresistibly expanding Rome" wrote Roberts and Bennett (Roberts and Bennett, 2012).

Essay 8: Leadership and change

One of the basic tenets of effective leadership is the leader's ability to bring about, and manage, change. Here below are some examples of triumph and failure in this area:

Yeltsin: Yeltsin provides us with a perfect example of a leader that could not manage change and as a result brought near-disaster to Russia. Yeltsin, apparently suffered from excessive consumption of alcohol amongst his other failings, and often brought embarrassment to Russia as a result. For long periods he could hardly control what was going on in Russia and this brought about chaos and thievery and near collapse of the defences of Russia. But, the Russians can only be grateful to him for giving then Putin that quickly went to work and brought about stability, particularly in the defence area, and helped Russians discover their great potential as a nation.

Jiang Zemin: As example of a leader who managed change brilliantly I chose the Chinese leader Jiang Zemin. Jiang led China during a very dangerous period and managed to bring about change without endangering his country. Jiang proved adept at keeping the country together in times of turbulence. China was expected to follow in the heels of Russia and the chaos of the Yeltsin era but Jiang held his nerve and instead of buckling under pressure to abandon socialism overnight, as Russia had done under the incompetence of Yeltsin, he instead adopted a long-term approach to change. This proved to be liberating for his country that is now a global economic powerhouse.

I am referring to the time when the Soviet Union and communism had collapsed and threatened China with unplanned change that would have spelt disaster for the country had it not been for Jiang's leadership. Had the Chinese structure fallen at the time the Soviet Union fell, the effects on Chinese society would have been calamitous to say the least. The Tiananmen Square protests of 1989 provided the fuse for a potential uncontrolled change at the time the Soviet Union was in the process of falling. These two events (collapse of the Soviet Union and the Tiananmen Square protests) taken together could have triggered an avalanche of uncontrolled changes for China.

Jiang Zemin had replaced Zhao Ziyang as General Secretary at the time the two massive changes described above were taking place. In other words he took over at a time when the odds were in favour of China following in Russia's footsteps. Zhao made the error of declaring support for the student movement and this proved lucky for the Chinese as he was bundled out and replaced by Jiang. Regrettably, the student movement was harshly dealt with by the authorities raising justifiable complaints from outside and inside China. At the time, and fortuitously for China, a vacuum had been created because of the diminishing influence of the aging "Eight Elders". Under the circumstances described above Jiang was quick to consolidate his power even if he was considered by most pundits as a stop-gap leader. In no time he became the paramount leader of China for most of the 1990s. He came at a time when political upheaval was on the rise because of the protests and the collapse of the Soviet Union, when behind-the-scenes infighting inside the party was on the rise, and when some outsiders were feverishly fomenting trouble for China.

Jiang showed his mettle when he got the military on his side and quickly dealt with and dispatched troublesome political competition. China is known for having leaders that eliminate opposition quickly and then take full control. The expected purges followed once Jiang assumed the chairmanship of the Central Military Commission. Gradually he managed to replace anyone whose loyalty was suspect. In this way he had his men (many of whom came from Shanghai) in the most critical positions. In his approach he used sound diplomacy and manipulation, successfully wooing those in need of wooing and showing strictness towards those that responded to strictness. This led ex-US Ambassador James Lilley to say that Jiang, "…[is] a good consensus builder, he's a good manipulator."

Let us now see how China faired under Jiang: First. The Chinese economy experienced higher than expected growth. Second. Reforms were introduced to the economy. Third. Hong Kong was returned to China peacefully by the British who were powerless to refuse the return of Hong Kong. Fourth. China regained control of Macau from Portugal. Fifth. China remained stable internally whilst its relationships with outside countries continued to improve. Sixth. External relations were strengthened with the Chinese head of state visiting the USA and the US president visiting China and declaring that there was a non-adversarial relationship between the two countries. Jiang continued his non-confrontational foreign policy until the end; even during the Third Taiwan Straits Crisis, the bombing of Serbia and the Chinese embassy, and the Hainan Island incident in 2001.

China's average GDP growth rate of 8% in the latter part of Jiang's term astonished the world and in many ways opened the path for China to develop into a major economic player in the world. His success rested greatly on the fact that he supported the transformation of China into a market economy without maddeningly destroying the old structures. In other words he thus avoided a Yeltsin-type catastrophe. Unavoidably he had his detractors. He was accused: First. Of causing environmental damage that was the result of his drive for economic growth, and Second. Of accelerating income disparity between the rich and the poor and for creating special interest groups. He was also accused of fomenting corruption inside the class of bureaucrats and party officials. When all is considered, however, the BBC credits Jiang with lifting the pariah slander from China and for bringing social stability whilst pursuing change and economic growth (BBC News, 2004).

> *China under Jiang was a paragon of "dynamic stability",*
> *demonstrating in this way how change and stability can coexist.*

References

BBC News. (2004). Profile: Jiang Zemin. [online] Available at: http://news.bbc.co.uk/2/hi/asia-pacific/1832448.stm [Accessed 8 Nov. 2018].

Burleigh, M. (2018). We must not alienate Turkey's strongman. [online] thetimes.co.uk. Available at: https://www.thetimes.co.uk/article/we-must-not-alienate-turkeys-strongman-vf972nsdf [Accessed 20 Sep. 2018].

Cain, Á. (2018). A look at the daily routine of James Madison, who owned 4,000 books, was too embarrassed to be seen without a hat, and drank up to a pint of whiskey a day. [online] Business Insider. Available at: https://www.businessinsider.com/james-madison-daily-routine-2017-7 [Accessed 24 Jan. 2019].

Cartledge, P. (2005). Alexander the Great. London: Pan Books.

Chaney, O. (1996). Zhukov. Norman, Okla.: University of Oklahoma Press.

Character. (n.d.). In: Merriam-Webster. [online] Available at: https://www.merriam-webster.com/dictionary/character [Accessed 18 May 2018].

Chou Locke, C. (2014). Asking Whether Leaders Are Born or Made Is the Wrong Question. [online] Harvard Business Review. Available at: https://hbr.org/2014/03/asking-whether-leaders-are-born-or-made-is-the-wrong-question [Accessed 1 Sep. 2018].

Ferguson, A. and Moritz, M. (2016). Leading: Learning from Life and My Years at Manchester United. New York: Hachette Books.

Hannay, T. (2014). Nature Versus Nurture. [online] Edge.org. Available at: https://www.edge.org/response-detail/25365 [Accessed 26 Mar. 2019].

InfoPlease. (n.d.). Clones Aren't Exact Copies. [online] Available at: https://www.infoplease.com/science-health/cloning-facts-and-fallacies/clones-arent-exact-copies [Accessed 7 Feb. 2019].

Karlgaard, R. (2019). Peter Drucker On Leadership. [online] Forbes.com. Available at: https://www.forbes.com/2004/11/19/cz_rk_1119drucker.html [Accessed Jan. 2018].

Kennedy, P. (1987). The rise and fall of the great powers. New York, NY: Vintage Books, p.325.

Lepore, J. (2018). These Truths: A History of the United States. New York: W. W. Norton & Company.

MacDermott, J. J. (ed.) (1981). The philosophy of John Dewey. Chicago: University of Chicago Press.

Melakopides, C. (2016). Russia-Cyprus Relations: A Pragmatic Idealist Perspective. New York: Palgrave Macmillan

McDougall, W. (1912). An introduction to social psychology. 4th ed. Boston: John W. Luce et Co.

McLynn, F. (2016). Genghis Khan: His Conquests, His Empire, His Legacy. Boston, MA: Da Capo Press.

Norris, S. T. (2016). Rome Across Europe. [online] Rome Across Europe. Available at: http://www.romeacrosseurope.com/?p=5044 [Accessed 27 Jan. 2019].

Plato. (1958). Socratic Dialogues. Translated and edited by W. D. Woodhead. Introduction by G. C. Field. Edinburgh: Nelson.

Plato. (2009). Phaedo. Translated and edited by D. Gallop. Oxford: Oxford University Press.

Psychology Today. (2019a). Extroversion. [online] Available at: https://www.psychologytoday.com/us/basics/extroversion [Accessed 7 Feb. 2019].

Psychology Today. (2019b). Intelligence. [online] Available at: https://www.psychologytoday.com/us/basics/intelligence [Accessed 7 Feb. 2019].

Realpolitik. (n.d.). In: Merriam-Webster. [online] Available at: https://www.merriam-webster.com/dictionary/realpolitik [Accessed 20 Sep. 2018].

Roberts, M. and Bennett, B. (2012). Twilight of the Hellenistic World. Havertown: Pen and Sword.

Rousseau, J. (1991). The Social Contract and Discourses. Norwalk, CT: Easton Press, p.163.

Statehouse.go.ug. (n.d.). President Apollo Milton Obote | State House Uganda. [online] Available at: http://www.statehouse.go.ug/past-presidents/president-apollo-milton-obote [Accessed 29 Jan. 2019].

Takala, T. (1998). Plato on Leadership. Journal of Business Ethics, 17(7), pp.785-798. Available at: https://www.jstor.org/stable/25073123

The Guardian. (2018). 10 of the best words in the world (that don't translate into English). [online] Available at: https://www.theguardian.com/world/2018/jul/27/10-of-the-best-words-in-the-world-that-dont-translate-into-english [Accessed 23 Nov. 2018].

Tocqueville, A. and Heffner, R. (1956). Democracy in America. New York: New American Library, p.105.

Ulrich, D. (2019). What Is an Effective Leader? [online] Amanet.org. Available at: https://www.amanet.org/training/articles/what-is-an-effective-leader.aspx [Accessed 2 Jan. 2019].

Waterfield, R. (2011). Dividing the Spoils: The War for Alexander the Great's Empire. Oxford: Oxford University Press.

Plato. (1958). Socratic Dialogues. Translated and edited by W. D. Woodhead. Introduction by G. C. Field. Edinburgh: Nelson.
Xenophon. (2012). Cyropaedia: The Education of Cyrus. Translated by Henry Graham Dakyns. Edited by F.M. Stawell. CreateSpace Independent Publishing Platform.

Book 3

The three pillars of leadership

Leadership supposes: a) a leader that is willing to lead, b) leader competence to ensure positive results and c) leader morality to ensure a virtuous milieu.

In this chapter I attempt to simplify leadership down to its basic component parts which are: a) the will to lead, b) leader competence and c) leader morality.

1.) Will to lead. Societies and organisations get their leaders from the ranks of those who are willing to come forward and lead. Not all that have leadership potential come forward to lead nor do all that come forward have the wherewithal to lead effectively. Because the will to lead is driven by many diverse motives one should not, therefore, assume that those coming forward are necessarily driven by pure and selfless motives, that they are competent, or that they are moral.

2.) Leader performance. For a leader to stay in power and to be given a chance to continue leading he ought to demonstrate high levels of performance and ability to meet at least some of the core needs of the led. Otherwise he will fail no matter how willing and moral he proves to be. An incompetent elected leader may hold on to power for the remainder of his term of office but this will not guarantee him respect. In time he will join the ranks of the ignominious.

3.) Leader morality. Willingness to lead and high leader performance are likely to elevate a leader to stardom but are unlikely to keep him there in the memories of the led. In the long term, good leadership needs leader morality. Leaders that fail the test of morality also fail to leave a legacy of good leadership. Because morality is not an easy construct to define and because the lines between moral, amoral and immoral are sometimes blurred some amoral and immoral leaders get away with their wicket practices; but not for long. In the end history calls their bluff and as soon as this happens they speedily glide down from their pedestal into the ranks of the disdained.

Three leaders that in my view personify each of these three virtues are: Xenophon (willingness to lead), Marshal Zhukov (competence) and Nelson Mandela (morality). In fact, each of these three great men meets, to varying degrees, all three criteria of leadership and not just one. I assigned each of the above three leaders to one specific criterion for purposes of highlighting the specific criterion via an example from history.

Essay 1: The will to lead

The March of the Ten Thousand

"The true test of a leader is whether his followers will adhere to his cause from their own volition, enduring the most arduous hardships without being forced to do so, and remaining steadfast in the moments of greatest peril" Xenophon (Xenophon quotes, 2019)

Here is leadership par excellence, particularly as regards the quality of coming forward to lead.

Xenophon: The life of Xenophon is a favorite subject of mine. In my public lectures I never tire of talking about the Athenian Xenophon because I am of the view that his feat must be made known in every corner of the world, to help people learn how to take control of their lives. Xenophon (a friend of Socrates) was a remarkable man. He was born circa 330 BC, at the start of the Peloponnesian War between Athens and Sparta, and grew up during Greece's worst period of internecine conflict. When he came of age he probably (or certainly, rather) took part in this terrible civil war. The war lasted for nearly 30 years and saw brother fight brother. Xenophon loved both his native Athens as well as Sparta. So, one can imagine Xenophon's torment as he saw two Greek cities fighting each other, and indeed when he himself had to engage in action, fighting on the side of Athens against Sparta, the city he admired and loved. (Kagan, 2003)

Xenophon. Leader of men par excellence! Volunteered to lead to safety some 10,000 fellow-Greek warriors that were trapped in the lands of the Persian Empire and who had literally no hope. Any other leader in Xenophon's position would most likely have surrendered but this never crossed Xenophon's mind. The fact that he was in his twenties when he undertook this gargantuan task takes his achievements beyond the human. He was a very decent and fair man and of an exemplary character. Friend of Socrates the philosopher as well.

Here is what Xenophon did that catapulted him to the heights of leadership and keeps him there to this day. After first consulting with Socrates and after putting a loaded question to the Oracle, he got permission to join the expedition of about ten thousand Greek mercenaries to fight on the side of Cyrus, the younger brother of the newly-installed King of Persia, Artaxerxes. Cyrus was the governor (satrap) of Asia Minor and its environs and had good relations with the Greeks. When he invited them to help him he never told them that his real aim was to overthrow his brother Artaxerxes (with the tacit approval of their mother Queen Parysates). Instead, he told the Greeks that he was preparing to fight some rebellious tribes.

At any rate, Xenophon joined the Greek mercenary force and gave battle on the side of Cyrus. Cyrus was killed right at the start of the first engagement, at Cunaxa. Then the two Persian senior officers that were with the Greeks and Cyrus played dirty and changed sides. As such, after the death of Cyrus the Greeks were stranded in enemy territory, without money, without supplies, without allies, and with the King's mighty army ready to have a go at them. It is important to note that despite Cyrus' death the Greeks were undefeated and with their command structure intact. The Persian governor (or satrap) of the territory in which the Greek army was stranded pledged peace to the Greeks. The perfidious satrap then invited the Greek generals to his tent. A total of five Greek generals, twenty captains and two hundred soldiers went to the meeting. The five generals were immediately arrested, "tried" and executed. The captains were murdered and the soldiers cut down. So, the Greeks were basically headless, destitute and abandoned by everyone except their weapons and their bravery. Most importantly, even if stranded they were undefeated. They were now in great need of new leadership.

Xenophon, probably 26–28 years old at that time, stepped forward and was elected as one of the five new generals. Xenophon in the rear and the Spartan General Chirisophus in the van succeeded in taking the Greeks back to Greece over a distance of about 1,600 kilometers through enemy territory, freezing weather, with low and inadequate food supplies and sicknesses. Of the ten thousand soldiers about eight thousand six hundred made it back. The rest fell victim to death (in action), frost bite and sundry illnesses including blindness. This was an extraordinary feat for such a large force to achieve, particularly as they had lost their original generals and had just voted in new leadership. (Xenophon, The Persian Expedition)

How did Xenophon achieve this daunting feat? Well, this is what he did:

1. He spoke to the troops and made them believe that the only way to survive was to win every challenge and every skirmish and battle and to overcome every threat and obstacle. This they did.

2. He managed to form alliances with local tribes as he marched out of Persian territory. He employed diplomacy and a heavy dose of common sense. In this way he avoided unnecessary fighting and enmity.

3. Although in a position of military leadership, he never abandoned his belief in democratic polity, putting most controversial decisions to the vote, and winning the outcome on account of his power to convince.

4. He created harmony and, with the exception of one incident, he never came to conflict with his fellow general, the able Spartan Chirisophus.

5. He employed impeccable management and leadership skills that saved the day; particularly whenever the Greeks experienced a reverse.

6. He displayed honesty, transparency and speckless behaviour.

7. He showed valour and the will to lead and win.

8. He was a model of selflessness. He never kept anything just for himself, and in fact by the end of the campaign he ended up as one of the poorest of the lot though much loot was gathered by the Greek army after so many victories.

> *Xenophon refused to surrender and came forward to lead his people out of a totally hopeless situation which would have caused anyone else in his position to capitulate.*

Essay 2: Leader performance

Here is another example of leadership par excellence particularly as regards performance:

Georgy Zhukov. It took more than two thousand years before the world could see through Zhukov a military leader of the likes of Alexander the Great. Words of praise for this great leader seem superfluous; his actions speak volumes. The world will probably have to wait for a long time before another Zhukov comes along.

Marshal Zhukov. Zhukov was about 45 years old when the Soviet front was first attacked on 22 June, 1941. Seeing he was born to relative poverty in a peasant family one can imagine what he had to endure and what leadership skills he needed to display to end up as the Soviet Union's supreme soldier. Not only did he have to escape poverty, he also had to escape Stalin's hatchet men. He did so through a miraculous appointment away from Moscow, just as he was about to be arrested during that horrible period of the purges in the mid-late nineteen-thirties. The Soviet military establishment thought that he was the right man to break the stalemate between the Soviet and the Japanese armies and as such was sent from Moscow to Khalkhin-Gol. Not only did he break the stalemate but he also crushed the Japanese forces. This catapulted his career to dizzying heights and began his unique relationship with Stalin, who envied Zhukov but at the same time was fond of him.

Soon after WWII, and whilst at the top of the military hierarchy, he found himself accused (vengefully) of Bonapartism. As a result he was demoted by Stalin to the Command of the Odessa Military District. All this happened about one year after Zhukov's triumphant military parade on victory day in Moscow at the end of WWII. He was slandered by some but more so by the Soviet Union's perhaps most loathed pair: Lavrentiy Beria and Victor Abakumov who headed internal security. Both these two were executed soon after their protector, Stalin, died. Zhukov was accused of "...plotting with others against the Soviet leader (Stalin); he unjustly relieved senior commanders; he sanctioned 'vicious' regulations; he conferred on himself credit for many wartime victories and played down the role of Stalin. They also denounced him because several well-known generals—Chuikov [Vasily Ivanovich Chuikov of Stalingrad fame] and Mikhail Katukov and others—called themselves 'Zhukov men' rather than 'Stalin men' ". (Chaney, 1996: 369)

Stalin was envious of Zhukov as Zhukov was the only man in the Soviet Union Stalin could not touch without fear of fatal consequences. Zhukov earned great loyalty from his fellow officers, some of whom proved to be great strategists in their own right. One such loyal fellow officer was General Vasily Chuikov, Zhukov's friend and comrade at Stalingrad. Here is what the New York Times had to say about Vasily Chuikov in an obituary column, "Marshal Vasily I. Chuikov, who led his troops in the defense of Stalingrad that turned the fortunes of Hitler's army, died Thursday at the age of 82, his family said today." And the New York Times continued, "The German defeat was a turning point in the war. Soviet morale soared. General Chuikov went on to lead his troops into the Donets Basin, then the Crimea and on into Byelorussia before spearheading the Soviet drive on the Eastern Front that ended in the heart of Berlin." (The New York Times, 1982)

During WWII Zhukov was the man of the hour and the marshal who would not surrender an inch unless this was part of a strategy. He would be called to go anywhere there was danger and anywhere where the Soviet forces found it difficult to stop a Nazi offensive: Leningrad, Moscow, Stalingrad, Kursk, etc. Hardly ever did Zhukov entertain the thought of retreat. He began to show his mettle from a young age and from the time he was called to do military service (conscripted) in 1915 during WWI. He was wounded a year later and again in 1919. At 33, he attended the advanced senior officers' course at Frunze Academy in Moscow. He then rose to the position of Chief of General Staff of the Soviet Army and later Deputy Defence Commissar. In the same year he became member of the Stavka (Supreme Command). In 1943, some two years into the war, he rose to the rank of Marshal of the Soviet Union just before he had organised the counter offensive in Stalingrad. In 1943, he coordinated action in the Central, Bryansk, and Western fronts and oversaw the battle of Kursk. In the next year he was in Ukraine to coordinate the First and Second Ukrainian Fronts as well as the

First and Second Belorussian Fronts and assumed command of the First Polish Army in preparation for his advance to Berlin. Zhukov was literally everywhere. He was the first to enter Berlin with his troops and after the fall of the city he became a member of the Allied Control Council. Then he became commander of all Soviet forces. Later he was briefly Minister of Defence until he retired in 1958. (Chaney, 1996: 485–488).

Writing about the siege of Leningrad, which according to the New York Times was one of the most horrific and heroic episodes in human history, Harrison E. Salisbury noted, "By the second of September [1941] von Leeb's Army Group Nord was driving on Leningrad for the kill...von Leeb felt victory within his grasp. The Fuhrer seemed pleased and graciously honoured him with awards and congratulations on his sixty-fifth birthday. The ageing Field Marshal had every reason to believe that he was on the verge of a success which would crown his earlier achievements in breaking the Maginot Line and occupying the Sudeten...The role of Army Group Nord had been clearly spelled out. It would wheel south after capturing Leningrad and approach Moscow from the rear." (Salisbury, 2000: 316). But, von Leeb's hopes were to be dashed since he first had to overcome the strategies of a military genius in the form of Georgi Zhukov. Unluckily for von Leeb, Stalin had sent Zhukov to Leningrad to take over in the midst of crisis. "The arrival of Zhukov and the change in command did nothing to lessen the threat to Leningrad." (Salisbury, 2000: 322). The arrival of winter convinced von Leeb to retreat from the area of Leningrad. Hitler relieved him of his post soon after, on 18 January, 1942.

Things gradually began to change and the city of Leningrad was ultimately saved. Zhukov put his customary tough and even ruthless command to work. He reorganized his command with indescribable efficiency and without much regard to feelings. Only one thing was on his mind: to save Leningrad. So, one of the first things he did was to pack off to Moscow the chief of operations,

Colonel Korkodin. He soon fired the commander of the 42nd army, Major General F. S. Ivanov. He then removed those he felt were not up to the job and assigned tasks to others. Some pages later Harrison E. Salisbury writes, "Zhukov had won. Leningrad had won. But no one knew this yet. von Leeb was still trying frantically to grasp victory, to break into the city..." (Salisbury, 2000: 348)

Zhukov was omnipresent and Leningrad was simply one of his stops, "...Zhukov had won the military battle of Leningrad. Within weeks troops from Leningrad would be on their way to help stem the German tide before Moscow." (Salisbury, 2000: 351). "The next evening the telephone rang in Zhukov's offices in Smolny. It was Stalin...'turn your command over to your deputy and come to Moscow' Stalin ordered." (Salisbury, 2000: 351). And, "In the early morning hours Zhukov flew off to take over command of the Battle of Moscow." (Salisbury, 2000: 352).

> *Zhukov was a results-oriented leader of massive capabilities that had only one thing in mind: to save his country from military defeat and destruction.*

Essay 3: Leader morality

"While the lion prevails with its claws, and the ox through its horns, man does by his thinking" Anaxagoras of Klazomenae, 5th century BC
(In Greek: "Λέων μὲν ὄνυξι κρατεῖ, κέρασι δὲ βοῦς, ἄνθρωπος δὲ νῷ")

Here is an example of leader morality and how one man saved a country from civil war and potential catastrophe.

Nelson Mandela. His enormous leadership qualities saved South Africa from almost certain civil war and as such averted a catastrophe that was in the making. Big-hearted, high-minded and magnanimous.

Nelson Mandela: Mandela's greatest accomplishment was the simple fact that he always behaved as expected and had no pretences. No theatre, no show and no facade. Mandela is now synonymous with overcoming oppression and adversity. He did not shelter hatred and vengeance against his former oppressors. He was one of the finest leaders in the ANC that was fighting to bring apartheid to an end, though much of his leadership was from the Robben Island prison where he was incarcerated for most of his productive years. He was the shining example of a virtuous leader, even if at times he was accused of incompetence and of turning a blind eye to ANC excesses. His erstwhile opponent and at times tormentor, the last white president of South Africa Frederik de Klerk, called Mandela in 2013 a humane and compassionate man. He then went on to say, "Uniting South Africa was Mandela's greatest accomplishment." (Reuters, 2013)

Undoubtedly Mandela's thinking gravitated towards morality and fairness despite some of his failings and the controversial positions he adopted at times. Mandela started off as a pacifist, and then graduated into a militant revolutionary. He then went back to pacifism and ultimately became one of the 20th century's most revered statesmen. The late Nelson Mandela was a man of forgiveness and held the highest standards of fairness. On this score he would probably put in the shade many other presidents and world leaders of his generation. His greatest achievement was first transiting the country into a pluralist state, avoiding civil war in those first difficult years and convincing as many whites as he could not to leave South Africa, taking their skills with them. The Truth and Reconciliation Commission which he established to investigate human rights abuses under apartheid was instrumental in averting civil war and certain bloodshed. In the end, most people from all ethnic groups in South Africa saw Mandela as their father. As president of South Africa he worked openly and steadily with all sides and this gave him the high moral ground vis-à-vis those who were conniving. We can reasonably say that he had, "... no fellowship with the unfruitful works of darkness, but rather reprove[d] them." (Ephesians 5:11, King James Version)

According to Anthony Sampson, Mandela's official biographer, Mandela accomplished some great things for his people in post-apartheid South Africa and helped them lead better lives. His administration connected poor people's dwellings with telephone lines, gave them safe drinking water, got children into the education system, organized clinics and improved housing amongst many other things. (Sampson, 2000)

> *Mandela displayed great moral leadership. He saw every man as equal in the eyes of God and helped turn a country full of social disparities and hatred into one of equal opportunities, after first saving the country from the prospect of catastrophe.*

Developments in South Africa since Mandela's retirement from politics are beginning to take a toll on his legacy. What is happening now in South Africa certainly would not have made Mandela proud of most of his successors. The country is now riddled with corruption and violence in towns and remote farms that are ruining people's lives and confidence in government and the country. Many whites are migrating to safer and more stable places taking their skills with them. The country's annual homicide numbers are staggering and frightening as these hover around 20,000 killings per year. These figures are typically seen in times of war; certainly not in times of peace. The language of hatred is beginning to be heard loud and clear from the mouths of hotheads, with the government unable to stop this. Mandela preached love and understanding which are now both in short supply in certain sectors of South African society. This is clearly not what Mandela had in mind when he talked about a new beginning of inclusiveness and prosperity. Do all these developments point to poor leader succession that this treatise considers a bad leader quality? Has Mandela failed to groom a worthy successor or is South Africa merely experiencing the effects of a faulty democratic polity that breeds corruption and incompetence?

Essay 4: Courage—the platform on which the three pillars stand

Anyone who bet money on Themistocles, Pausanias, Xenophon and Zhukov prevailing must have made millions from each bet.

With the caveat that "no leader is without blemish" I just noted above my admiration for Xenophon stressing his willingness to lead, Zhukov for his effectiveness and Mandela for his morality. But, I admire many other leaders as well, and more particularly those who show exemplary courage as they face daunting challenges and threats. Below I will mention a handful of my leadership heroes just to demonstrate the importance of courage in leadership. I will mention these leaders in historic sequence: Themistocles (leader at the battle of Salamis), Pausanias (leader at the Battle of Plataea), Xenophon (again). Later I will mention Parmenion (Alexander's legendary general). Jefferson (third president of the United States) and others. Courage is a necessary condition for good leadership, but not sufficient.

> *The pillars of leadership stand on courage because without courage there's simply no outstanding leadership.*

Great leaders display fortitude. They are not discouraged or disheartened when the odds are stacked heavily against them. Two such leaders of fortitude were Themistocles of Salamis and Pausanias of Plataea. These two great leaders were instrumental in successfully defending Western civilization some two and half millennia ago. Their victories allowed us to enjoy Western values to this day. Here is how things developed in these two epic battles under two great leaders.

Themistocles: The place was Salamis. It was the first time that the Persians heard from Greek ships what Aeschylus called 'a mighty battle cry' that was the paean (lyric poem expressing triumph and thanksgiving). Admiral Evriviades of Sparta (ally of the Athenians) sounded his trumpet signalling the start of the battle. This was repeated by the trumpets of the generals and echoed back by the crews of the Greek triremes (ships). This is how the Battle of Salamis started in 480 BC in which the Persians were the odds on favourites (1,000 to 1 perhaps) to win. (Strauss, 2005: 157). This is the paean in English and Greek that fired up the Greeks:

"O sons of the Greeks advance:

Liberate the fatherland, liberate

Your children, your women, and the abodes

Of your ancestral gods and the graves

Of your ancestors. Now is the battle for them all!" (Strauss, 2005: 163–164)

(Greek: «Ω, παίδες Ελλήνων, ίτε, ελευθερούτε πατρίδ', ελευθερούτε δε παίδας, γυναίκας, θεών τε πατρώων έδη, θήκας τε προγόνων` νυν υπέρ πάντων αγών». (Aeschylus, Persians: 402–405)

An assembly of about one thousand Persian ships and an army from a Persian alliance of some forty countries, according to Herodotus in his 8th book, descended on Greece to teach the Greek upstarts a lesson. The Athenians fled Athens and congregated on the small island of Salamis off Athens with some 200–300 triremes; all in the narrow straights of Salamis. The Persians got word that the Greek navy would escape at night so they, "...expected to catch the cowardly Greeks in the act of sneaking out of their harbour on Salamis during the night, which is why the entire Persian fleet has been deployed in darkness in the straits. Not a Greek ship had budged..." (Strauss, 2005: 157)

"On the far side of the straits, the first sign of trouble for the Persians was an unexpected sound from the Greek harbours. 'A song-like shout sounded triumphantly from the Greeks,' reports Aeschylus, 'and at the same time, the island's rocks returned the high-pitched echo. This was the paean." (Strauss, 2005: 160) The Persians had heard the paean before at Artemisium and Thermopylae and they were destined to hear it again a year later at Plataea. The Persians beat defenceless foes in Euboea, Phocis, and Attica; now they were up against a cunning and more determined foe. In the end the Persian King Xerxes, who was viewing the battle from his throne on a nearby hill, turned to go back to Persia after witnessing the humiliation of his navy and that of his allies, the Phoenicians.

With the help of a modern metaphor I would say that any person that had visited a betting shop in those days and placed a wager in favour of the Greeks winning this battle would have made millions. The odds were totally stacked against the Greeks: a small Greek force versus the largest military machine in the world at the time, that was supported by some Greek traitors including a former Spartan king, Demaratus, that had accompanied the Persians to Greece hoping to be reinstated on the Spartan throne. Artemisia was another Greek traitor who proved to be the best fighter on the Persian side. The Greeks looked trapped inside the straits of Salamis with no room for retreat or escape. So how did the Greeks manage to defeat the powerful Persians? Here is the answer: The Greeks won mostly on account of the brilliance of one man who refused to surrender: the Athenian admiral Themistocles whose name we mention several times in this treatise.

> *Themistocles refused to surrender despite the heavy odds against him.*
> *He met the danger head on, fought, and won.*

Having been humiliated by the Greeks in the battle of Salamis (480 BC) the Persian king and much of his army left Greece leaving behind, in the territory north of Athens, General Mardonius of Persia (nephew and son-in-law of King Cyrus) to continue what they thought would be an easy fight on land, considering the strength of the Persians relative to that of the Greeks. Mardonius and his army had their opportunity at Plataea in the summer of 479 BC, a year after the battle of Salamis. Here again the Persians were crushed by the Greeks under the leadership of Pausanias the young Spartan general and nephew of King Leonidas. The Persian fleet that had retreated to the eastern Aegean Sea after the defeat at Salamis was also crushed in the same year (479 BC).

Pausanias. The despicable traitors of the Greek cause at Plataea were the Theban leadership, that were more than happy to help Mardonius establish his base at Plataea, in the general vicinity of Thebes. The Greek army assembled on the hills not far from the Persian camp. Neither of the two sides were willing to make the first move but in the end the battle was forced on the Greeks when Greek supply routes were blocked and water supplies were put in danger due to Persian activity. The Greeks moved to a new position but the move was not a total success leading Mardonius to attack what he saw as a disorganized Greek army. This was exactly the chance the Greeks needed: a fight at close quarters. Mardonius was killed by the Spartans. As was the case in other similar situations the leaderless Persians took to flight. In the ensuring chase by the Greeks the Persians suffered huge and horrific losses and probably lost one-third to one-half of the Persian army, which at the start of the battle was at least three times that of the Greeks. Fighting between Greeks and Persians continued for many more years, but the Persians never invaded Greece again after Plataea. Salamis and Plataea were enough to teach the Persians what the spirit of a free and determined people can do.

How did this happen? Again it was mostly down to one man and his leadership: General-regent of Sparta, Pausanias. Pausanias was acting in place of his first cousin Pleistarchus, son of Leonidas who was still a minor. Herodotus tells us that the Greek combatants numbered nearly 110,000. "The Barbarians...numbered 300,000. The number of Greeks allied to Mardonius [Greek traitors and those Greeks that were forced to side with Persia] ...at a guess, I would estimate there to have been some 50,000 of them gathered there." (Herodotus, trans. 2013): 602–603). Therefore, a total of 350,000 on the Persian side.

Here is what Herodotus had to say about Pausanias, "...the fairest victory of any known to us was won by Pausanias, the son of Cleombrotus, the son of Anaxandridas." (Herodotus, trans. 2013: 616). Pausanias commanded the largest Greek force ever assembled until that time, and fought an army at least three times the size of his own army, and with massive assets and reserves at the disposal of the Persians.

> *General Pausanias assumed the leadership of the Greeks when he was still in his mid-late twenties and not for a moment did he shy away from responsibility. His victory at Plataea is deemed by many to have saved western civilisation.*

Effective leadership takes courage. There comes a time when leaders have to decide existential matters for their country, their organisations and their teams. Under such conditions some are overtaken by fear and anxiety which leads them to surrender to the forces that threaten them. Others stand up to the threat and meet the challenge; they refuse to surrender. In modern history Churchill owes his reputation to the fact that he refused to surrender during WWII. The President of tiny Cyprus Tassos Papadopoulos made his mark as leader in April, 2014 when he stood up to powerful forces that pressured and indeed threatened him and his people to force him to agree to support a sham plan that would have meant the demise of the Republic of Cyprus and the surrender of the indigenous population of Cyprus to outside forces and more particularly to Turkey. This single courageous act earned him a special place in the history of Hellenism.

References

Strauss, B. (2005). The battle of salamis. New York: Simon & Schuster.

Herotodus. (2013). The Histories. A new translation by Tom Holland. Introduction by Paul Cartledge. New London: Penguin Classics.

Xenophon quotes. (2019). BrainyQuote. [online] Available at: https://www.brainyquote.com/quotes/xenophon_144993 [Accessed 15 Jan. 2019].

Kagan, R. (2003). The Peloponnesian War. London: Penguin Books.

Xenophon. (1972). The Persian Expedition. Translated by Rex Warner. Introduction by George Cawkwell. London: Penguin Books.

Chaney, O. (1996). Zhukov. Norman, OK: University of Oklahoma Press.

The New York Times. (1982). Marshal Vasily Chuikov, 82, Dies; Commanded Stalingrad's Defense. [online] Available at: https://www.nytimes.com/1982/03/20/obituaries/marshal-vasily-chuikov-82-dies-commanded-stalingrad-s-defense.html [Accessed 4 Jul. 2018].

Salisbury H. E. (2000). The 900 Days: The Siege of Leningrad. London: Pan Books.

Reuters. (2013). Uniting South Africa was Mandela's greatest accomplishment: de Klerk. [online] Available at: https://www.reuters.com/article/us-mandela-deklerk/uniting-south-africa-was-mandelas-greatest-accomplishment-de-klerk-idUSBRE9B41DZ20131205 [Accessed 27 Oct. 2018].

Sampson, A. (2000). Mandela: The Authorized Biography. New York: Vintage Books.

Book 4

Morality is routinely sidelined for the sake of performance.

> *Leaders that are consumed by a desire to win at any cost routinely sideline morality.*

In this book I will attempt to demonstrate the ease with which high performing leaders put morality by the side once they begin to engage in what they view as a life or death contest for supremacy. Morality, in effect, is turned into collateral damage for as long as the contest lasts. In rare cases morality is restored after the contest is won. I have written four essays in this book. The first two essays cover Stalin as a high performer but in many ways an amoral autocrat. The other two cover Mao, a highly successful leader who was mesmerised by the need to bring about change at any cost. Both these leaders mellowed once their objectives were achieved [largely] through cruelty. In fact, at the end of their lives both began to revisit morality which they had earlier thrown out of the window.

Efficiency and despotism

One does not have to be highly moral to be an effective leader. But, morality is essential not only for its own right but also as a teaching tool for future generations. Stalin serves as a good example of a largely amoral leader that was the cause of some of the world's greatest excesses against his fellow men but who was at the same time the personification of efficiency under the most daunting conditions during WWII. What he achieved during his long reign as head of the Soviet Union stands out as a monument to his ability to perform great feats. In his time the Soviet Union's achievements began to raise doubts in the minds of some of the staunchest supporters of capitalism over whether a command economy was superior to a free market one. After Stalin's death the country found it hard to continue in his path; and the post-Stalin Soviet administrations were, on balance, more humane. In the end, and in just over three decades after Stalin's death, the country began to show severe signs of strain that ultimately led to the Soviet Union's demise and break-up. The question of whether the Soviet Union could have survived had a "new" Stalin replaced the "old" Stalin remains unanswered and will probably remain so forever.

Efficiency and revolutionary leadership

Among Stalin's supporters some put forward the argument that Stalin needed to employ harshness because the country was going through life or death challenges that had to be met one way or another. An irreversible military loss during WWII would have meant the end of the Soviet Union. China had different but equally daunting experiences to those of the Soviet Union. China was the victim of a catastrophic invasion by the Japanese that lasted for more than a decade. China also had to content with internecine contests and in-fighting between warlords who were trying to protect their own selfish interests, caring little about China. Stalin had to defend the country against external enemies that were poised to capture the Soviet Union. Mao had to content with foreign occupation, recessionary activities that were fomented by warlords and, worse perhaps, widespread poverty which plagued the majority of the population, many of whom died of starvation. Both Stalin and Mao fought a revolution and also a war against invaders and then indulged in serious nation-building exercises. In this regard Mao employed some of Stalin's cruel practices to achieve his three objectives. Like Stalin, he managed in the end to bring to the country many positive economic and other social changes. In fact, he laid the foundations for China's future. Unlike Stalin, Mao managed to give China prospects and continuity and a momentum for economic growth hardly seen before. Now China is an economic powerhouse, and by all forecasts will soon lead the world financially for decades to come. Stalin's Soviet Union is now history but Russia is still a major world power and a military giant.

Essay 1: Leader performance and morality

"In the Soviet army it takes more courage to retreat than advance." Joseph Stalin.

Not many leaders put morality before performance, especially if they consider morality to be an impediment to performance.

Stalin: Debate.org ran a digital questionnaire with this question: "Was Stalin a good leader?" The responses to this question were an impressive 62% yes and 38% no. What were more interesting were the comments and justifications that followed these findings. The following comment by a "yes" respondent summarises well how many saw Stalin as leader: "Sometimes you have to be bad" wrote a respondent. In other words Stalin had to be bad for the sake of performance and for the benefit of the Soviet Union.

Lenin died in 1924. From 1929 to 1953 Joseph Stalin was the undisputed leader of the USSR. He took a poverty-stricken Soviet Union and turned it into an industrial and military superpower using deplorable cruelty and cunning, but also employing practices that led to high performance. In the period in which Lenin was incapacitated and coming to the end of his life, Stalin manoeuvred himself into the best position to 'outwit' his opponents to the leadership. In the end he succeeded. Lenin had described Stalin as brash and arrogant; that is exactly what Stalin was. He continued to employ cunning throughout the rest of his life. Many people admire Stalin not for his ethics, but for his performance and effectiveness as leader. In the view of many the Soviet Union's power during the era of Stalin stands as monument to his stewardship of the vast Soviet Union. (Debate.org, 2018)

In our drive to demonstrate the chasm between performance and morality in leadership what better place to start than Stalin? When Stalin was asked by Lenin to carry out what in our days is known as 'organisational restructuring' and 'rationalisation', the latter's instructions to Stalin were, 'replace intelligence with efficiency'. Not much different to William F. Buckley Junior's memorable and remarkable contempt for theoretical and impractical approaches, "I'd rather be governed by the first 2,000 names in the Boston telephone directory than by the faculty of Harvard." (Robinson, 2008)

Here is the profile of one of Stalin's appointees, Lazar Kaganovich: aged thirty, profession: shoemaker (Stalin's father was a cobbler), education: semi-literate. Main virtue: extremely hard working. This selection tells us right at the outset about Stalin's great concern with efficiency and his aversion to too much sophistication. Another great in the area of performance, former President Nixon, wanted first loyalty, which he saw as necessary if he were to be efficient as President. Nixon's lieutenants Ehrlichman and Haldeman recorded the President's orders on what to look for in people that were candidates for appointment, "Foreign Service appointments—based first on loyalty then competence." And, "Not brains, we want loyalty" (Reeves, 2001: 547).

A 2006 survey showed that 47% of Russians saw Stalin in a positive light, even if he was Georgian and not Russian, ruthless, an exterminator in the 1930s, exiler of innocent people to the gulags and deporter in cattle trucks of minorities of all forms. In time, and in more than two decades of rule, Stalin managed to put Lenin in the shade, rendering him of little contemporary relevance to the affairs of the Soviet Union. (Walker, 2008).

Here is what the New York Times had to say about Stalin and his qualities in an obituary:

Stalin, the high achiever: "During the second World War, Stalin personally led his country's vast armed forces to victory. When Germany was defeated, he pushed his country's frontiers to their greatest extent and fostered the creation of a buffer belt of Marxist-oriented satellite states from Korea across Eurasia to the Baltic Sea. Probably no other man ever exercised so much influence over so wide a region. In the late Nineteen Forties, when an alarmed world, predominantly non-Communist, saw no end to the rapid advance of the Soviet Union and her satellites, there was a hasty and frightened grouping of forces to form a battle line against the Marxist advance. Stalin stood on the Elbe in Europe and on the Yalu in Asia. Opposed to him stood the United States, keystone in the arch of non-Marxist states."

Stalin, the practical and results-focused leader: "Stalin took and kept the power in his country through a mixture of character, guile and good luck. He outlasted his country's intellectuals, if indeed, he did not contrive to have them shot, and he wore down the theoreticians and dreamers. He could exercise great charm when he wanted to."

Stalin and concern for psychological distance: "But the Stalin that the world knew best was hard, mysterious, aloof and rude. He had a large element of the Oriental in him; he was once called "Genghis Khan with a telephone" and he spent much of his life nurturing the conspiracies that brought him to power and kept him there."

Stalin the man of steel (Стал in Russian means steel): "Although he remained an enigma to the outside world to the very end of his days, Stalin's role as Russia's leader in the war brought him the admiration and high praise of Allied leaders, including

President Roosevelt and Winston Churchill. And, indeed, only a man of iron will and determination like Stalin's could have held together his shattered country during that period of the war when German armies had overrun huge portions of Russian territory and swept to the gates of Moscow, Leningrad and the Caucasus. Like Churchill in England, Stalin never faltered, not even at moments when everything seemed lost."

Stalin the masterful executive: "Surrounded by a galaxy of brilliant generals, whose names will go down in history as among the greatest of Russia's military leaders, Stalin was portrayed in the Soviet and foreign press as the supreme commander responsible for overall strategy. To what extent this was true will have to be determined by the future historian, but that his role in the conduct of the war was paramount is undeniable."

Stalin the transformer and innovator: "Not since the days of Peter the Great, who sought to westernise Russia by force, had the country witnessed so violent a transformation. In fact, nothing in the history of revolutions could compare with the gigantic social and economic upheaval brought about under Stalin." (The New York Times, 1953).

What else would a panel of judges need to have before declaring Stalin a brilliant planner and effective executive (and executioner most would say)? He could also be charming if this served his objective. Even President Harry Truman was taken by him and memorably stated that he liked old Joe, whom he saw as a decent fellow and more or less a victim of bad counsel coming from the Politburo.

For some, the most contemptuous act of Stalin was his appointment of a brutal man like Beria to lead his intelligence service which in the end was chiefly responsible for the execution of thousands of innocent people. But here again, Stalin was driven by efficiency when he appointed a workhorse like Beria, to whom he also assigned the task of developing the Soviet nuclear bomb after what had happened to Hiroshima in 1945. True to form Beria delivered the bomb before any harm could come to the Soviet Union from people like the Dulles brothers in the American Administration. Radzinsky writes, "It was to Beria and his secret departments that the Boss had thought it best to entrust the creation of the bomb. In this context Beria was like Molotov in his diplomatic activity—merely a workhorse driven by the Boss." (Radzinsky, trans. 1996: 513)

Stalin the amoral: Discounting exaggeration and bias that one sees in the following quote from The Daily Telegraph the objective observer understands that Stalin was poor on morality, "Posterity has been kind to Stalin. His crimes are already sinking into oblivion, whereas his great rival, Hitler, has rightly become uniquely synonymous with radical evil. We recall the Holocaust or Shoah in countless ways, and all the nations that fought or were occupied by the Nazis commemorate their dead. Where are the memorials to Stalin's nameless victims? Historians do not even agree about their numbers; more are constantly discovered as new evidence comes to light. At a conservative estimate, Stalin was directly responsible for the deaths of some 20 million. Indirectly, the totalitarian communism of which Stalin was the chief architect has so far killed up to 100 million around the world. By comparison, the Nazis' victims numbered about 25 million. Why is there still such an imbalance in our judgment of the two great tyrannies of the past century? In part, this has to do with Stalin's role in the victory over Hitler: the gratitude of the Western allies to 'Uncle Joe' was sincere. Another factor is the uniqueness of the Holocaust, which overshadowed all other crimes against humanity. Few consider that Stalin, too, was a racist, indeed an extreme anti-Semite. In the 1930s, he established a Jewish state, Birobidzhan, on the Chinese border. By 1953, Jews were being arrested, tried and shot throughout his empire, and it seems that he intended to deport the entire Soviet Jewish population to perish in Siberia and

Kazakhstan: a fate that had already befallen many others, including the Volga Germans, Crimean Tartars and Chechens." (The Telegraph, 2003).

Edward Radzinsky, an unkind biographer of Stalin, had this to say about the Soviet Union under the more than two decades brutality of Stalin. Though some of the events below do not fall directly under Stalin, the picture given is vivid enough to make the reader shudder. Radzinsky describes the plight of one distinguished family that was the victim of Soviet-era violence en masse. What happened to the members of this illustrious family will not leave the reader unmoved; I am sure of that from personal experience.

Radzinsky writes, "Perestroika arrived, Gorbachev came to power, people began reviewing what they had lived through. I received a letter: My name is Yuri Nikolaevich Pepelyaev. I have long been curious about my family. Can you possibly give me detailed information about my relatives, and in particular:

—Pepelyaev, N. M. Major General in the tsar's army, killed 1916, in the First World War.

–Pepelyaev, V.N. President of the Council of Ministers in Kolchak's government, shot in 1920 at Irkutsk.

–Pepelyaev, A. N. Lieutenant General, commanded Kolchak's First Siberian Army, then fought in the Far East, was forced to surrender. Sentenced to death and shot in 1938.

–Pepelyaev, L. N. White officer, killed during the Civil War.

–Pepelyaev, M. N. Staff Captain in the tsar's army, convicted in 1933, died in prison camp.

–Pepelyaev, A. N. Surgeon in Kolchak's army, tried and convicted 1942, died in Siblag [a prison camp] in 1946.

– Pepelyaev, A. I. Member of the Socialist Revolutionary Party, shot by the Cheka at Perm in 1918.

–Pepelyaev, M. E. My grandfather, resident at Blisk, tried and convicted in the thirties.

–Pepelyaev, M. I. Resident at Blisk, killed in the great Patriotic War [World War II]." (Radzinsky, trans. 1996: 581–582)

A poll by the Russian independent Levada Center showed Stalin and Putin both receiving positive ratings and majority approval. Stalin's shine comes mainly from his role in winning WWII and turning the USSR into a superpower. (Sharkov, 2017). It would of course be a travesty of justice to confuse Putin with Stalin. Putin won several democratically-run national elections by a large margin and his popularity is a matter of record and undisputed in the eyes of the independent observer. Putin's name amongst most Russians and an array of foreigners stands very high, considering the relentless harangue and polemic he is subjected to from some sources in the West. Also, Putin is considered by a plurality of people around the world as a man possessing enormous leadership qualities, which are in short supply in many countries.

Margaret MacMillan writes on Stalin, "The Tartars ruled over the Russian heartland for 250 years yet, unlike the Moors in Spain, said Pushkin, 'having conquered Russia they gave her neither algebra nor Aristotle.' Its vulnerability had left Russia another legacy in the centralized and authoritarian government which finally emerged. In the early twelfth century in the first work of Russian history, the people of Rus in today's Ukraine are described as inviting a potential ruler: 'Our whole land is great and rich, but there is no order in it. Come to rule and reign over us.' Putin has recently made the same justification for Stalin in Russian history— that he and his regime were necessary to hold Russia together in the face of the challenges from its enemies. A related consequence was Russia's unending search for security by pushing its frontiers outwards." (MacMillan, 2013: 194).

Indeed, Russian history is all about Russia's search for security, its fight to keep the country safe from aggressive enemies and its pursuit to maintain a common identity with the aid of institutions such as the church, the army, central government, etc. The

Stalin (L). Probably twentieth century's most controversial, fascinating, loved and hated at the same time figure, personification of efficiency but also of violence, master of incredulity who at the same time gave hope and caused despair to his people. A malevolent pragmatist who is credited with building a nation that struck feared in the hearts of all aggressors. In his time the economy of the Soviet Union registered one of the world's highest growth rates, yet, his people had to wait in mile-long queues just to buy a loaf of bread. Stalin (the man of steel/сталь) oversaw the liberation from Nazi occupation of most of Europe during the great Patriotic War (Вели́кая Оте́чественная война́) sacrificing in the process over twenty-five million Soviets. Yet he failed to get the West to admit to this glaring fact.

fatherland is above everything for Russians. President Putin is well aware of Russia's existential battles and the need to fight (see Napoleon's invasion of Russia, Operation Barbarossa, etc) and the difficulty of managing a vast country. Like former Russian leaders he sometimes adopts practices that look to outsiders (and insiders) as hard or even heavy-handed. But Putin is certainly not what some try to make him out to be. Evidently, he is not some dictator who came to power through the barrel of a gun. Nor is he running Russia like some dictator of the likes of the former Shah of Iran whom, incidentally, the West elevated to power as a suppliant ally of those who had set their eyes on Iranian oil. (On the elevation of the Shah into leadership and the overthrow in a coup of Mosaddegh read Kinzer, 2003).

Russia has a long history of assessing her leaders against performance measures and more particularly on their demonstrated ability to keeping Russia safe. More than two hundred years ago Peter The Great (1672–1725) asked one of Russia's most respected and objective advisors, Prince Jacob Dolgoruky (Russia's Cato) how his achievements as Tsar compared to those of his father Tsar Alexis. Prince Dolgoruky assessed father and son against three performance factors: a) administration of the country and the dispensation of justice. Apparently Alexis did better than Peter because he had more time to spend on these matters, b) organisation of a regular army. Apparently Alexis laid the foundations of the army until some misguided people undid his work and Peter had to start all over again. The outcome of the war (that was waged then) was to decide who was best, said Prince Dolgoruky, and c) building of the fleet, making treaties, and determination of relations with foreign countries (external relations). Apparently Dolgoruky rated Peter higher than Alexis on the third factor. So, here we see the Tsar being judged on largely measurable performance indices centring largely on defence. Security was clearly central to Dolgoruky's appraisal system. (Massie, 1980: 747–8).

Russia rarely shies away from adopting outside institutions to help her build a strong society and defend against outside invaders. The Greeks gave the Russians their religion which helped them stand together under the banner of the Eastern Orthodox Church and to fight invaders under this banner. The institution of the church is powerful in Russia and Greece to this day and gives both countries faith to suffer and overcome adversity. Faith is very strong in both these countries according to the Economist of June 2, 2017, "...the veneration of saintly remains is a huge phenomenon..." in both Greece and Russia. (The Economist, 2017)

In judging Stalin and his post-WWII image as portrayed by his detractors in the West, one ought to remember that some in the US administration and [most maybe] in the British Foreign Office viewed the Soviet Union with disdain and wished for its demise. Stalin and partners knew all about this and prepared for the worst, particularly in the period when America had monopoly of the bomb. The Dulles brothers (John Foster and Allen) were everywhere in the American establishment, planning some dreadful Nazi-esque acts against the Soviet people, just as Hitler had planned against the Jews; forgetting that the Soviets were allies of the USA during WWII. These were two brothers who ran in parallel US foreign policy, the CIA, and its covert operations. In fact, some believe that these two would not have blinked an eyelid dropping an atomic device on Moscow and other large Russian population centres just to prove who the boss was; reminding us of Hitler's plans for the total devastation of Leningrad and Moscow. The machinations of the Dulles brothers were enough to create paranoia in normal people, let alone in the super-suspicious and cunning Stalin.

General Eisenhower was in the main liked by the Soviet establishment and Zhukov in particular, who saw him as an honest partner. General Eisenhower in turn held Zhukov in high esteem particularly as a great Marshal of the Soviet Union. Writing within the spirit of the times Kinzer claimed that after the death of Eisenhower, "They [John Foster Dulles, incoming secretary of state and brother Allen, the incoming intelligence director] were among the fiercest of Cold Warriors. They viewed the world as an ideological battleground and saw every local conflict through, the prism of the great East-West confrontation. In their eyes, any country not decisively allied with the United States was a potential enemy. They considered Iran especially dangerous." (Kinzer, 2003: 4). "The Dulles brothers believed there was a serious danger that... [Iran] would soon fall to communism...their proposal to overthrow Mosaddegh and replace him with a reliably pro-Western prime minister..." (Kinzer, 2003: 4). "...on January 20, 1953, John Foster Dulles and Allen Dulles told their British counterparts that they were ready to move against [serving prime minister] Mosaddegh... To direct it, they chose a CIA officer with considerable experience in the Middle East, Kermit Roosevelt, a grandson of President Theodore Roosevelt." (Kinzer, 2003: 4). One last comment: Iran is in Russia's neighbourhood. (For further reading about the Dulles brothers read Kinzer, 2013)

Writing on 24 May, 2018, Andrew Glass said this about John Foster Dulles: "Although he advocated the doctrine of 'massive retaliation' against the Soviet Union, Dulles never believed it would come to that; he thought that the Soviets when faced with annihilation would back away from an intercontinental nuclear exchange." (Glass, 2018). Good to notice the term 'annihilation'" in the language of John Foster Dulles!

Essay 2: Efficient despot-leader

"You have your way. I have my way. As for the right way, the correct way, and the only way, it does not exist."
— Friedrich Wilhelm Nietzsche

Stalin. Under Stalin the Soviet Union was an undisputed superpower that had achieved epic feats in industry and industrialization, science, music, the arts, culture, and the military. In space, the first Sputnik was launched in the 1950s, and the Soviets were well on their way to becoming the custodians of a formidable nuclear arsenal. In many ways this was a clear victory of efficiency, often at the expense of morality. Of course, there were catastrophic errors of judgment as well; not to mention illusions and fantasies about the power of the command economy.

Here is what happened during Stalin's time, or soon after, mostly as a result of Stalin's relentless effort to make the country powerful:

Food supplies:

1. The world's first seed vault to fight starvation and recover lost seeds and plants was established, though the storage of crops was terribly inefficient.
2. Monster tractors made their appearance in agriculture and ploughed vast tracts of land, in this way spelling the

demise of horse energy that had dominated agriculture for hundreds of years.

3. In the post WWII period, the USSR was among the world's most industrially active countries.

Education:

1. The country was transformed into the world's most literate nation, marking probably the Soviet's most laudable achievement. Russia's 99% literacy rate of today bears testimony to the success of earlier programmes.
2. The density of tertiary educated people to total population was one of the highest in the world and continues to apply to this day. Many Moscow taxi drivers know more about Sophocles, Euripides and Pericles than some university graduates in other countries.
3. The level of military and aviation technology as well as the scientific prowess of the country continue to impress to this day.
4. Russia's legendary computer literacy levels are in many ways the product of the scientific ethos that was built during Soviet times.

Medicine and the sciences

1. Great advances in medicine and particularly virology were made in Soviet times.
2. Mortality rates were reduced significantly.
3. Universal health care was introduced for the benefit of every citizen.

Safety and security

1. With Zhukov in command, Stalin put an end to Japan's dreams of dominating Mongolia.
2. With the Great Patriotic War, Stalin, Zhukov and co put an end to aggressive Nazi expansion and saved Europe and Britain(!) from catastrophe. The Nazi army was destroyed in Belorussia, the Ukraine and the Russian Soviet Republic. The losses of the Nazis outside the USSR theatre were comparatively small.
3. The USSR welcomed Jews to fight the Nazis and gave them protection in Eastern Europe to the highest level possible.
4. Helped in the colonial liberation of many countries in Africa and Asia.

Social and religion

1. Safety in Soviet streets was the world's highest. Anyone could walk in the streets of Moscow at any time of the night, never having to worry about being mugged or molested.
2. The Muslim republics were convinced to shed any idea of religious fanaticism. This was an outstanding achievement.
3. Women were great beneficiaries of Soviet laws: equality of sexes, women in management positions, the military and medicine; at a time when many women in the West were fighting for their rights.
4. Work was guaranteed for all, and unemployment in the 1930s was unknown.
5. Fertility rates were up, and the population grew.

Space and technology

1. In the space race success followed success.
2. First man and woman in space: Yuri Gagarin and Valentina Tereshkova.
3. First to walk in space and first multiple crew.
4. First to exit earth's orbit and first to orbit the moon and Venus, and first to reach Mars.
5. First to put a space station into orbit.
6. First water spaceship recycling system.
7. First closed-water recycling system for space ships.
8. Many direct technological applications that improved people's lives and enhanced knowledge.
9. The Soviets had the world's biggest hydroelectric plant and truck factory, along with the trans-Siberian railroad. (Carey, 2011)

"The capacity of the Russians for suffering and sacrifice, whether in war or in the endless wait in long lines to buy food is something that still awes foreigners. The ability to focus enormous talent and energy on grand projects is equally awesome. These qualities lay behind the Soviet Union's impressive achievements in science, weaponry and construction." (Schmemann, 1991)

Serge Schmemann wrote in 1991, "And yet the Soviet Union was also an indisputable superpower, a state and a people that achieved epic feats in science, warfare, even culture. Perhaps all this was achieved despite Communism, not because of it. Yet by some combination of force and inspiration, the system begun by Lenin and carried out by Stalin unleashed a potent national energy that made possible the rapid industrialization of the 1930s, the defeat of Nazi Germany in the 1940s, the launching of the first Sputnik in the 1950s, the creation of a nuclear arsenal in the 1960s and 1970s. Even now, for all the chaos in the land, two astronauts, Aleksandr A.

Volkov and Sergei Krikalev, continue to circle the globe." (Schmemann, 1991)

The unprecedented surrender of Field Marshal von Paulus at Stalingrad in 1943 and the capture of Stalin's son Yakov by the Germans give us a first-class opportunity to see an important side of Stalin's leadership. Count Bernadotte of the Red Cross [murdered on 17 September, 1948 by members of the Jewish Stern Gang, some 70 years ago] approached Molotov with an offer to exchange Yakov for Paulus. Stalin refused to swap a marshal for a soldier; it did not matter that the soldier was his own son. Stalin said that all Soviet soldiers were his sons and that he could not discriminate. Stalin's detractors said that his reply was loveless cruelty. But this piece of propaganda does not detract from Stalin's exemplary act. One wonders what Churchill and Roosevelt might have done under such circumstances. The story of John McCain (son of Admiral McCain), who was given the opportunity of freedom after spending five and a half terrible years as a Vietnamese captive, is not the same. McCain responded that "I just knew it wasn't the right thing to do" then added: "I knew that they wouldn't have offered it to me if I hadn't been the son of an admiral." Irrespective of motive, John McCain's response was heroic and laudable, and helped raise the morale of his fellow fighters. (Rappaport, 1999: 72)

Stalin gave this explanation for the position he took over his son's captivity: "Just think how many sons ended in camps! Who would swap them for Paulus? Were they worse than Yakov? What would I have said to the millions of Party fathers if, having forgotten about them, I had agreed to swapping Yakov? I would no longer be Stalin." Yakov's daughter Gulia believes Stalin 'did the right thing". So does Stalin's daughter Svetlana. On 14 April 1943, in a POW camp near Lübeck Yakov, who courageously refused to cooperate with the Germans, committed suicide by throwing himself on the camp wire. Stalin was proud of the way his son behaved. But fate treated Yakov unjustly, said Stalin.

Stalin's position not to exchange a marshal for a soldier has other precedents, one of which is the American Civil War of 1860. After the First Battle of Manassas, in 1861, Garrison tells us, the leaders of the two sides wished to exchange prisoners, so they referred to an official agreement between governments in the War of 1812. In February 1862 the two sides agreed on the "Compensation of men and officers", which applied largely throughout the war and stipulated: "The basis for exchange is man for man and officer for officer, men and officers of lower grades to be exchanged for officers of a higher grade, and men and officers of different services to be exchanged." (Garrison, 2000: 105). This basically meant: one Commanding General = sixty privates. One Colonel = fifteen privates . One Major = eight privates . One Captain = six privates . One Lieutenant = four privates and One Sergeant = two privates . So it appears Stalin's position vis-à-vis his son was not about "loveless cruelty" but rather about bravery and laudable behaviour. One minor (or perhaps major) reason why many Russians still remember [cruel] Stalin fondly!

Essay 3: Efficient revolutionary-leader

"A revolution is not a dinner party, or writing an essay, or painting a picture, or doing embroidery; it cannot be so refined, so leisurely and gentle, so temperate, kind, courteous, restrained, and magnanimous. A revolution is an insurrection, an act of violence by which one class overthrows another." Mao Zedong (Mao, 1965: 28)

Mao Zedong. Here is Mao's story as leader. A Chinese poll on Mao Zedong and his legacy of 1,045 eighteen-year olds or older in Beijing, Shanghai, Guangzhou, Chengdu, Xi'an, Changsha and Shenyang by the Global Times newspaper, brought out some interesting facts. The results showed Mao mostly in a favourable light, but less so in the eyes of the young and more educated. About 85% of respondents said that "…his achievements outweigh his mistakes." Fairness and turning the country around ranked first and second as Mao's greatest achievements. It seems that people were ready to forgive him for the ten years of chaos in the 60s when he was implementing his Cultural Revolution and for the hardships that the revival of the spirit of the late 40s had caused. (Aljazeera.com, 2013).

Mao was a Chinese communist leader who founded the People's Republic of China. He was an efficient but ruthless leader who sometimes implemented disastrous policies at great human cost. Despite the element of inhumanity, often coupled with recklessness, his achievements are admired by many to this day. For some that reminisce about communism he continues to be an icon. Some of these achievements were:

1. Helped set up a state out of a half-colonised and feudal China.
2. Dealt with an assortment of greedy people who exploited and deprived the poor and brought them to the point of destitution.
3. Gave respect to the poor, who were treated by the privileged in China like landless animals: beaten and threatened by the landlords.
4. Gave respect to a nation that had been humiliated by the Japanese invasion.
5. Put an end to warfare and killing that was caused by warlords fighting for expansion of their landholdings. The

deaths of the poor at the hands of one or the other warlord were considered at the time as simple collateral damage.

6. On the one side was Chiang Kai-shek who was more interested in consolidating his position as the most powerful warlord rather than fighting or resisting the Japanese army. In effect, with his inaction Chiang had helped the Japanese plan for an invasion of Manchuria, China's North-Eastern province. On the other side was Mao who built a well-disciplined communist Chinese army that obeyed orders. Mao forbade the army from stealing from the peasants and stopped army rape, arbitrary imprisonment, beatings and atrocities. The contrast between the two men was glaring.

7. While the Nationalist Party of Chiang Kai-shek was fighting the Chinese Communist Party to keep them out of power, Mao was fighting the Japanese, who had invaded China (1931–1945). He then organised his army and defeated Chiang Kai-shek, who left the country soon after the Japanese defeat in 1945.

8. Mao achieved the unification of the country and established a central government that now controls all of China; a massive achievement considering the "tribal" history of China.

9. Introduced industrialisation and set up many infrastructure, engineering and energy projects just to mention a few of his achievements in the area of industrialisation.

10. Dealt successfully with the great problem of vaccination that in the end saved so many lives.

11. Managed to stay away from the West-East conflict.

12. Gained a seat for China in the UN Security Council while not being a major participant in WWII.

13. Partly on account of Mao's earlier work the poorly educated Chinese of earlier days today rank high in the PISA and TIMMS education performance tables.

14. Got the number of children attending school from 20% to 80%, thanks to literacy campaigns and the integration of the education system up to tertiary level. By the time Mao died in 1976 a billion Chinese could read and write.

15. Supported women's liberation at a time when women were a trader's item, and brought in gender equality.

In a 23 December, 2013 report under the title "China Media: Mao Zedong's Legacy" the BBC quoted Professor Ai who had earlier said in his lecture at the Taiyuan University of Science and Technology that, "During the Cultural Revolution, there was a satellite space launch, a successful missile test and a nuclear submarine launch. During the Cultural Revolution, we defeated Soviet revisionism, entered the United Nations and established diplomatic relations with more than 60 countries" (BBC News, 2013)

Here below are excerpts from Mao's obituary in The New York Times which highlights some of Mao's major achievements:

"In Chinese terms, he ranked with Chin Shih-huang, the first Emperor, who unified China in 221 BC, and was the man Chairman Mao most liked to compare himself to. With incredible perseverance and consummately conceived strategy, he harnessed the forces of agrarian discontent and nationalism to turn a tiny band of peasants into an army of millions, which he led to victory throughout China in 1949 after 20 years of fighting. Along the way the army fought battles as big as Stalingrad and suffered through a heroic march as long as Alexander's."

"A Chinese patriot, a combative revolutionary, a fervent evangelist, a Marxist theorist, a soldier, a statesman and poet... Like many Chinese of the past 100 years, angered by the insults of imperialism, he wanted to tear China down to make it stronger. He envisioned creating in China an egalitarian, revolutionary utopia in which mass enthusiasm provided the motive force." (Butterfield,1976)

Essay 4: A case of performance with reduced concern for morality

Mao. Though Mao's legacy divides opinion to this day he is generally considered to have been one of the most influential thinkers of the 20th century. Equally, despite his great achievements he is held responsible for the horrible consequences of the Cultural Revolution he launched in 1966 and which saw millions of people go into manual labour contrary to their will and thousands eliminated on the accusation of engaging in "counter revolutionary" activity.

The New York Times report to which we referred above continued, "At the same time he brooked no opposition to his control. To consolidate his new regime in the early 50s he launched a campaign in which hundreds of thousands were executed. In the late 50s, despite criticism from other party leaders, he ordered the Great Leap Forward, ultimately causing widespread disruption and food shortages. Throughout his years in power he toppled one of his rivals after another in the party. In the Cultural Revolution he risked throwing the country into chaos."

And "...above all Mao was a moralist who deeply believed, as have Chinese since Confucius, that man's goodness must come ahead of his mere economic progress." (Butterfield, 1976)

The Guardian made the following remarks about Mao in its 8 September, 2016 report,

"The economy was crippled and up to 45 million people are believed to have died in The Great Famine caused by Mao's catastrophic Great Leap Forward push for breakneck industrialisation in the late 1950s. Up to two million more lives are thought to have been lost in the tumultuous decade-long Cultural Revolution..." (Phillips, 2016)

Tom Phillips reported in 2016 that despite what Mao did in the Great Leap Forward and the Cultural Revolution which saw millions killed, people remember him as a revolutionary who led the drive to make China great. The resurgent China we see today and the pride this engenders in the Chinese is to a large extent the result of Mao's past work. (Phillips, 2016). (See also Wasserstrom, 2016)

Speaking in 1956 of the future of China 45 years after 1956, Mao said: "She [China] will have undergone an even greater change. She will become a powerful socialist country. And that is as it should be...But we must be modest — not only now, but forty-five years hence as well. We should always be modest. In our international relations, we Chinese people should get rid of great-power chauvinism resolutely, thoroughly, wholly and completely." (Mao, 1996: 144–145). Good advice from Mao and very prophetic as well considering what is going on in China today.

References

Aljazeera.com. (2013). Mao's achievements 'outweigh' mistakes: poll. [online] Available at: https://www.aljazeera.com/news/asia-pacific/2013/12/mao-achievements-outweigh-mistakes-poll-2013122553410272409.html [Accessed 26 Dec. 2018].

Butterfield, F. (1976). Mao Tse-Tung: Father of Chinese Revolution. [online] The New York Times. Available at: https://archive.nytimes.com/www.nytimes.com/learning/general/onthisday/bday/1226.html [Accessed 18 Jun. 2018].

Carey, G. (2011). Why Russia won the space race. [online] The Telegraph. Available at: https://www.telegraph.co.uk/culture/tvandradio/8437995/George-Carey-Why-Russia-won-the-space-race.html [Accessed 12 Oct. 2018].

Debate.org. (2018). Was Stalin a good leader? [online] Available at: https://www.debate.org/opinions/was-stalin-a-good-leader [Accessed 11 Oct. 2018].

Garrison, W. (2000). The Unknown Civil War. Nashville, Tennessee: Cumberland Publishing House.

Kinzer, S. (2003). All the Shah's Men: An American Coup and the Roots of Middle East Terror. Hoboken, New Jersey: John Wiley & Sons.

Massie, R. (1980). Peter the Great his life and work. New York: Ballantine Books. 1980.

MacMillan, M. (2013). The war that ended peace. New York: Random House.

Mao, T. (1965). Report on an Investigation of the Peasant Movement in Hunan. In: Selected Works of Mao Tse-tung:

Volume 1, 1st ed. Peking: People's Publishing House, pp.23–59. Also available online at: https://www.marxists.org/reference/archive/mao/selected-works/volume-1/index.htm.

Mao, T. (1996). Quotations from chairman Mao Tse-tung. Introduction by Maurice Meisner. Norwark, Connecticut: Easton Press.

Phillips, T. (2016). Great Helmsman or ruinous dictator? China remembers Mao, 40 years after death. [online] The Guardian. Available at: https://www.theguardian.com/world/2016/sep/08/great-helmsman-dictator-china-anniversary-mao-40-years-after-death [Accessed 18 Jun. 2018].

Radzinsky, E. (1996). Stalin: The First In-Depth Biography Based on Explosive New Documents from Russia's Secret Archives. Translation by H. T. Willetts. New York: Doubleday.

Rappaport, H. (1999). Joseph Stalin: A Biographical Companion. Santa Barbara, California: ABC-CLIO Publishers.

Reeves, R. (2001). President Nixon: Alone in the White House. New York: Simon & Schuster.

Robinson, P. (2008). Milton Friedman, Ronald Reagan And William F. Buckley Jr. [online] Forbes.com. Available at: https://www.forbes.com/2008/12/11/friedman-reagan-buckley-oped-cx_pr_1212robinson.html [Accessed 11 Oct. 2018].

Sharkov, D. (2017). Stalin more popular than Putin, Russians say. [online] Newsweek. Available at: https://www.newsweek.com/putin-behind-stalin-top-russias-most-outstanding-people-poll-629032 [Accessed 26 Jun. 2018].

The Economist. (2017). In Greece and Russia, the veneration of saintly remains is a huge phenomenon. [online] Available at: https://www.economist.com/erasmus/2017/06/02/in-greece-and-russia-the-veneration-of-saintly-remains-is-a-huge-phenomenon [Accessed 1 Feb. 2019].

The New York Times (1953). Stalin Rose From Czarist Oppression to Transform Russia Into Mighty Socialist State. [online] Available at:

https://archive.nytimes.com/www.nytimes.com/learning/gener al/onthisday/bday/1221.html [Accessed 18 Jun. 2018].

The Telegraph. (2003). Stalin's legacy. [online] Available at: https:// www.telegraph.co.uk/comment/telegraph-view/3588394/Stalins -legacy.html [Accessed 18 Jun. 2018].

Walker, S. (2008). The Big Question: Why is Stalin still popular in Russia, despite the. [online] The Independent. Available at: https://www.independent.co.uk/news/world/europe/the-big-question-why-is-stalin-still-popular-in-russia-despite-the-brutality-of-his-regime-827654.html [Accessed 16 Jun. 2018].

Wasserstrom, J. (ed.). (2016). The Oxford illustrated history of modern China. Oxford: Oxford University Press.

Book 5

Self-induced fall from grace

It is remarkable how easily leaders induce their own fall from grace by being hubristic, thinking that they are untouchable and that the world owes them and their families.

In this Book I will attempt to show through examples how remarkably easy it is for leaders (even great leaders) to fall from grace through their greed for money and power and/or hubristic behaviour, inviting many people to disrespect them and to even wish them ruin. Hubristic behaviour can continue even after the period the leader is in office. In fact, some such leaders become haughtier once they leave office than they were before, considering that there is less public scrutiny over their behaviour.

Leader achievements and vices

Even leaders that have all three of the fundamentals for leadership, that is: a) willingness to lead, b) performance and c) morality can in

Alexander the Great. The Greek legendary king Alexander that fully deserves the title of Great. Through his successful campaigns he spread Hellenistic thought and ideals to the "ends of the world and the Great Outer Sea".

the end fall from grace if they are not careful. Somehow, they manage to leave a shadow over their leadership as if destined to fall from grace. They simply fall victim to their vices considering that hardly any leader can claim to be vice-free. Alexander the Great was generally of a good nature and was not amoral yet his tendency to drink heavily, his apparent envy of the successes of other leaders in his team and his wish to remain as 'the one and only', a god, tarnished his image even if he continues to be considered as probably the greatest leader of all time. His achievements speak for themselves and defy imagination. His strategic mind, speed and boldness go beyond human bounds, his single-mindedness and his focus on objectives are beyond belief. Alexander was a man of nous but with strong and often catastrophic vices.

Achievement and love of money

Money can easily corrupt the consciousness of great men and in the end ruin their legacy that was built on their great successes. Depending on one's view of the corrupting effect on leaders of greed for money, one could even go as far as to say that the relentless search for money and personal wealth and power touches the bounds of moral profligacy. This explains why leaders with substantial wealth that was gained during or after they had assumed office are looked down upon by people with high (and sometimes pure) moral standards. On the other hand there are those who do not mind leaders growing wealthy after leaving office and do not care that these leaders are exploiting the influence which they have on account of formerly holding high office. Some even consider such leaders smart, even if laden with greed, forgetting that what these leaders do is capitalise on the mantle their followers provided them by voting them into office in the past. They are in a way exploiters of the favour extended to them by the voters and their supporters. Be this as it may and considering the arguments on both sides, the fact remains that in the minds of those with very strict standards of morality, the practice of leaders capitalising financially on the platform the voter provided them is, certainly in this author's mind, unsavoury to say the least and in most cases a blot on the leader's personality and legacy.

Hubris, pride, vanity, and modesty

"Pride goeth before destruction, and a haughty spirit before a fall." (Proverbs 16:18 King James Version). It is amazing how much this piece from the Proverbs applies to so many leaders. History is full of examples of leaders with great achievements who ultimately fell from grace because of their own less-than-intelligent, and almost morose, actions whilst in office or after leaving office. I am writing about leaders that fell victim to pride and to a feeling of being "untouchable". In fact, the mind boggles at the ease with which otherwise smart leaders fall into this trap.

Here are a few examples of hubris.

Richard Nixon. Richard Nixon was a political genius, as judged from his work. Yet, Richard Nixon fell victim to hubris and pride and got punished for that. Nixon could have gone to gaol had he not resigned in time and received a pardon. Other US presidents before him did worse things but were lucky enough to not be caught and as such escaped the ignominy and embarrassment Nixon had to endure up to his last days.

Pausanias. Pausanias of Sparta literally saved Western civilization from being overrun from the East and won a battle of unthinkable and unimaginable proportions. Yet, in the end he was disgraced through his own actions such as adopting Persian dress and enjoying most of what was prohibited by mother-Sparta and the Greek fatherland. The man that was brought up on a Spartan diet of two plates of wheat soup a day and nothing else so that he could strengthen his Spartan discipline through frugality, ended up enjoying Persian banquets and dress. This unacceptable behaviour of this magnificent leader was exploited by those who had an axe to grind against him and his family of kings. This kind of recklessness is not limited to politicians or generals. We regularly see heads of commercial businesses and financial institutions end up in prison on account of overstepping their authority, routinely and stupidly thinking that they are "untouchable".

Essay 1: Leader achievements and vices

"...Alexander became in various countries and at various times a hero, a quasi-holy man, a Christian saint, a new Achilles, a philosopher, a scientist, a prophet, and a visionary." (Cartledge, 2005: 3)

Here is an example of hubris that was displayed by a leader that has been an icon to millions over the last two millennia.

Alexander the Great. Alexander is for many the epitome of leadership as measured by achievement. But he also did some terrible things in his time. He fell victim to the soul-destroying vice of envy and was prey to "the one and only" syndrome that often afflicts great leaders. (Cartledge, 2005). Alexander had it all and behaved in an exemplary manner towards his friends and associates until hubris engulfed him. Alexander had all he needed to become a successful hereditary Macedonian leader: education, guidance and counsel, except that he was envious not only of his deceased father King Philip, but also of other powerful and able generals in his own army. He was also of a suspicious nature, maybe because assassinations were the rule in his time. Suspicion caused him to betray in the most revolting fashion the trust of his close comrades and brothers-in-arms. His victims were his childhood friends and classmates and not lesser than him in leadership qualities. They were his greatest asset at a time of continuous warfare far away from their Greek fatherland.

But Alexander became intoxicated by victory, and pride overtook him. Most importantly he was consumed by envy and fear. After all his father was assassinated in his early forties and this would have weighed heavily on him. Here is what happened as regards Alexander's change in character.

1. At the start of the Persian campaign Callisthenes praised Alexander, but as the army moved on into Asia Callisthenes began to have second thoughts about Alexander. He saw that Alexander was fickle in some things and enjoyed praise and glorification.

2. Once the aggrandizement process set in, Alexander allowed more and more flatterers to surround him. Flatterers then began to foul-mouth Alexander's real or imagined "antagonists", gradually turning him vengeful against them.

3. Now full of himself, Alexander went into a state of hubris, envy and hatred against those that actually or presumably posed or could pose a challenge. Gradually but steadily Alexander was becoming neurotic and paranoid.

4. Ultimately he lashed out at the targets of his envy (Philotas and Parmenion for example) with catastrophic long-term results for the Greeks.

5. Philotas' assassination set in motion negative emotions in the rank and file which culminated in the death of Perdicas, who had played a treacherous role in the Philotas affair. Perdicas was later killed by his own troops in revenge for his treachery against the brave and able Philotas.

6. Alexander did not stop after killing Philotas. Almost immediately after he went on to assassinate Philotas' distinguished and universally esteemed father for fear of a rebellion against him on account of the injustice he had committed against his son.

These internecine killings set the trend for Alexander's successors after he had died. The results were disastrous for the long-term future of the Greek nation.

This hubris that overtook Alexander as he progressed with his triumphs seems to be under-reported in the plethora of books written about Alexander and his leadership. Many business executives, others in management education, and scholars in and outside academia continue to study Alexander's leadership and ascribe to him mostly virtues. Some, as expected, are out to desecrate his memory. Alexander and his leadership style now feature in books assigned to students in MBA programmes. (see Kets de Vries and Engellau, 2004). Alexander is credited with having had, among others, these qualities: a compelling vision, unsurpassed execution, a well-rounded executive team, walked the walk, encouraged innovation, fostered group identification, encouraged and supported followers, invested in talent management, consolidated gains, carried out succession planning (sic) and created mechanisms of organisation and governance. All these sound good business/management language. Yet, Alexander failed to make succession plans which literally every book on business and management stresses as being vital to good management. He knew that one day he would die and that he ran the risk of being incapacitated. Yet he did nothing on this front even though he knew that great generals such as Philotas were more than capable of succeeding him. In fact, and as if by design, he made sure not to have people like Philotas and his father General Parmenion around. He arranged to have them killed. Alexander viewed himself as 'the one and only' and not as 'first amongst equals' as he ought to. (Arrian, trans. 1893)

No matter how great a leader Alexander was and how much he achieved and how many accolades he earned, in the end he was a man who betrayed his close friends' trust and had some of his best generals killed. I never forgave Alexander for this treachery to his brothers. Whenever I read about Alexander's undoubted achievements I am also reminded of his follies, the worst of which was the elimination of his closest friends. In fact, he killed one of them with his own dagger. When I first found out about this side of Alexander I was horror-struck because I realised that success often comes at a price and often wreaks havoc on the personality of the leader.

> *In the end, success can create terrible psychological turmoil in leaders and a desire to become the infallible "one and only".*

The 'one and only' syndrome reigns supreme to this day in some places. Of course, modern-day democracies and corporate settings will not allow physical violence (as was the case in Alexander's time) but many of the other practices of the past can still be found today to enable leaders to stay in power. These include psychological violence, isolation from the network, lowering of status, use of surreptitious, vitriolic and high-falutin language that in practice is meant to humiliate, and so on. A competitor for leadership can be defamed, besmirched, besmeared, undermined, belittled and can fall victim of character assassination! All it takes is for the leader to fall prey to the "one and only" syndrome that will inevitably lead to jealousy and malice.

My conclusion is that Alexander was largely driven by envy that led him to murdering some of his close friends and his mentors. Alcohol and quick temper might have played a role in the killing of Cleitus but certainly not of Philotas and Parmenion, whose killings were planned. These two killings were premeditated murder. Throughout history envy has been known to consume many a leader; with sycophants, like Perdicas, playing their treacherous role behind the scenes. Perdicas boosted sky-high Alexander's feeling of importance, in the process making him envious of anyone that was good enough to be his equal. These murders were the biggest blemishes on Alexander's otherwise great legacy. Worse, these murders brought to light Alexander's ingratitude to those who helped make him great.

It is widely accepted that Alexander killed General Cleitus the Black (Κλεῖτος ὁ μέλας) in a frenzy of drunkenness. But, the question that needs to be answered is this: "what had caused Alexander to become so angry with Cleitus in the first place?" In the eyes of Alexander Cleitus "sinned" when he compared Alexander to his illustrious father King Philip. In some ways Alexander came second best in this comparison against Philip. Flatterers were telling him otherwise. The comparison of Alexander to his father was the real cause behind the killing of Cleitus. Cleitus was his father's friend and general and as such, knew well the strengths of both. The killing of Cleitus, even if under the influence of alcohol, brought to the fore Alexander's unremitting feeling of envy whilst at the same time it showed his ingratitude to the person that saved his life at the battle of River Granicus at the start of the campaign. Had it not been for Cleitus, Alexander would have been just a short note in the history books. He also had Philotas inhumanely tortured and then killed. Philotas was his boyhood friend and commander of the elite Companion Cavalry and probably the ablest and most talented Greek general. Philotas was his friend but also the son of his army's supreme commander, Parmenion, whom Philip held in high regard, and brother of General Nikanor (Νικάνωρ in Greek).

Alexander accused Philotas of "conspiracy" and more specifically of hearing about a conspiracy against Alexander and not taking it seriously enough to report it to him. The culmination of his all-consuming envy was the killing of Marshal Parmenion, who was the icon of everybody in the Greek military. Parmenion was seventy at the time Alexander schemed and planned his assassination in 330 BC. Parmenion was of noble blood and the 'General of Generals'. No wonder Philip though of Parmenion as the equal of ten Athenian generals put together. Parmenion was killed for no reason other than the fact that he was the father of Philotas who was a victim of sham court proceedings and the torturers that Alexander unleashed on him with ferocity. Worried that after killing Philotas the troops would rally around the popular and time-tested Parmenion, Alexander had him killed as well. (Arrian, trans. 1893)

Parmenion. A few words about the great man Parmenion, who never ceased to fascinate me since the first time I came across his name as a child. The tragic and totally unfair end of his life could be the subject of many books, one would presume. Deservedly the Greeks of today honour Parmenion by giving his name to the largest annual military exercises in modern Greece. These carry the codename "Parmenion" in honour of this great general who served the Greek cause more than two thousand years ago. Equally, at the time of writing the people of Greece were demonstrating en masse in favour of the protection of the name of Macedon from usurpation by a Greek neighbour that insisted on naming the neighbouring country "Northern Macedonia". In the end, unfortunately, the name of Macedonia was betrayed by a handful of Greeks in power that failed to resist foreign pressure coming from the West to deliver the name of Macedonia that Greeks hold so dear to their hearts. When challenged to put the issue through a referendum the government chickened out, knowing what a crashing defeat they would have suffered at the hands of patriotic Greeks that are proud of their heritage.

One can, of course, easily brush aside as sentimentalism any reference I make today to what happened to Parmenion two-and-a-half thousand years ago. After all, horrible acts of violence were the rule in those times as were palace rebellions, coups, succession quarrels, and court intrigue. But, in my view, what happened to Parmenion should serve as a reminder that envy has no limits once it engulfs a leader. Injustices ought to be reported from time to time to help us stay away from them in the future.

> *Injustice is the sledgehammer that can destroy the rule of law and demolish the platform on which all that is good rests.*

Parmenion. By the time Philip died in 336 BC Parmenion was the foremost general in Macedon (and of the world one would assume) and the one Alexander had to chiefly rely on for military tutoring and support. There were other generals as well but Parmenion was the general supreme whose support Alexander needed (and in fact received) when struggling to secure his throne after Philip's assassination. At the time of Alexander's death Parmenion was in action against the Illyrians, whom he defeated. Parmenion and his family's contributions to the Macedonian and Hellenic cause were massive. Here is how savagely Alexander treated this august family and icon of Hellenism: a) Parmenion's son-in-law and military commander Attalus was arrested, accused of treason and executed, probably on Alexander's orders at the time of Philip's death. Alexander simply suspected that Attalus did not support him with all his heart and mind for succession to the throne, b) Parmenion's sons Philotas and Nicanor were the commanders of the Companions (Alexander's élite unit) and the Hypaspists respectively, c) Coenus, Parmenion's new son-in-law, who had married Attalus' widow, commanded a battalion of Pezhetairoi (the backbone of the Macedonian army). He was the one bold enough to voice the army's grievances to Alexander in 326 BC and when Alexander was at his height. Nicanor died of natural causes shortly before Philotas was executed by Alexander for treason. Parmenion's other son Hector died in an accident whilst the army was in Egypt and d) Parmenion was assassinated on Alexander's orders.

So therefore, having reached the supreme heights of military glory, Parmenion saw his family either decimated by Alexander or hit hard by misfortune. He then suffered assassination himself. Parmenion experienced the best and the worst of life and died tragically. Parmenion was instrumental in the three major Macedonian set-piece victories at Granicus, Issus and Gaugamela as commander of the left wing of the army and the famous Thessalian cavalry that was positioned on the left. Maybe Alexander's most despicable and shameful act was not the killing of Parmenion and his family but the defamation campaign against Parmenion that followed after he had him killed. Alexander's press core accused Parmenion of bad counsel, even though Parmenion's sterling career was a matter of public record considering that he was seventy at the time of his assassination and had all his life on record. We read, "Diodorus describes the death of Philotas as a 'base action' that was 'quite foreign' to Alexander's good nature. There is certainly no doubt that we are dealing with an episode in the great king's life that is every bit as murky as the plot to kill his father." (Diodorus, trans. 1963)

Equally, Alexander killed his teacher's (the philosopher Aristotle's) great-nephew Callisthenes, who accompanied Alexander as historian of his campaigns. Callisthenes' deadly mistake was to harangue Alexander for adopting Persian customs and for demanding that the Greeks bow before him. The ritual of proskynesis or prostration was an absolutely foreign and demeaning custom for the Greeks. In typical fashion Callisthenes was accused of "conspiracy" (just as were Philotas and Parmenion)!

If we put aside all of the above treacherous act and failures of character and concentrate on Alexander's triumphs we will learn much about effective leadership.

Alexander the Great. Alexander had leadership galore and the fact that his name still reverberates two and a half thousand years later is testimony to his greatness. He never lost a battle in more than eleven years of fighting far away from home base; Napoleon got smashed up in Russia in 1812 and his capital, Paris, was overrun and occupied by the Russians and allies a year later. Clearly:

1. Leading by example and maintaining morale were probably Alexander's two most heady gifts. His charisma helped morale and his valour helped the Greek army's fighting spirit.

2. Alexander's ability to design and execute great strategy and tactics was a blessing for the Greeks which helped them capture an area many times the size of Greece, including Macedonia. The odds he faced were formidable and these tested his generalship to the limit. He employed successful strategies and tactics both in set-piece battles and when on the march or giving chase to the enemy.

3. Alexander's siege strategies and tactics were unparalleled. All one has to remember is the siege of Tyre in 334 BC which lasted for more than seven months before the defenders' fortifications were breached leading to the city's capture. Equally, the siege of the Rock of Aornos in 327 BC was a great feat considering the impregnability of this natural stronghold that blocked Alexander's route to India.

4. d.) Alexander favoured international friendship and as such tried to bring everyone in the fold sometimes angering those Greeks that disagreed with such practices. The marriage of his officers with oriental women serves as good example of his desire to bring people and nations together. This particular experiment failed in the end as the vast majority of these marriages came to an end after Alexander's death.

Essay 2: Achievement and love for money and fame

"Man's welfare then lieth not in obtaining or multiplying any external thing, but rather in despising it, and utterly rooting it out from the heart. And this thou must understand not only of income of money and riches but of seeking after honour also, and the desire of vain praise, all which pass away with this world." (Kempis, trans. 1900: 153).

There is nothing wrong in being rich. Many people have made it to the ranks of the wealthy through sheer hard work, good risk management and ability to offer the market good products of services that satisfy the market's legitimate needs. Some rich people can be very generous as well making sizeable contributions to worthy causes and helping others in need. In the essays that follow there is no intention of accusing the rich or to vilify wealth creation. Greed in layman's language is all about wanting more and more; wanting more than what is necessary to stay comfortable and relatively secure economically. I guess greed is present in most of us human beings. Many of us want to make more and more and even admire those that are outstandingly rich. Greed is a disturbing issue for most and as such featured prominently throughout human history. Greats of antiquity, and in fact greats of every era, talked about the subject often from different vantage points including the philosophical and theological. More recently in history thinkers such as Tocqueville, Max Weber and Galbraith tried to help us understand greed and its root causes bringing into the equation economics and sociology.

Here in this treatise our concern is not with greed in a general sense and as expressed above. Rather, our concern is with greed that engulfs some leaders (but certainly not all) once they are out of office and away from the glare of the lights the press shine on them and after their political opponents lose interest in following and criticizing their every action. Why do some former leaders escape the temptation to exploit the status their former position gave them to make money and why others fail to do so and ultimately tarnish their image. Why under the same roof and in the same society one finds both the humble Jimmy Carters (USA) and the Harold Wilsons (Britain) but also the opposites the Bill Clintons (USA) and the Tony Blairs (Britain) pair appearing to have made it a life's mission to accumulate wealth after leaving office?

Money made during the leader's tenure or after vacating his post is a serious issue that touches on the leader's perception of what is proper behaviour and what is not. We are of course talking about making money through methods that most people consider to be distasteful

The Lebanon is well-known as a fine example of wealth and politics. A cursory review of the wealth of some of the top politicians of this country makes interesting reading. Two of the former top politicians are worth more than $3 billion and $2 billion respectively. Other former politicians hold net assets in the hundreds of millions. The lowest net worth of the top ten richest politicians in the country is a "meagre" $49 million. Leader wealth touches all religious denominations in the Lebanon. (TopRichests.com, n.d.). Is this bad? Obviously one cannot tell from just reading the figures but clearly there is a perplexing element to the picture considering that the country's per capita GDP is a paltry (circa) $10,000. Is this proof that poor people prefer voting the rich into positions of leadership? As regards money and power it is interesting to see some politicians around the world entering politics with strong socialist views and becoming great lovers of money as their political career progresses.

Take the example of Luiz Inacio Lula da Silva (known as Lula) of Brazil.

Luiz Inacio Lula da Silva. Lula was a labour union man and later president of Brazil. To get elected he brandished his credentials as a socialist/communist. But he soon discovered the sweetness of power and the opportunity that power gave him to enjoy money. In the end he was sentenced to jail on account of his love for things that pushed him to acquire property under apparently suspicious circumstances. He started as a man beyond reproach seeing he rose from the ranks of the poor and illiterate (he learned to read when he was ten). This former peanut seller and shoe-shine boy was caught up in a scandal and was convicted of corruption. He was sentenced to more than nine years in prison. He maintains his innocence and claims the judge was biased and did not wish to see him running for president in the 2018 elections.

Whilst on the surface there is nothing laudable in being poor while holding a position of leadership, the reality is that the led feel more comfortable knowing that their leader does not become too friendly with riches that could ultimately have a debasing influence on him.

Alexandros and Demetrius Ypsilantis. These two brothers and generals of the army are the epitome of leaders that had little love for money, and from rich ended poor, as a result of sacrifice. The Ypsilantis family and its immense wealth disappeared, all gone to the Greek cause of liberation from the Ottomans that started in 1821. The Ypsilantis family lost all its wealth, but in the end won eternal memory and became an object of reverence for many. The formerly outstandingly wealthy brothers, Alexandros and Demetrius Ypsilantis died literally penniless by the end of the Greek War of Liberation from the Turks in which both played leading roles. The same for many other Greeks, most notably the wealthy princess Mando Mavrogenous who died in utter poverty after the 1821 war came to a close. Many American Founding Fathers died poor and many former American Presidents died in penury. Some apparently remained poor because of a spiritual conviction against materialism, others fell on hard times, others experienced bad luck and others managed their affairs poorly.

But here again it depends on one's definition of wealth. Here are some examples to highlight the wealth of former holders of high office and how they came to be rich.

Obama. Obama is a poor-rich former president with a few million. This obviously does not put him in the ranks of the super wealthy and does not give him club membership! But here again Obama made his money from writing a couple of successful books before his presidency began and then after his presidency ended. Book writing can be a very lucrative business for some, particularly when these books end up in the best-seller lists, owing to folks' fascination with people in power and leadership positions. Obama had no inherited wealth but I do not think that many would argue against Obama having made some money considering his overall good behaviour with money.

Kissinger. Then there are the benefactors who intervene at some point to sustain the politically powerful, until money begins to flow their way and until they hit the jackpot through paid lectures or peddling influence. In an article in Politico (20 January, 2018) Niall Ferguson and Laurence A. Tisch, professor of History at Harvard University, reminded us of Kissinger's connection to the powerful Nelson Rockefeller, "His [Kissinger's] appointment as Richard Nixon's national security adviser in December 1968 nevertheless came as a surprise to many people (not least Kissinger himself), because for most of the previous decade he had been so closely identified with [the influential and powerful] Nelson Rockefeller...". And Ferguson and Tisch continue, "While in office, Kissinger appeared on the cover of Time magazine no fewer than 15 times." He was, according to one of the magazine's Kissinger profiles that was published in 1974, "'the world's indispensable man'—though one who stood accused by his critics of 'paying more attention to principals than principles.'" And, "Kissinger's power, still based on a network that crossed not only borders but also professional boundaries, endured long after he left government in 1977, institutionalized in the advisory firm Kissinger Associates, maintained by almost incessant flying, meeting, mingling, dining. By contrast, the executive branch after Nixon saw its power significantly curtailed by congressional scrutiny and greatly emboldened newspapers. No future national security adviser or secretary of state, no matter how talented, would ever be able to match what Kissinger had achieved." (Canellos, 2018)

Tony Blair. Under the title, "Tony Blair and his 'greedy' wife are laughing all the way to the bank", Geoffrey Levy wrote on 11 January, 2008 in the Daily Mail, "Some men leave the highest public offices and devote their lives to helping others. Tony Blair, aided and abetted by his 'greedy' wife, is making copious arrangements to help himself." Levy makes it clear that there is nothing wrong from profiting from one's experiences and knowledge. After all, Margaret Thatcher did so with lectures east and west of the Atlantic. Levy added this to the Blair story, "They [the Blairs] needed money — and fast — to ease the problems of paying some £20,000 a month on an estimated £5 million mortgages on their five properties." And Levy illuminates us on the money Blair earns from lectures, "One recent month he earned almost £500,000, and the bookings stretch ahead. Many will find it thoroughly distasteful that Blair is now making millions out of talking to bloated after-dinner audiences about the war, especially at a time when the care and treatment of our wounded Iraq and Afghanistan heroes has been under severe question." (Levy, 2008)

The Clintons. Victor Davis Hanson wrote in the National Review on 26 July, 2016 under the witty title, "How the Clintons got Rich Selling Influence while Decrying Greed", "Most presidents, before and after holding office, are offered multifarious opportunities to get rich, most of them unimaginable to Americans without access to influential and wealthy concerns. But none have so flagrantly circumvented laws and ethical norms as have Bill and Hillary Clinton, a tandem who in little more than a decade went from self-described financial want to a net worth likely over $100 million, or even $150 million." And, "No president, however, sought to create a surrogate nonprofit organization to provide free private jet travel for the former first family while offering sinecures to veteran operatives between campaigns. The worth of both the Clinton family and the Clinton Foundation (augmented by a recent ten-month drive to raise $250 million for the foundation's endowment) is truly staggering, and to a great extent accrued from non-transparent pay-for-play aggrandizement" (Hanson, 2016).

Reporting from Washington on BBC News on 15 April, 2019 Jude Sheerin under the title, "The Mental Rigours of Being US President" highlighted the mental and emotional challenges many former US presidents had to face. Here is an excerpt, "A 2012 study by psychologists from Emory University in Georgia found several presidents exhibited psychopathic traits...." The two former presidents that were most psychopathic, as reported, were Lyndon Baines Johnson and Andrew Jackson. Here are the attributes of psychopathic behaviour that the Emory team identified, "... superficial charm, egocentricity, dishonesty, callousness, risk-taking, poor impulse control and fearlessness." (BBC News, 2019). Clinton's superficial charm, egocentricity and poor impulse control are not new to the reader.

Once former leaders start engaging in what is seen as greedy behaviour, the ethical side of the leadership equation gets disturbed, causing great damage to the former leader's legacy as good and righteous. Giving some of this money to charity for the sake of public relations and often as a decoy does not contain the damage in the long term.

Admittedly US presidents make relatively little money when in office, compared to the magnitude of the work they are expected to carry out and the complexity of the role of president. Executives in the top ranks of any serious global job grading system earn millions a year for their labours. Surely the job of President of the USA is much more complex and demanding than any other top level executive job? The current US president's salary of $400,000, that includes a $50,000 expense allowance, clearly does not reflect the job's complexity, and underpays the president.

But surely the presidency is not just another job; presidents ought to serve their country even on an under par package. I am sure some idealists would be ready to undertake the job of president for nothing just as Prince Capodistrias did, right after Greece was freed from the Turks and the country faced financial despair. US presidents do not earn exorbitant pensions either. At the time of writing after leaving office a US president could expect to earn a taxable pension of $199,700 per year (about half his annual salary when serving as president). This pension is roughly eight times the value of the annual salary of $25,000 of a 19th century American president. From this paltry annual salary of $25,000 the 19th century American presidents had to pay for their travel, entertainment and the salaries of their staff. This explains why some of the first presidents of America such as Thomas Jefferson, who was by nature generous with his money and enjoyed expensive things, died poor. On the opposite side, when Truman's annual salary rose to $1,000,000, in today's values, this was enough to take him out of near-bankruptcy and to elevate him into the ranks of the well off. (Berman, 2012)

Being above money or Χρημάτων Κρείσσων

"The man who dies rich, dies disgraced," Andrew Carnegie.

Here are some examples of great leaders that stayed away from the temptation of using their public position to hoard or amass money. The list could of course be extended significantly.

John Adams. John Adams (US president: 1797–1801) was "...never a rich man, always worried about making ends meet, John Adams in his long life had accumulated comparatively little in the way of material wealth. Still, as he had hoped, he died considerably more than just solvent." (McCullough, 2001: 648)

Thomas Jefferson. Thomas Jefferson (US president: 1801–9) "Jefferson, by sad contrast, had died with debts exceeding $100,000, more than the value of Monticello, its land, and all his possessions, including his slaves." (McCullough, 2001: 648). Jefferson failed one of his own axioms, that of "Living within one's means." He was heavily in debt until the day he died. In a letter to James Madison in 1789 Jefferson wrote: "No generation can contract debts greater than may be paid over the course of its own existence." Jefferson made many such statements. So how does one explain what happened to the finances of this great leader? As we said above, his annual compensation was a meagre $25,000 for each of the eight years of his presidency, and from this amount he had to cover the salaries of his staff, travel and entertainment. He even paid out of his own pocket, White House entertainment for dignitaries visiting him. When he retired he could not hope for a pension, because there wasn't one at the time. No wonder in the years after the end of the American Revolution the US presidency was the fast lane to poverty.

Jefferson had to make up the difference between his expenses as president and his salary as president. No chance, considering Jefferson's generosity, high standard of living, love for things good and pretty, and his little concern for money. Above all, he was an honest man, a philosopher, a man of ideals who could not dirty his hands to line his pockets, "my hands are as clean as they are empty" he confided to a friend. He had land but little cash because his

Thomas Jefferson. Former President of the USA and author of the Declaration of Independence. Outstanding champion for democratic polity. Through his "no foreign entanglements" he was amongst the first to express concern about the dangers of America getting involved in the affairs of other countries in foreign lands as is happening now. He stands out as a magnificent president, thinker, innovator and for his achievements in many other endeavors. He was a leader of massive proportions.

income from Monticello was nowhere near covering his cash shortfall. Added to that were the unstable prices of commodities and management deficiencies. The lottery that was run to help him cover his debts was not enough to prevent the sale of Monticello or to stop the bill collectors of pecuniary America. Thus another great man with little love for money died poor. What a great president Jefferson was, what a great democrat and what a great model of an idealist philosopher-president. I am fascinated with Jefferson.

James Madison. (fourth US president: 1809–1817) was an intellectual genius not many can match to this day; especially on constitutional matters. He was a scholar and a man who could think deeply. His breadth and depth of thought helped establish a new type of government; America owes Madison a debt of gratitude for establishing the constitutional rights they continue to enjoy to this day. Above all, he was a great man with little interest in money.

James Monroe. (US president: 1817–1825). Monroe was the fifth president of the USA who on retirement went out as a poor man following a great American tradition (in the post-revolution era) of having presidents spend their post-presidency time with little money. Monroe needed some $1.5 million in today's terms to stay solvent. He could not even do that with a gift from Congress that though helpful, was not enough to take him out of poverty. He had to live the last year of his life with the family of his daughter in New York City.

Abraham Lincoln. (US President: 1861–1865). The sobriquet "honest Abe" says it all about former President of the USA Abraham Lincoln. He made the list of American presidents who did not lust for money. He came from humble origins and once managed a store which ultimately went bankrupt. The bankruptcy was debited to Lincoln rather than to the owner of the store. He also had bad luck with a store he owned with a partner who died and left no assets. As a decent man, Lincoln took on his partner's debt as his own and paid the debt off in good time.

He later made some money as a successful lawyer, and pushed his financial standing ahead of that of his early beginnings. He had financial reverses, but was a great leader who is revered around the world to this day. The way he dealt with the American Civil War that started at the beginning of his presidency was exemplary.

Harold Wilson. (Wilson was British Prime Minister in the periods 1964–1970 and 1974–1976). He died a poor man. "...Denis Healey is wrong in his assessment of Wilson as a man who had 'neither political principle' nor 'sense of direction.'" In fact, Wilson had both. Plus, "...he possessed an intuitive sense of decency which he tried to spread around the country and to his fellow citizens. He had a profound belief in what he was doing particularly in the direction of establishing social fairness. He was also a modest man despite his gifts and intellectual prowess. There was another curious aspect to Harold Wilson — a strange modesty." (Goodman, 1995)

Wilson was smart and responsible enough to keep Britain out of the meaningless Vietnam War but without in the end ruining his relationship with the Americans. He did not toe the line, but did not go far enough to anger his perennial allies. Maybe his most insightful moment was when he realised that Great Britain was a power in decline, as she withdrew from east of Suez (for more on how the Suez British calamity ended in the time of Wilson's successors read Kyle, 2011). He was not a rabid anti-Soviet and was generally friendly in his relations with the Soviets. It is said that he attended the House of Lords meetings regularly until a year before his death, just to receive the stipend to make ends meet. What an example of decency Wilson was.

Essay 3: Haughtiness, Pride, Vanity, and Modesty

We need to revisit hubris considering how important it is in the destruction of leaders that show haughtiness, pride and vanity. The world hubris has its origins in ancient Greece. The English language picked up the word and "turned" it to mean a special brand of cockiness which ultimately ends with backlash against the proud person. Hubris is a dangerous character flaw, which in the end attracts the wrath even of the gods. It is a fatal shortcoming that can even lead to death. Typically, overconfidence can lead someone to overstep the boundary and to think of himself as God. Inevitably, the gods humble the offender with a sharp reminder of his frailty and mortality. Here is what Merriam-Webster says about hubris: "...extreme pride, especially pride and ambition so great that they offend the gods and lead to one's downfall." Hubris was a character flaw often seen in the heroes of classical Greek tragedy, including Oedipus and Achilles. 'Pride goeth before a fall', which is often employed in modern parlance, is about hubris. (Hubris, n.d.).

And now a few sentences on the difference between "vanity" and "pride". "Vanity and pride are different things, though the words are often used synonymously. A person may be proud without being vain. Pride relates more to our opinion of ourselves, vanity to what we would have others think of us."

— Jane Austen, Pride and Prejudice

In Luke we find one of the best pieces on pride and vanity and its consequences, "For whoever exalts himself will be humbled, and he who humbles himself will be exalted" (Luke 14:11, New King

James Version). (in Greek: «πᾶς ὁ ὑψῶν ἑαυτὸν ταπεινωθήσεται καὶ ὁ ταπεινῶν ἑαυτὸν ὑψωθήσεται» [Κατά Λουκάν, ιδ´ 11]). Socrates makes it easy for us to understand, "Τοὺς μὲν κενοὺς ἀσκοὺς ἡ πνοὴ διίστησι, τοὺς δ' ἀνοήτους, τὸ οἴημα...". (see below the English version).

> *"Wind fills the empty bags and haughtiness fills the idiots."*

Talking of the Greco-Persian wars and the vanity of the Persians who thought they would crush the Greeks by just showing up, Grote notes, "The disproportion between the immense host assembled by Xerxes, and the little which he accomplished, naturally provokes both contempt for Persian force and an admiration for the comparatively small handful of men by which they were so ignominiously beaten," (Grote, 1864: 239–240). "...the men indeed, individually taken, especially the native Persians, were not deficient in the qualities of soldiers, but their arms and their organization were wretched—and their leaders yet worse. On the other hand, the Greeks, equal, if not superior, in individual bravery, were incomparably superior in soldier-like order as well as in arms: but here too the leadership was defective, and disunion a constant peril." (Grote, 1864: 240). He then goes on to say that Greece owns its liberation as much to Xerxes' cowardice and imbecility and in this way takes some of the gloss off the magnificent display of valour and love for liberty of the Greeks. Here again we visit Pausanias' haughtiness.

Pausanias. Hubris and pride typically afflict either the very successful or those who lead autocratic administrations and get funny ideas about their infallibility. George Grote notes this on hubris, which he calls 'being spoiled by success':

"In recounting the history of Miltiades, [the victor at Marathon] I notice the deplorable liability of the Grecian leading men to be spoiled by success: the distemper worked with singular rapidity on

Pausanias. As conqueror of Plataea, he had acquired a renown unparalleled in Grecian experience, together with a prodigious share of the plunder: the concubines, horses, camels, and gold plate, which had thus passed into his possession, were well calculated to make the sobriety and discipline of Spartan life irksome, while his power also, though great on foreign command, became subordinate to that of the Ephors when he returned home. His newly-acquired insolence was manifested immediately after the battle, in the commemorative tripod dedicated by his order at Delphi, which proclaimed himself by name and singly, as commander of the Greeks and destroyer of the Persians: an unseemly boast, of which the Lacedaemonians were the first to mark their disapprobation..." (Grote, 1864: 253–254)

Antidotes to haughtiness and pride

Humility. The antidote to haughtiness and pride is humility. On this, Chrysantas, one of Cyrus' generals, commented: " 'Gentlemen this is not the first time I have occasion to observe that a good ruler differs in no respect from a good father...If obedience (humility to accept other's power over you) is the one path to win the highest good, remember it is also the one way to preserve it...And we, to what do we owe our triumph, if not to our obedience?...If obedience is the one path to win the highest good, remember it is also the one way to preserve it...And just as you wish your subjects to obey you, so we must obey those who are set over us.'" (Xenophon, trans. 2012: 164)

But the great generals Pausanias, Themistocles and Miltiades felt that they were above everyone and behaved with little consideration for controls. They felt "untouchable". Pausanias' behaviour gave the Ephors, who bore a grudge against his royal family, the opportunity to use his behaviour after his great triumph at Plataea against him and to carry out a despicable judicial killing, thus humiliating his family of kings and princes. Themistocles ran for his life and just made it into exile in Persia, while Miltiades died in prison. This was the fate of these great men and staunch defenders of liberty who suffered the ingratitude and envy of their co-citizens. It is maybe axiomatic that hubris almost inevitably brings with it nemesis.

Piety. The terms 'piousness' ('εὐσέβεια' in Greek) have been around since Homer's time (εὖ + -σεβής , e.g. θεο-σεβής). I adopt the synonyms and antonyms suggested by the Merriam-Webster dictionary, for the word 'pious' which are: synonyms: constant, dedicated, devoted, devout, faithful, fast, good, loyal, staunch (also stanch), steadfast, steady, true, true-blue and antonyms: disloyal, faithless, false, fickle, inconstant, perfidious, recreant, traitorous, treacherous, unfaithful, untrue. (Pious, n.d.)

"The Greeks performed the sacrifices required before they could join battle with Mardonius and his army...Then Pausanias turned his face towards the temple of Hera at Plataea and prayed to the goddess, begging her to not let them be disappointed in their hopes. As he prayed, the Tegeans got to their feet, stepped out in front of the rest [probably because they had their own omens] and advanced towards the barbarians. And, at the right moment, just after Pausanias had said his prayers, the omens from the sacrifices at last became favourable, and the Lacedaemonians charged the Persians as well." (Herodotus, trans. 2013: 611). Pausanias showed great piousness before the battle, but soon fell victim to pride just as the Greeks were out of danger. It is not unusual for a 26-year-old to fall victim to pride after a massive achievement. In our day, we see young, successful, and rich sportsmen and actors displaying wayward behaviour that often far exceeds the bounds of haughtiness and hubris.

Cyrus The Great. Cyrus, the great leader of antiquity, had "an abiding love for piety", Xenophon tells us, that protected him from bad deeds. Those that read Xenophon's Cyropaedia are aware of the qualities that Xenophon says a good leader ought to have: seeking consensus, sharing and generosity, good manners, decisiveness, righteousness, friendship. In our day, piety does not seem to be a highly valued quality for many, particularly in secular Europe. This contrasts with the promotion, in the past, of piety as a central quality of a good leader. Cyrus thanked Zeus before and after giving battle and sacrificed to him, secured Zeus' advice and asked for his goodwill and help to enable him to refrain from impious actions. Divination was part of Cyrus' forecasting tools. "Thus, he [Cyrus] took pains to show that he was the more assiduous in his service to the gods the higher his fortunes rose" (Xenophon, trans. 2012: 166). Xenophon warns that, "...the Persians of today and their allies are less religious than they were of old, less dutiful to their kindred, less just and righteous towards other men, and less valiant in war." (Xenophon, trans. 2012: 194).

Piety is an all-beneficial trait which was cherished by the ancient Greek leaders such as Pausanias, Agesilaus, Socrates the philosopher, Pericles (he built an altar to the goddess Athena). Alcibiades was condemned for impiety and later chased out of Athens because of treachery. A leader without piety is likely to perceive himself as the Almighty, and is more than likely to fall into committing hubris and acting hubristically in his dealings with people and followers. Oftentimes piety works as antidote to haughtiness and hubris.

"Therefore I exhort first of all that supplications, prayers, intercessions, and giving of thanks be made for all men, for kings and all who are in authority, that we may lead a quiet and peaceful life in all godliness and reverence." (I Timothy 2:1–2, New King James Version). In Greek, « Παρακαλῶ οὖν πρῶτον πάντων ποιεῖσθαι δεήσεις, προσευχάς, ἐντεύξεις, εὐχαριστίας, ὑπὲρ πάντων ἀνθρώπων, ὑπὲρ βασιλέων καὶ πάντων τῶν ἐν ὑπεροχῇ ὄντων, ἵνα ἤρεμον καὶ ἡσύχιον βίον διάγωμεν ἐν πάσῃ εὐσεβείᾳ καὶ σεμνότητι.» (Πρὸς Τιμόθεον Α 2:1–2).

Two national heroes that are victims of hubris

Sadat and Mubarak. As mentioned earlier hubris is more likely to afflict the very successful and/or others who work in a less than perfect democratic polity that allows them to get away with a lot of things before catastrophe strikes. Our examples here are going to be Sadat and Mubarak, former presidents of Egypt, a country I know well and with which I have close emotional links, and whose progress I follow closely.

Michaud refers to an earlier piece by Newhouse, who saw compelling parallels between the latter years of Sadat's and Mubarak's reigns. In particular, the anger and intolerance people felt for them because of their ostentatious lifestyles and aloofness from people's problems, and most importantly the problem of poverty. Here is what Michaud wrote, "Relief is the main reaction to Mubarak, that one senses in most Egyptians, of whatever political bias. Sadat had stretched their tolerance too far. In the latter years of his rule, he seems not just to have been out of touch with popular sentiment but to have completely misread it." (Michaud, 2011)

Mary Anne Weaver tells us that just before the end of his tenure and subsequent imprisonment, and when it was first mooted that Mubarak would have to leave office, "Mubarak, normally a man of stolid demeanor and few words, looked genuinely startled. 'Impossible! he replied. No president ever steps down!' ". I take it that 'no president ever steps down' referred to the two former presidents of Egypt, Nasser who died in office, and Sadat who was assassinated and as such did not step down.

"During Mubarak's rule the real arbiters of power changed little. Ever since he took over the presidency in 1981 (after militant Islamists assassinated his predecessor, Anwar Sadat), Mubarak has led Egypt as the head of a narrow ruling circle of military officers and security and intelligence men. Sadat was part of that same circle." (Weaver, 2003)

In the above piece one sees in Mubarak arrogance, wilfulness, the "I am Egypt," syndrome and other similar syndromes; thus, the signs of hubris that allow one to feel free to act at will and with little regard for the feelings of the community. As regards Anwar Sadat we read, "At the time of his death, Sadat had amassed the majority of his wealth through politics. According to a statement released by his brother, the net worth of their family was only $2 million... However, this $2 million is still over ten times the net worth his family declared to avoid taxes." (Famous People, n.d.)

Again, we see the syndrome of, "let the laws apply to others and not to me" wrapped in hubris. It was general knowledge in Egyptian streets that the Sadats dressed in the latest fashion. Sadat's wife tried to conceal this, saying in an interview "'...she and her husband used to sew only one dress and suit a year.'" And, Mrs Sadat continued, " 'I usually bought clothes from the wholesale markets in European cities when I travelled abroad, contrary to what was alleged by some people that I bought brand clothes from the finest shops,'". I am sure that Mubarak and Sadat both meant well, particularly when they first entered politics. Both Sadat and Mubarak were for a time Egyptian national heroes and patriots, who put their lives on the line for their country. Sadat was the mastermind of the successful crossing of the Egyptian army into Sinai in the 1973 war. Mubarak was central to the role of the Egyptian air force in the same war. Sadat tried hard to bring about peace in the region and even lost his life in the process. But, both had fallen victim to a high lifestyle and desire for power that gradually drove them away from the common man and his daily problems; maybe without even realising that they were veering off course. Both were victims of the beguiling tunes of hubris. Of course they were neither the first nor will they be the last to suffer from such flaws.

An extreme case of hubris

Idi Amin Dada. Idi Amin Dada of Uganda personifies the extreme of hubristic behaviour which some explain as being the result of some form of paranoia. On 25 January, 1971, General Idi Amin Dada overthrew the government of Milton Obote, (using some murky reason) with support from the British, as Obete was seen to be moving to the left. Amin became one of the first Ugandans to gain an officer's commission whilst serving in the British Colonial Army. Here are some of the things that made Idi Amin notorious: a) he gave refuge to hijackers who were later killed at Entebbe airport; b) he invaded Tanzania, only to retreat soon after; c) he promoted himself [flippantly] to Field Marshal without any justification or merit and d) he often resorted to arbitrary violence to maintain his position. Encyclopaedia Britannica notes: "In one incident, he destroyed the one potential centre of effective opposition by a wholesale slaughter of senior army officers loyal to Obote." (Encyclopaedia Britannica, n.d.). (see also: South African History Online, 2012)

He died in exile, while his country refused to allow his remains to be returned to his birthplace. Idi Amin is now considered a laughing stock.

References

Arrian (1884). The Anabasis of Alexander. Translation by Edward J. Chinnock. London: Hodder & Stoughton. Available online at https://en.wikisource.org/wiki/The_Anabasis_of_Alexander [Accessed 8 Apr. 2019]

Austen, J. (1813). Pride and prejudice. London: T. Egerton.

BBC News. (2019). The mental rigours of being US president. [online] Available at: https://www.bbc.com/news/world-us-canada-47671986 [accessed 16 April 2019]

Berman, D. (2012). 7 US Presidents Who Flopped Financially | ThinkAdvisor. [online] ThinkAdvisor. Available at: https://www.thinkadvisor.com/2012/09/06/7-u-s-presidents-who-flopped-financially-3/ [Accessed 11 Oct. 2018].

Canellos, P. (2018). The Secret to Henry Kissinger's Success. [online] POLITICO Magazine. Available at: https://www.politico.com/magazine/story/2018/01/20/henry-kissinger-networking-216482 [Accessed 18 Feb. 2019].

Cartledge, P. (2005). Alexander the Great. London: Pan Books.

Diodorus Siculus (1963). Library of History. Vol. VIII, Book XVII. Translated by C. Bradford Welles. Boston, Massachusetts: Loeb Classical Library. Ch. 79, 80.

Encyclopedia Britannica. (n.d.). Uganda — Tyranny under Amin. [online] Available at: https://www.britannica.com/place/Uganda/Tyranny-under-Amin [Accessed 14 Oct. 2018].

Famous People. (n.d.). Anwar Sadat Biography. [online] Available at: https://www.thefamouspeople.com/profiles/anwar-sadat-3642.php%20oretrieved%20%2014.10.2018 [Accessed 14 Oct. 2018].

Goodman, G. (1995). Harold Wilson obituary. [online] The Guardian. Available at: https://www.theguardian.com/politics/1995/may/25/obituaries [Accessed 17 Jun. 2018].

Grote, G. (1864). A history of Greece. Vol. 5. New York: Harper & Brothers.

Hanson, V. (2016). Clintons Got Rich Selling Influence While Decrying Greed. [online] National Review. Available at: https://www.nationalreview.com/2016/07/clintons-got-rich-selling-influence-while-decrying-greed/ [Accessed 11 Oct. 2018].

Herotodus. (2013). The Histories. A new translation by Tom Holland. Introduction by Paul Cartledge. New London: Penguin Classics.

Hubris. (n.d.). In: Merriam-Webster. [online] Available at: https://www.merriam-webster.com/dictionary/hubris [Accessed 25 November 2018].

Kempis T. A. (1900). Of the Imitation of Christ. Revised Translation, London: Oxford University Press

Kets de Vries, M. and Engellau, E. (2004). Are Leaders Born or Are They Made? The Case of Alexander the Great. London: Karnac Books.

Kyle, K. (2011). Suez: Britain's end of empire in the Middle East. London: I.B. Tauris.

Levy, G. (2008). Tony Blair and his 'greedy' wife are laughing all the way to the bank. [online] Daily Mail Online. Available at: https://www.dailymail.co.uk/news/article-507518/Tony-Blair-greedy-wife-laughing-way-bank.html [Accessed 11 Oct. 2018].

McCullough, D. (2001). John Adams. New York: Touchstone, Simon & Schuster.

Michaud, J. (2011). From Sadat to Mubarak. [online] The New Yorker. Available at: https://www.newyorker.com/books/double-take/from-sadat-to-mubarak [Accessed 14 Oct. 2018].

Pious. (n.d.). In: Merriam-Webster. [online] Available at:
https://www.merriam-webster.com/dictionary/pious [Accessed
25 November 2018].

South African History Online. (2012). General Idi Amin Dada
overthrows Ugandan President, Milton Obote. [online] Available
at: https://www.sahistory.org.za/dated-event/general-idi-amin-
dada-overthrows-ugandan-president-milton-obote [Accessed 14
Oct. 2018].

TopRichests.com. (n.d.). Top 10 Richest Politician of Lebanon.
[online] Available at: https://toprichests.com/top-10-richest-
politician-of-lebanon/ [Accessed 11 Oct. 2018].

Weaver, M. (2003). Pharaohs-in-Waiting. [online] The Atlantic.
Available at:
https://www.theatlantic.com/magazine/archive/2003/10/pharao
hs-in-waiting/302811/ [Accessed 14 Oct. 2018].

Xenophon. (2012). Cyropaedia: The Education of Cyrus. Translated
by Henry Graham Dakyns. Edited by F.M. Stawell. CreateSpace
Independent Publishing Platform.

Book 6

Select qualities for aspiring leaders

In my seminars on leadership I often ask participants to list for me four central qualities they would like nature to bless them with as aspiring leaders. I am not surprised when I hear them include the qualities of 'oratory', 'charisma', 'luck', and "ability to read the situation". I must admit that I am taken slightly aback with their insistence on "luck" as an absolutely necessary quality, saying that without luck the leader would always be at a disadvantage and would run the risk of catastrophe. I have chosen the above four qualities as the themes of this book.

Needless to say, the seminar participants did not say that the above four qualities were the only ones that could make a leader successful. Nor did they insist that without the presence of "oratory" and "charisma", aspiring leaders would be condemned to failure. Most felt however, that by its very nature, "luck" was a "make or break" quality. They also felt that without sound judgement ("reading the situation") the leader would sooner or later end up in a cul-de-sac that would force him to give up. The order in which the four qualities appear below does not suggest their relative importance. Equally, no single quality should be seen as self-determining, considering the importance of interdependence and holism in every aspect of life.

Oratory. Oratory continues to stand out as a major catapult to leadership without necessarily saying that without oratorical skills aspiring leaders are likely to fail. Oratory certainly helps in a major way in most cases. But, oratory can be a double-edged sword.

Charisma. Charisma is probably one of the most overrated qualities of leadership, though I admit that it is a powerful quality that has proved its worth over time. Though charisma certainly helps, a leader should perform and deliver results, otherwise charisma will mean little. As such, no measure of charisma can save an incompetent leader, certainly in the long term. Again, charisma too can be a double-edged sword.

Luck. Luck always played a major role in leaders' lives though not all leaders would admit to this. A stroke of bad luck at the start of a leader's career can ruin his chances for ever. But, the importance of the quality of luck lies in the eyes of the beholder. Some people simply refuse to acknowledge "luck" as a determinant of leadership while others consider it as absolutely essential. At the one end are those with a strong internal locus of control who typically tend to underrate the importance of "luck" because it is an external factor while on the other end are those with a strong external locus of control that tend to overrate luck's importance. The concept of locus of control explains how much control people believe they have over matters that affect their lives. Leaders with an external locus of control believe that outside, uncontrolled forces such as luck play a significant role in their life's fortunes. Leaders with a strong internal locus of control believe that they control their life's fortunes, and not outside forces.

Ability to read the situation and take action. Unless leaders can identify correctly and then meet adequately the needs of the led they will almost certainly fail in their task. They will simply lose legitimacy. Leaders must be able to satisfy the needs of the led at a reasonable cost. Here I am talking about legitimate needs such as the need for protection of the people by the security forces, the need for the leader to provide medical care and schooling, etc. Cognition and a "good sense" are central to the process of "reading the situation" correctly. Leaders ought to take correct decisions; in fact that is their main role. But, to take a correct decision the leader needs first to identify the problem correctly and to read the situation well if he is to hope to take the right decision in solving the problem. Thus, reading the situation and taking decisions go together and are inseparable.

Essay 1: Oratory

"I know that men are won over less by the written than by the spoken word, that every great movement on this earth owes its growth to great orators and not to great writers." —Adolf Hitler, "Mein Kampf," 1925

Aristotle was certain that oratory is central to leadership. But, just as is the case with other human qualities, oratory can be used for good or evil. It can be the instrument in the hands of good people to convince others to do something superior and laudable, or it can be the vehicle of the unprincipled to fool people and to put them in the path of evil. Churchill was a worthy orator who used oratory brilliantly and for a good cause. But after the end of WWII oratory failed him and he lost the election to the drab and dreary Attlee. Oratory is known to have been used by pernicious, evil and shameless liars and by the impudent to fool constituents. Mussolini was one such example. "In the annals of recorded history, there are few examples of rulers who relied as much on the art of oratory to achieve and to maintain control of their countries as did Benito Mussolini" (Lezzi, 1959). Bad men show contempt for the public and employ every trick in the book including oratory to put their vile message across convincingly.

Oratory's significance: "...to teach the art of public speaking to their fellow citizens in the Greek republics and later, to the children of the wealthy under the Roman Empire. Public performance was regarded as the highest reach of education proper, and rhetoric was at the centre of the educational process in western..." (Baird, n.d.)

Oratory is important for several obvious reasons: first of all it is through oratory that typically the public first gets to meet and hear the leader. So in this way first impressions, that are difficult to erase, are created. Even with social media and the explosion of other communication mediums, oratory is still the king of persuasion. Good orators typically use precise, short, and powerful messages that are easy for the public to remember. Oratory can hide a lot of leader imperfections including the shortfall of not knowing the subject matter well. Oratory can also be a good vehicle for liars who fool their listeners through high-faluting language. Through oratory leaders can make themselves look better than they are and in this way fool the public. In ancient times oratory was a cherished quality which appears to be losing some of its lustre these days, though illustrious educational centres such as the University of Oxford, for example, do an excellent job of keeping this fine art alive.

Mussolini. Mussolini was a powerful orator with great charisma who put his skills in the service of his objectives during WWII. He cannot be compared to Pericles though, because of the simple fact that his oratory was geared towards badness and wickedness; he urged people to indulge in war and domination rather than freedom. There was nothing virtuous in his speeches during WWII. This raises the question of whether bad people that speak well and mange to enthuse the crowds to do bad are true orators or charlatans with strong language skills in the service of mischief.

Pericles. One of the best orators of all time was Pericles of ancient Athens. He employed powerful speech to help him make Athens the greatest city of its time whose ancient light still illuminates the civilised world. Here is what Britannica tells us about oration: "An oration involves a speaker; an audience; a time frame, place, and other conditions; a message; transmission by voice, articulation, and bodily accompaniments; and may, or may not, have an immediate outcome." (Baird, n.d.)

Good oratory typically entails:

a) brevity and clarity.

b) a well-defined and relevant message.

c) capture of the audience's attention.

d) speaking freely and with little stress, though with passion.

e) employing informality and some humour where possible.

f) a balanced message so as not to sound extreme.

g) controlled speed of delivery to make the orator understood.

h) good use of body language.

i) creation of enthusiasm to influence the audience in favour of the orator's message.

Ronald Reagan. Former president Reagan ("the great communicator") used simple messages in his oratory; almost nothing complicated came from the lips of this capable person. He was not exactly the personification of a sophisticated politician such as Pericles or Cimon. Reagan's oratory appealed to the average man, considering that brevity and clarity are essential to understanding. The well-known Reagan Doctrine (apropos communism) was simple, "Communists and their sympathizers were bad, anticommunists and their supporters were good." In its manifestation this doctrine led to America supporting the contra rebels in Nicaragua against the leftist government and to American support for the El Salvador government against a leftist insurgency. (Brands, 2015: 532)

Alexander's speech to his rebellious troops: oratorical masterpiece

Alexander the Great. Alexander was Aristotle's student. Early in his life Alexander understood the need for oratory in convincing his troops to lay down their lives in foreign lands in pursuit of his dream to Hellenize (spread the Greek culture) to the East and to punish the Persians for their past invasions of Greece. I have chosen Alexander's speech as an example of sublime and clever oratory at a time when Alexander was about to suffer a rebellion with terrible consequences. He used oratory to contain rebellion and employed all he had learned from Aristotle to inspire and galvanize his army and followers: a) to continue and not to give up in the face of adversity, and b) to complete the task as planned. (Aristotle, trans. 2006)

Alexander never lost a battle except the one against his troops' will to continue. They had rebelled and refused to go forward. All was therefore dependent on Alexander's oratorical skills to convince the troops to change their minds and save his project. Using additionally, some strong-arm tactics which were the rule of the day in the 4th century BC! This is how things happened. Alexander and his troops advanced into the Punjab to fight the most costly battle of his career at the Hydaspes River. He fought against the Indian King Porus and won, but at great cost. As a smart politician and wily strategist he immediately reassigned Porus to his earlier post, but under Alexander's command.

Alexander's troops were growing weary and tired after some ten years of continuous fighting. They refused to go any further and expressed their wish to return to their homes. His mutinous soldiers put him on the spot at Opis, near modern Baghdad, in the summer of 324 (a year before his untimely death). Alexander "... delivered a shaming harangue. He contrasted the greatness of their achievements under his leadership with their intended, thoroughly ignoble, desertion of him and dereliction of their duty." (Cartledge, 2005)

Here is part of his speech in which he makes reference to the great achievements of the army under his leadership. In this way he makes his troops feel proud of what they had achieved as a unit with him in command. But, he also employs a conciliatory tone. He shamed them by telling them that they were ready to abandon him to the hands of the barbarians who they, under his command, had humiliated before. In this way, he made them feel shame for what they were about to do.

"You all wish to leave me — well, get going then! And when you get back home, tell them that your king, Alexander, conqueror of Persians and Medes and Bactrians and Sacae, destroyer of Uxii and Arachotians and Drangians, who added to this empire Parthians and Chorasmians and Hyrcanians as far as the Caspian Sea, who crossed over the Caucasus beyond the Caspian Gates, and over the Oxus and Tanais and Indus, which none but Dionysus had crossed before him, and the Hydaspes and Acesines and Hydraotes — yes, and the Hyphasis too, if you hadn't shrunk back in fear; who broke through to the great ocean beyond by both mouths of the Indus, and traversed the desert of Gedrosia, where no one had previously been with an army, and acquired in addition Carmania and the land of the Oreitae as he passed through, while the fleet had already sailed along the coast from the land of the Indians to Persia; who was brought back by you to Susa — tell them it was him you deserted and left to the mercy of the barbarians..." (Cartledge, 2005)

> *While moral leaders use oratory to promote virtue, crooked salesmen, charlatans, shenanigans, tricksters, and amoral leaders use language and oratory to fool people.*

Essay 2: Charisma

> *"A personal magic of leadership arousing special popular loyalty or enthusiasm for a public figure (such as a political leader)" Merriam-Webster dictionary (Charisma, n.d.). Notice in the definition the words "personal magic" which summarise well what charisma is basically all about.*

Charisma and leadership go together in the minds of many people. This of course is not entirely true. Suffice to remember that Harry Truman, who some consider to have been an effective leader, hardly had a modicum of charisma. On the other side of the spectrum there was Maria Eva Duarte de Peron, known as Evita of Argentina, who was charisma par excellence.

Maria Peron. Maria Peron was of peasant origin with little education but with much charisma. Evita, as she was known to the world, rose to become Argentina's First Lady as wife of Argentine President Juan Peron. She died young in 1952 aged 33 after having been declared "Spiritual Leader of the Nation". Her early death helped her image and gave her less time to make mistakes and of course less time to [potentially] do more good things as well. Charisma can certainly help someone climb to a position of leadership but will not guarantee effective leadership. Historically some charismatic leaders were good, but others proved to be a disaster and the cause of great harm to other people. As Peter Drucker wrote, "The most charismatic leaders of the last century were called Hitler, Stalin, Mao and Mussolini. They were mis-leaders! Charismatic leadership by itself certainly is greatly overstated." (Karlgaard, 2004).

Pericles and Cimon. I would agree with Drucker that charisma is an overrated and overstated quality, though I would also argue that charisma can be very helpful to leaders that use it for good purposes and are genuine. Fake charisma is dangerous, deceptive and offensive. One such leader with genuine charisma was Pericles of Athens who had all the attributes of charisma: good communicator, good looks, family background, ability to charm, smart, aggressive at times, decent and so on. An even better example was Cimon of Athens, some twenty years Pericles' senior. Charismatic leaders are gifted people who possess what Marston calls "Inducement," or ability to use friendly persuasion. Inducement does miracles when in "perfect alliance between the interests of inducer and induced". (Marston, 1928: 109). Effective charisma ends up with, "...persuading someone in a friendly way, to perform an act suggested by the subject." (Marston, 1928: 109) Where, "The power of inducement in evoking alliance from the induced person lies entirely in the extent to which the inducer is able to serve the other's interest..." (Marston, 1928: 109). In the case of politicians I would say, "...alliance between the interests of the inducer and what the inducer promises to the induced, and not necessarily on what the inducer delivers." Marston gives us some popular terms to describe inducement: persuasion, attraction, captivation, seduction...alluring, luring, attractive personality, personal charm, personal magnetism, appealing...convincing, selling an idea or oneself. (Marston, 1928: 272–273).

It seems that above all, charismatic leaders possess a particularly sharp [sound as well as weird] understanding of human behaviour. Some charismatic leaders indeed can play havoc with people's emotions and thought processes and in the end even 'own' them in the way cult leaders do. Jim Jones had 900 people commit mass suicide in Guyana; all members of his "People's Temple".

Napoleon Bonaparte. Upon hearing the word charisma many people bring to mind Napoleon Bonaparte, forgetting that Napoleon was a soldier of fortune and an opportunist who hijacked the French Revolution for his own ends, and in the end died in disgrace. Napoleon was just 1.57 meters tall with a burning need to prove himself. He was also smart and daring and could talk well even though his French was not what one would describe as "high French", seeing as he came from Corsica. But by the age of 34 he managed to become emperor. So, it was a case of charisma plus cunningness, maybe!

Despite standing just 5 feet, 2 inches (1.57 meters) tall and mocked as a child in Corsica because he couldn't speak proper French, Napoleon Bonaparte was phenomenal in many respects. As a young officer in the French army, he proved to be smart, aggressive and fearless, and inspired great loyalty in just about anyone he met. Call it charisma. Because of these traits, Bonaparte's soldiers won numerous battles for France, and by the age of 34 he was emperor (1804). But here is what happened in the eight years after becoming emperor. He sent his army to capture Russia, only to be mauled by Kutuzov's army with nearly all of Napoleon's expeditionary force killed, injured, taken into captivity, or dead from illness. He was lucky to end his life on Saint Helena instead of experiencing the hangman's noose for recklessness and for using his charisma to convince people to lay down their lives in adventurism. Using his charisma he led people to great victories and ultimately to their destruction. The same goes for Hitler who in the end committed suicide.

Fidel Castro. Charismatic Fidel Castro did some truly amazing things as leader of a small nation. He kept his people together and thumbed his nose at America, which never stopped trying to intimidate Cuba to join the American cause. But what happened in the end? He left Cuba in poverty for far too long and isolated by all the countries that had succumbed to American pressure and went against Cuba.

Winston Churchill. Winston Churchill was an amazing figure with great charisma. He had all the qualities except that in later years he grew overweight. Bombastic and a show man (but not transparent), he had an amazing gift of galvanising people and enthusing them, particularly in times of crisis just as happened during WWII. He used charisma mostly for the good of Britain. "Let us therefore brace ourselves to our duties, and so bear ourselves that, if the British Empire and its Commonwealth last for a thousand years, men will still say, 'This was their finest hour'" is one of his most memorable pieces of oratory (Lewis, 1965).

The Great Man Theory speaks of the impact of "great men" on history. "Great men" are strongly influential because amongst other virtues they bring with them the gift of personal charisma and the ability to influence (to "induce" in Marston's language). Different times, different societies, and different social conditions and societal threats give rise to the unique charismatic individuals of their times. Weber's political leadership theory identifies three types of political leaders: a) bureaucratic, b) charismatic and c) traditional. (Mommsen, 1993)

Stalin and Churchill. The charismatic leader theory can be helpful in analysing the styles of leaders such as Stalin and Churchill who had their charismatic authority partly resting on their personal distinguishing characteristics. These helped them stand out amongst the crowd with ordinary men the first to be influenced by such exceptional persuasive powers. In the case of Stalin, his charisma even gave him the aura of 'cult of personality'. The same goes for Churchill who could do no wrong in the eyes of those who believed in him. Both were above the common man and both had great achievements in their CVs (more in the case of Stalin, some of which were notorious, of course). Both were seen as prophets, as liberators and as God's gift to man (though seminarian Stalin gradually turned into an atheist!). Both were seen as protectors of their people, as inspirers of liberty, and as the personification of doggedness and refusal to surrender. People felt proud to be living in the times these two lived, even if frightened by events such as Stalin's purges. Churchill's presence was overwhelming, even though he operated in a democracy that typically discourages one-man dominance. Stalin's presence was overwhelming as overwhelming can be. It helped that he operated in an autocratic environment that allowed for such behaviour. Of course, he had full control of the State media, which allowed him to monopolise news, information and propaganda.

Though at the height of their leadership both lacked striking physical characteristics, such as impressive good looks like those of John Kennedy for example, both had attractive attributes and mannerisms which the masses generally liked. Churchill donned a cigar and Stalin sported a moustache and had a pocked face as well. Was it then a matter of Weber's manufactured charisma? Not in the case of Churchill, whose eloquence and wit overshadowed most of his peers. Stalin had a rugged look that made him attractive to many. Plus, he was efficient, clever, cunning, and with a powerful personality to match. (see Oleynik, n.d.)

On this charismatic man Stalin, Semyon Kvasha and Vladimir Yerkovich of RBTH reminiscing sixty years after Stalin's death told us, "For many, Stalin's death was akin to the assassination ten years later of US President John F. Kennedy — Russians old enough to remember that time know exactly where they were when they heard the news." Here is what one older woman (seventy-two at the time the report was written) had said, "We were home listening to the radio when we heard the news of Stalin's death. Everyone cried — my mum, my sister and I. Our leader, the person everyone loved more than their own mother and father — our god — had died. I went to school the next day. We gathered together to mourn Stalin's death, and everyone sobbed there too." (Erkovich and Kvasha, 2013)

This is the message Queen Elizabeth II sent to Lady Churchill upon the passing of the charismatic Churchill:

"The whole world is the poorer by the loss of his many-sided genius while the survival of this country and the sister nations of the Commonwealth, in the face of the greatest danger that has ever threatened them, will be a perpetual memorial to his leadership, his vision, and his indomitable courage." (Lewis, 1965). Notice that little was said about Churchill's political leadership that was deficient to say the least.

John Kennedy. John Kennedy's charisma was so plentiful that it even overshadowed his other great achievements as president according to Strober, "John F. Kennedy was noted for his charismatic personality, which, to some observers, overshadowed his performance as president". (Strober and Strober, 1993: 50)

In a farewell address to the Massachusetts legislature on January 9, 1961, President-elect John F. Kennedy gave the world a good indication of the standards of oratory a charismatic leader, like him, needed to have, "Of those to whom much is given, much is required. And when at some future date the high court of history sits in judgement on each one of us—recording whether in our brief span of service we fulfilled our responsibilities to the state— our success or failure, in whatever office we may hold, will be measured by the answers to four questions: First, were we truly men of courage—secondly, were we truly men of judgment...third, were we truly men of integrity, dedication...these are the qualities which, with God's help, this son of Massachusetts hopes will characterize our Government's conduct in the four stormy years that lie ahead. Humbly, I ask His help in this undertaking. But aware that on earth His will is worked by man, I ask for your help and your prayers, as I embark on this new solemn journey." (Strober and Strober, 1993). In summary, here is what Kennedy considered as the four major leadership attributes:

a) courage,

b) judgement,

c) integrity, and

d) dedication.

These four requirements encapsulate well all that is largely required of leaders.

> *In the mists of drought, charismatic leaders can come either as life-giving rain or as burning simoom.*

Charisma in enigmatic leaders

Andreas Papandreou. Andreas Papandreou (known to most Greeks simply as Andreas) studied at Columbia University and earned a doctorate in economics from Harvard University. He was the son of a popular, fatherly and affable former prime minister who was overthrown by the palace through intrigue and apostasy. For Andreas this meant imprisonment by the Greek Junta. He was subsequently freed, courtesy of the celebrated American economist John Kenneth Galbraith, who intervened with the American administration on his behalf. Here is how Galbraith describes what happened in A Life in Our Times, as reported by Christopher Hitchens. The US President Lyndon Johnson instructed one of his senior assistants as follows, "'Call up Ken Galbraith and tell him that I've told those Greek bastards [meaning the Greek Junta that America mostly supported] to lay off that son-of-a-bitch — whoever he is [meaning Andreas Papandreou].'" (Hitchens, 1997). President Johnson's expletive-laden language is clearly descriptive of the contempt with which the American administration held the major actors in NATO ally Greece.

Andreas was a brilliant academic and his work was respected by his colleagues including Nobel Laureates who spoke highly of him and his academic merits. But, Andreas' first wife, a Greek-American psychiatrist, was less than enthusiastic about Andreas' behaviour. Here is what Dr Rassias, former wife of Andreas, had to say about him according to Marlise Simons as reported in the New York Times on June 23, 1996, "Dr Rassias, a psychiatrist, said she often felt bullied by her husband... [who] lied all the time. She wrote an unpublished autobiography in which she described Mr Papandreou as... dishonest." (Simons,1996). Because he was a controversial politician his faithful supporters would disagree strongly with what his former wife had said about him whilst his detractors would obviously be pleased. Of course what former spouses say about each other ought to be considered with extra caution!.

He was a brilliant and a powerful orator even if his Greek language vocabulary was less than extensive. He brimmed with charisma and confidence. He was a maverick politician who could captivate audiences and as such managed to change the political map of Greece. He was voted in for three terms as prime minister but was also accused of corruption along with colleagues of his, two of whom were found guilty. Many of his colleagues are viewed with suspicion by the general public to this day. "Few other politicians in modern Greece have inspired as much love and loathing at home and as much bewilderment and irritation abroad. The tall figure with bushy eyebrows fascinated Greeks with his compelling oratory and his unpredictable and volatile ways, and he remained hard to fathom even for his friends.", said Marlise Simons in her obituary column in the New York Times. (Simons, 1996).

Papandreou was good at applying in practice Hayek's advice, "The most effective way of making people accept the validity of the values they are to serve is to persuade them that they are really the same as those which they, or at least the best amongst them, have always held, but which were not properly understood or recognised before." (Hayek, 1944). Papandreou appeared to take a position that seemed not totally pro-American even if Greece continued to be a client state of the USA. Yet, he gave America what others, whom he accused as being subservient to America, found difficult to give the USA for fear of being labelled sell-outs. Importantly, he gave the USA a five-year renewable agreement for their bases in Greece. These bases were meant to be used against the Soviet Union which Papandreou apparently admired, considering that he claimed to be a 'non-dogmatic Marxist'. At the tail end of his career the 'non-dogmatic Marxist' Papandreou and supposed champion of equality and socialism lived in a $1,000,000 house with his third wife and former air hostess who was half his age! No wonder many of his former supporters now feel cheated.

Papandreou brought about some positive and long overdue changes to Greece which included the abolition of censorship and other liberty-constraining practices. He was not against Greece's EU membership, but his administration (in which no one dared to question his authority) squandered the $12 billion the European Community lent Greece to modernise the country. Apparently he used most of this money to enhance his image amongst his voters and to stay in power. Not that he did anything out of the ordinary within the context of Greek politics, considering that many Greek politicians behaved in this way and continue to do so to this day. He suffocated the civil service with superfluous staff and party apparatchiks and supporters, many of whom in the end had little work to do other than sip coffee and discuss politics aimlessly and meaninglessly! The system remains unchanged under the socialist (by name only) administration at the time of writing. By the end of the second term his administration was mired in scandal he could not control. He was indicted on charges of bribery and embezzlement. His supporters accused the Americans (to whom he had given the five-year renewable lease for their bases!) of being behind the scandal that aimed, in their view, to destabilize Greece. (Simons, 1996) Admittedly, most of those who knew him would agree that he was a larger-than-life leader.

The charming, highly intelligent, and gifted Andreas left a terrible legacy in the form of successors, some of whom were incompetent, others corrupt, and others totally unsuited for the job. One of his senior lieutenants was the person behind the massaging of statistics that were sent to the EU in support of Greece's drive to join the Euro zone and which were the cause of much economic hardship to the Greek people after the economy collapsed. Two of his lieutenants were largely responsible for the catastrophic, and traitorous to most Greeks, management of the sovereignty of two Greek islets that were basically abandoned by Greece as a way of "diffusing" a tense situation with Turkey over them. Another of his senior lieutenants was instrumental in passing a law absolving Ministers (including the initiator of the bill) from financial crimes committed by Ministers whilst holding office. Another of his blue-eyed boys was convicted for fraud involving defence projects and for receiving massive kick-backs. Prior to his incarceration this particular blue-eyed boy of Papandreou splurged with his new young wife whilst Greek Navy sailors and defenders of the country's territorial integrity had to make do with net €600 a month because of defence fund shortages!

It is a shame that the legacy of such an intelligent and charismatic person that had so much to offer his country, and indeed offered a lot, particularly in the area of personal liberties, had his image tarnished by his inability to recruit and appoint people of sound and patriotic character. He made disastrous management selection mistakes, primarily because few if any of his advisors dared question his decisions. I had never intended to include Papandreou in my essays but did so at the insistence of one of his former students and dedicated follower, a well-meaning distinguished academic who truly loves Greece and who once opened one of his speeches on energy that I had attended not long ago with a declaration of admiration for Andreas. I promised him that I would look into the matter. I researched the topic and came up with what I wrote above.

> *Most charismatic leaders also carry the seed of their downfall. Once their charisma goes to their head the feeling of exceptionalism sets in, often leading them to their downfall.*

Essay 3: Luck

Luck is a major factor in leadership, which if absent can wreck a leader's path, right from the start sometimes. Here is how luck saved two of the worlds greatest warriors: Zhukov and Alexander the Great and whose lives play a prominent role in this book.

Here is how luck worked in the case of some great leaders

Zhukov. One of Zhukov's greatest 'attributes' was luck, which came to his rescue at critical junctures in his military career. Absence of luck would have spelled the end of his brilliant rise to great heights. One must remember that Zhukov reported to the brilliant and competent, but cunning, Stalin. Stalin was at the same time violent and did not hesitate to put people on the executioner's list. Also, Stalin kept company with some of history's most unsavoury characters, such as Lavrentiy Beria, who apparently was behind many of Stalin's cruellest actions. Others included Genrikh Yagoda, Nikolai Yezdov and Victor Abakumov. These were Stalin's hatchet men and were perhaps equally culpable as Stalin for the execution and disappearance of thousands of innocent men and women, some of whom were brilliant army officers, scientists, doctors, men of letters and so on.

Equally, the above bruisers oversaw confiscations, deportations, wholesale arrests and executions. Of course, we now know that Stalin himself never listened to intelligence reports on impending attacks because he feared angering and provoking the Nazi command but more than listened to informers. As such, he failed in the area of preparedness to counter the Nazi attacks that were certainly coming. Beria, Yagoda, Yezdov and Abakumov were also responsible for supplying names to Stalin to carry out his purges. The 1930s purges saw thousands of army officers fall victim to Stalin's army of informers, that mostly served under the above three. A lie from one of the four was enough to send someone to his death. Beria was formerly chief of police in Georgia and in 1938 took the reigns of the NKVD (secret police) stationed in Moscow. He composed and managed the target list of political enemies earmarked for execution. He also ran the gulag network. Admittedly he was very competent and amongst his achievements is the successful evacuation of the Soviet defence industries to the east during WWII, when these were under threat from the Nazis. Most importantly he oversaw the development of the atomic bomb, which brought great relief to the Soviet people.

Many of these great officers were put to death charged with seditiousness and of being "enemies of the people". General Dmitry Pavlov was executed (as a scapegoat) at the start of operation Barbarossa for alleged neglect of duty and for failing to contain the initial Nazi attacks. He was later exonerated posthumously in 1952. The Stalin purges of the 1930s were among the worst extrajudicial killings in history. Yet, because of sheer luck Zhukov managed to escape the firing squad at the last moment. He was saved by the bell because the war at Khalkhin Gol in Manchuria against the Japanese was not going well for the Soviets. The Soviets needed someone extra-competent to contain and then crush the enemy. Zhukov was the man of the hour. Indeed, Zhukov saved Stalin from defeat in the East at the hands of the Japanese. Zhukov was hurriedly sent to the East just before he was due to be arrested, charged and executed. He was saved by leaving Moscow on assignment; a sheer stroke of luck! Had he been executed his name would have simply been added to the long list of victims and his death would have been just a statistic and maybe a footnote in world history books. Russia would have lost a great leader, the world would not have seen the achievements of a brilliant general and history would not have documented his military greatness. Worse still, WWII might have had a different outcome without Zhukov's strategic brilliance. The West would in all likelihood have been crushed had Russia fallen. Certainly England would have fallen to the Nazis. (For an interesting incident around Zhukov and his strategic thinking read Montefiore, 2003: 387–388).

Alexander the Great. At the very start of his expedition into Persia-dominated territory, Alexander had to give battle at the Granicus River. In the fighting that followed and as Alexander was personally battling against the enemy a Persian soldier was about to give Alexander a deadly strike with his sword. Alexander was saved at literally the last moment. As if by divine intervention one of Alexander's generals, whom Philip had bequeathed to Alexander, General Cleitus ("the Black") cut the Persian down just as he was about to strike. Alexander lived to conquer the East. Again, a stroke of luck saved a great leader, and the Greeks from certain Persian revenge. In a tragic twist, and as we have seen earlier, Cleitus was later killed by Alexander's sword in a frenzy of drunkenness and fury. (Cartledge, 2005: 209).

One now wonders whether these two great men (Zhukov and Alexander) would have lived to tell the story of their successful and glorious campaigns had they not been so lucky to escape death in the early stages of their careers.

John Kennedy. The two Kennedy brothers provide history with two examples of terrible luck falling on promising leaders. John (the 'Camelot') was assassinated just as he passed the halfway mark of his first term in office only to become later a figure of folklore and the subject of conspiracy theories. How Kennedy would have turned out as leader had he lived we do not know and we will never know.

In a speech at the American University in June, 1963 Kennedy promised that the United States would do "its part to build a world of peace where the weak are safe and the strong are just." (Bacevich, 2010: 88). He also vowed that, "The United States, as the world knows, will never start a war. We do not want war. We do not now expect a war. This generation of Americans has already had enough—more than enough—of war and hate and oppression." (Bacevich, 2010: 88). But, did America never start a war as Kennedy promised before his death? Did Kennedy signal a new policy shift at the time? What happened to this policy. Would the world have been any better had John Kennedy lived? How about Vietnam? There are many questions that still hang in the air to this day. Nixon wrote, "In his Inaugural Address, John F. Kennedy vowed 'to pay any price, bear any burden, meet any hardship, support any friend, oppose any foe, in order to assure the survival and the success of liberty.' " (Nixon, 1994: 38). But, would Kennedy have honoured his pledge to serve liberty had he lived? How about the meddling of the military-industrial complex and the influence of the neoconservatives of those days? The world will never know.

Robert Kennedy. Robert Kennedy suffered the same bad luck as his brother John at the hands of a deranged killer. He was assassinated just as his brother had been assassinated before him. We now all ask how the admittedly brilliant Robert Kennedy would have fared as president and world leader. Unfortunately for the Kennedy family bad luck did not stop at Robert's door and continuous to this day.

Kennedy depended a lot on ideas from a wide spectrum of people. On that basis one assumes that his presidency would have been balanced and his decisions the result of debate among people of knowledge. "In similar fashion, the cabinet consisted of individuals who had achieved success in a varied area of disciplines, including elective politics, business, and diplomacy" say the two Strobers. (Strober and Strober, 1993)

> *Good luck and bad luck are facts of life. By failing to acknowledge the element of good luck in their success, leaders hubristically declare that they are masters of their own destiny; this simply cannot be the case.*

Essay 4: Reading the situation correctly

The ability of a leader to read the situation well at an early stage and without full information is a great quality. History is full of examples of leaders that were unable to read the situation well that subsequently failed in their project. Equally, history is full of examples of accurate reading of the situation by leaders resulting in successful outcomes and victories.

Time magazine described for us how some "autocrats" are able to read the situation well and go on from there. In one of its issues (May 3, 2018. Vol 191. No 18) Time came out with this heading on its cover page, "Rise of the Strongman". The cover page was adorned with the photos of a handful of world leaders whom Time called "strongmen". Ian Bremmer, the writer of the piece, gave us names though the list did not include some of the most notable "strongmen" that are supporters of the West. (Bremmer, 2018). But I guess, one short article cannot possibly cover every conceivable strain of "strongman" in the world. It is clear from the article that leaders who Bremmer calls "strongmen" have the ability to read the situation well and act accordingly.

Vladimir Putin. Among the Time's list of "strongmen" was Vladimir Putin of Russia. According to Time, Putin's emergence as leader is owed to the fact that he promised to, "…wave away Western vultures that would pick Russia clean by making trouble in neighboring states like Ukraine" (Bremmer, 2018: 29). In other words Putin was able to read the situation very accurately and to define the problem well. Once the problem was defined Putin took the next step which was to convince people that he could solve Russia's major concerns. Bremmer continued, "Putin… [aged 65 when the Time article was written!] embodies an image of Russian virility and swagger." I say, good for Putin seeing he had the ability to clearly identify the number one problem Russia faced and to promise to address this. Of course Putin emerged in the midst of the crisis and chaos that Yeltsin had thrust on the people of Russia and which threatened the very integrity of the country as a unitary state. Russians saw the danger and, as one would have expected, wished to see in place someone like Putin. They wanted someone, with leadership qualities galore and with a firm hand to take over. Those that enjoy berating Putin conveniently forget that Putin rose to power through the ballot box with the Russians voting him in with an overwhelming majority more than once. Putin got his position democratically. Apparently, "[President Trump] has expressed sincere admiration for the likes of Putin, Xi Jinping of China, al-Sisi (of Egypt) and Duterte." (Bremmer, 2018: 31).

Just before Operation Barbarossa Stalin failed to read Nazi intentions accurately and the Soviet people paid a heavy price as a result. Equally, Hitler paid the price for failing to appreciate the fighting spirit and resolve of the Soviets and paid the price as well. Did Hitler really believe that the Russians would be easily defeated and that they would have left the Nazis in peace had they suffered occupation? Elsewhere in this treatise I write about how the Vietnam and Afghanistan disasters engulfed America and Russia. Were these two tragedies not the result of bad reading of the situation by leaders that ought to have known better?

Robert Mugabe. In the period leading up to the granting of independence to Rhodesia by Britain, the wily and violence-prone Robert Mugabe read British intentions correctly when Lord Soames arrived in Rhodesia as Governor for a short while after the country reverted back to a British Colony transiting to black rule. Mugabe was convinced that he could intimidate and traumatise voters and that the British under Soames would not lift a finger to protect the black electorate. So, he let loose his armed militias who went on the rampage and rigged the election through violence and intimidation. We now know that, "The British Chief of Defence Staff, Sir Terence Lewin, confirmed that the British Governor, his support staff and the ceasefire monitoring force were to 'get the hell out of it' if the ceasefire broke down." (Frame, 2018: 499). Mugabe literally broke every ceasefire rule and behaved with dishonesty knowing that in the end he would get away with anything and win the elections through violence. As such the people of Zimbabwe were robbed of the opportunity to choose their government freely. So, here we can see how a leader can read the situation well with the aim of cheating and doing bad things to his people. Mugabe masterfully followed these steps to power:

Robert Mugabe: Former Prime Minister and later President of Zimbabwe. Hard to find something good to say about him except that he helped in the area of mass eduction. Hated those not of his ilk especially those of a different: tribe, colour or political party. The British were his favourite scapegoats. He is accused of being behind the killing of tens of thousands of people in Matabeleland and for amassing extraordinary wealth through corruption. From being landless before taking office he is said to now own twenty-one farms some of which he took from white farmers whom he forcefully and violently evicted from their farms without compensation. In the end he was overthrown by his own army.

a) diagnosed the weakness quickly and accurately. He knew that the British were there as just a formality and that all they cared for was to get rid of the Rhodesia problem with no regards as to what would happen to the people.

b) defined the weakness in concrete terms considering that the British had only sent a small ceasefire monitoring force that was there only as a façade and had no power to intervene.

c) came up with the solution of using violence since his men were everywhere armed and willing to employ violence. He made sure that thousands of armed men stayed outside the Assembly Points, free to roam rural Rhodesia and strike fear and terror.

d) promoted his candidature as the only attractive solution using a convincing narrative and promises that were never to be fulfilled. He gave people false hope to the point of them accepting violence as a means to "democracy" Mugabe style!

The infuriating thing is that at the time Robert Mugabe was hypocritically hailed in both East and West as an enlightened and moderate leader.

Some business leaders are adept at reading the situation accurately and acting on that. Unless a business can define correctly what the market wants the business is unlikely to succeed. This is what business schools and MBA programmes teach students: a) find out what the consumer wants, i.e. read the situation well, b) develop a product that will satisfy the consumer's needs, c) price the product competitively, d) sell the product for profit/surplus and e) aim for repeat and new customers. This fits well with what Philip Kotler, the [generally accepted] "father of marketing", says about the subject, "[Marketing is] The science and art of exploring, creating, and delivering value to satisfy the needs of a target market at a profit. Marketing identifies unfulfilled needs and desires. It defines, measures, and quantifies the size of the identified marketing and the profit potential." (Kotler and Keller, 2003)

Reading the situation well is a skill everyone in leadership ought to have. Businessmen need this skill just as politicians and military leaders do. In fact every decision-maker needs to have this skill otherwise his decisions are going to be wrong. Cyprus has failed to read the situation correctly and as such is going around in circles trying to find a solution to a problem that does not exist. The Cyprus problem is a matter of: a) Turkish army occupation of 37% of the country and the pouring in of colonisers to change the population mix of the country and b) the fact that the EU principles of democracy are not applied throughout Cyprus because of occupation. The problem is not about a misunderstanding between communities, which forty years of negotiations are trying to 'solve', whilst leaving the two major issues outside the agenda.

Powerful countries are adept at reading what autocrats need if they are to stay on their side, and as such pour praise on them in the full knowledge that corrupt and incompetent leaders only need recognition, praise, protection, and cover for their many inequities. Western leaders such as Reagan and George H. W. Bush for example read well what Mobutu needed to keep Zaire on America's side. As such they paid tribute to Mobutu who was cordially received by President Bush in the White House as the first African head of state to visit Bush. Reagan went further and praised corrupt and autocratic Mobutu as "a voice of good sense and goodwill" keeping silent about Mobutu's human rights abuses and the millions of dollars he siphoned off from the public coffers and into personal offshore accounts. Interestingly, the rhetoric changed when Mobutu stopped being useful to the USA. Yeltsin, who once ordered a tank platoon to attack his country's parliament, was, at the time, also hailed by some in the West as a Russian democrat.

> *Politicians, business leaders, educators, and others need first to read the situation well and define the problem accurately, otherwise they will not be able to go forward and meet their objectives.*

References

Aristotle (2006). On Rhetoric: A Theory of Civic Discourse. 2nd ed. Translated by George A. Kennedy. Oxford: Oxford University Press.

Baird, A. (n.d.). Oratory | rhetoric. [online] Encyclopedia Britannica. Available at: https://www.britannica.com/art/oratory-rhetoric [Accessed 25 Dec. 2018].

Bacevich, A. (2010). Washington Rules America. New York: Henry Holt & Co.

Brands, H. W. (2015) REAGAN the life. New York: Doubleday.

Bremmer, I. (2018). The 'Strongmen Era' Is Here. Here's What It Means for You. Time Magazine (Vol 191, No 18), pp.29–31. Available online at: http://time.com/5264170/the-strongmen-era-is-here-heres-what-it-means-for-you/ .

Cartledge, P. (2005). Alexander the Great. London: Pan Books.

Charisma. (n.d.). In: Merriam-Webster. [online] Available at: https://www.merriam-webster.com/dictionary/charisma [Accessed 23 November 2018].

Erkovich, V. and Kvasha, S. (2013). Russians remember how they felt the day Stalin died. [online] Russia Beyond. Available at: https://www.rbth.com/society/2013/03/05/russians_remember_how_they_felt_the_day_stalin_died_23521.html [Accessed 26 Oct. 2018].

Frame, J. (2018). The Rhodesian Civil War. New Generation Publishing.

Hayek, F. (1944). The road to serfdom. London: Routledge.

Hitchens, C. (1997). Hostage to History. New York: Verso.

Karlgaard, R. (2004). Peter Drucker On Leadership. [online] Forbes.com. Available at: https://www.forbes.com/2004/11/19/cz_rk_1119drucker.html [Accessed 1 Jan. 2018].

Kotler, P. and Keller, K. (2003). Marketing Management. Cambridge: Pearson.

Lezzi, F. (1959). Benito Mussolini, crowd psychologist. Quarterly Journal of Speech, 45(2), pp.166–170.

Mommsen, W. (1993). The Political and Social Theory of Max Weber: Collected Essays. New York: Wiley.

Montefiore, S. S. (2003). Stalin. London: Phoenix.

Nixon, R. (1994). Beyond Peace. New York: Random House.

Oleynik, Y. (n.d.). The Roles of Stalin and Zhukov in World War II: Who led the USSR from Defeat to Victory?. [online] Academia.edu. Available at: https://www.academia.edu/24262369/The_Roles_of_Stalin_and _Zhukov_in_World_War_II_Who_led_the_USSR_from_Defeat_ to_Victory [Accessed 11 Apr. 2019].

Strober, G. and Strober, D. (1993). "Let us begin anew". New York: Harper Collins.

Simons, M. (1996). Andreas Papandreou Dies at 77; Fiery, Ambiguous Premier DominatedGreek Politics. [online] The New York Times. Available at: https://www.nytimes.com/1996/06/23/world/andreas- papandreou-dies-at-77-fiery-ambiguous-premier- dominatedgreek-politics.html [Accessed 23 Nov. 2018].

Book 7

Developing into a leader

There are many ways leaders can learn to lead and add to what nature already provides them. Considering that we have already agreed that nurture is critical to the development of the leader I chose four relevant essays to include in this book. I selected these particular four because I believe that together they provide the aspiring leader with much of what he needs in order to improve on what nature provides him. Two of these themes have to do with training, which can either come through third parties and coaches or through the family. The other two relate to learning through surviving negative experiences, which in the end help fortify the leader and make him more resilient. When the aspiring leader goes through bad experiences, he runs the risk of things going wrong and marking him for life, and in extreme cases even destroying him as a potential leader. But, once aspiring leaders survive these dangers they invariably come out as winners having learned much from their tribulations.

Training. Training and development are ubiquitous paths to improved chances of success in almost any field and more so in the case of leadership; provided of course that the developmental activities are targeted and are sound. And here, one would need to see training within the "nature vs nurture" spectrum which I address elsewhere in this treatise. What training can do to advance leadership is best exemplified by the habits and traditions of ancient Sparta that showed the world how even the timid can be turned into servants and leaders of their country. Roughly at the age of seven Spartan male children were subject to compulsory training in the Agoge. There they learned about discipline, obedience, courage, daring, self-control, endurance, tenacity, and above all virtue (αρετή) to prepare the student for service. Even the King's male offspring were liable for training in the Agoge, apart from the one that was first in line to succeed him. The legendary King Leonidas had to go through the Agoge (and in fact excelled) because his two older brothers Cleomenes and Dorieus were ahead of him in the line of succession. Cleombrotus (Pausanias's father and Leonidas' twin brother by some accounts) and Pausanias certainly went through the Agoge. The young that demonstrated capacity for leadership were selected for service in the elite Crypteia, Sparta's secret police. At twenty all Spartan men were turned into full-time soldiers. Active duty continued until they reached sixty. Discipline was at the centre of all military activities. Now compare what you have just read to how George W. Bush, president of America, served his country during the Vietnam War. Bush served in the Texas Air National Guard and also secured a Harvard deferment and as such apparently maneuvered to avoid the dangers during those horrible days of the Vietnam War.

Parents. It goes without saying that parents exert great influence on their children and help them form their character, which in turn helps guide their actions in later life. Parents' influence, particularly on a child's will to lead, has been demonstrated throughout history even if parenting conventions varied in line with the expectations of the times. One expects that parental influence will continue in the future unless the structure of the family unit changes drastically and for the worse.

Tenacity and dealing with failure. The ability of a leader to stay on course when barriers are thrown in his path is an undoubted quality strong leaders ought to have. Here we are talking mostly about the leader's capacity to deal with failure and to bounce back after disaster. Failure can be a great learning experience if managed properly. Personal adversity is just one type of barrier that a leader may be called upon to deal with. But that is just one type of adversity. Unless we see how a leader manages problems, bad decisions, bad results and adversity we will never be able to judge him fully as a leader. True tenacity is tested largely under conditions of adversity. Personal adversity is discussed later in this book as a separate issue.

Personal adversity. Leadership development that comes via the road of adversity is painful and sometimes linked to luck. Some leaders are very lucky never to experience severe adversity, which allows them to go through the exercise of leadership unchallenged by great reverses; others are not so lucky. Adversity can turn into a terrible calamity if not dealt with prudently and correctly. But it can also be character building if dealt with correctly. In managing adversity leaders often call on faith and spiritual guidance to help them navigate the dangers and pains of adversity. It appears that there is a limit after which just reason ceases to be of help to leaders facing enormous adversity. When this point is reached, belief, faith and spirituality take over. When faced with extremities and conditions of great distress, reason can take leaders up to a poing but not beyond.

Essay 1: Training and leadership

On the road to wise headship leaders ought to keep educating themselves consistently and benefiting in this way from the experiences and advice of others. Most importantly, leaders with potential ought to seek to serve under model leaders of integrity who can help them develop the skills of effective and honest decision-making. Lucky is the potential leader that serves under an enlightened mentor and guide; starting from first assignment.

> *I tell young promising graduates whom I am honoured to mentor that fortunate is the man who at the start of his career serves under an effective leader of integrity whom he can then adopt as a role model.*

Poorly read and poorly educated leaders are likely to rely overly on luck, intuition, improvisation and gut feeling. I remember once asking a former Head of Government whether his top lieutenants had the habit of reading history, philosophy, politics and economics particularly to help them with their task of serving their country well. I got this response, "The reality is that they are too busy with their day to day work." I pressed the issue telling my interlocutor that reading and education should be a serious part of every politician's job description and as such top priority should be given to continuing education. We both knew, of course, that some of his lieutenants were there on account of political expediency and nothing more. Encouragingly he reiterated his belief that politics is a serious business requiring in-depth knowledge and understanding of issues. He stressed to me his belief that frivolity and flippancy are no substitute to continued and life-long education.

Some leaders have the false impression that just because they earned a university education their obligation to self-development ends with the completion of their formal studies. Formal education helps but it should be just the beginning because life-long reading, continuing education and research are critical to a leader's understanding of complex issues, particularly in our ever-changing world. College education should just be the start. I remember vividly an experience I had soon after earning my bachelor degree and when I returned to my village to visit my parents. At the time I felt that I "knew it all". My father, a former school teacher, asked me to tell him how many books I had read at university. This was before the internet had entered the lives of university students and at the time we were required to read set textbooks (required reading) for each subject plus recommended reading as additional side material. Typically, we were examined on our knowledge of the set textbooks. "Fifty to sixty books" I responded off my head but after a few speedy calculations (5–6 subjects for each of 8 semesters —at one set textbook per subject plus recommended reading). Roughly 20,000–30,000 pages of reading which we had to understand and prepare for exams. "With this paltry reading do you consider yourself an educated man?" my father asked. Startled, I responded, "no, certainly not". "Good, now you are on the path of learning; remember to continue reading classics and always mix with decent people from whom you can learn good things", he told me. To this day I remember the exact place we both stood, the date and time, as this conversation served as a strong reminder in my later life.

Earlier in the treatise we cursorily touched on Plato's ideas on leadership. Plato suggested that the leader ought to be trained [more] specifically in these three subjects: a) mathematics, to enhance reasoning and logical approach to problem-solving, b) physical education, considering the Greek maxim of, "healthy mind in a healthy body". Physical education strengthens the leader's body and brings him closer to nature and other people. In team sports one learns to mingle with others and to cooperate, and in boxing athletes learn to compete and to defend, and c) music, which helps to develop the feeling of harmony and beauty. (Plato's Republic 398b-412b, 522c-e, 525b-526c). Music is also an excellent tool to help advance reasoning and logic and to strengthen our ability for discernment. Pythagoras, the ancient Greek mathematician, was probably also the world's first music authority. (Tan, 2014).

Music for leaders and all others

I remember when some friends of mine from university paid me a visit in Cyprus. Over lunch in a restaurant by the sea we debated plenty of issues and in particular the need for more education in the liberal arts (which incidentally some of us in the team supported strongly). My friends all came from the sciences. We debated under conditions that we tried to approximate to an ancient Greek symposium and as such our discussion took place over after-meal drinks. I was asked this question, "Suppose you were given the authority by God to introduce quickly one (just one) innovative idea to the world. What would that be"? Without hesitation, I responded that I would introduce music everywhere; preferably soft and soothing music (instrumental but also voice); no wild and noisy stuff! Music everywhere: in the skies, in the waves, in the mountains, in the streets, on trees, in cellars; everywhere. When asked why I would prefer this idea over so many other great ideas, which in our time would include technology, I defended my choice saying that I expected music to help tame passions, reduce aggression and make people kinder to each other which in turn would, maybe, improve society. I added that I expected music to encourage the return to the world of lost beauty, rhythm, balance and harmony in our day-to-day lives and in our relationships, and in the way we lead and follow. From there we would try a reboot, not forgetting to keep the good things we now have.

For lo and behold, if we allow uncouth and foolish people to rule over us arbitrariness and brute force will prevail over reason and prudence. A group of foolish people, Plato tells us, do not necessarily equate with one wise (and cultivated I would add) person. (Plato's Crito 47a-b).

> *Uncouth and rough-in-character leaders ought to have no role to play in the leadership of a civilized society except, maybe, when society is faced with conditions of grave danger where the only thing that would count is deliverance from danger, by anyone who can.*

Classics

Whenever a young man or woman asks for my opinion on what to study at university I unfailingly advise him to start out with a considerable dose of classics if he aspires to a position of true leadership. From there he can then move on to his preferred field which he would in the end make his career as: physician, scientist, engineer, teacher and so on. One reason why I am a strong admirer of the American tertiary education system is the requirement that all freshman year students go through some general education that allows them to rethink their major field of study, and also provides them with the opportunity to take a snippet of classical education. Three-year programmes leading to a first degree do not provide students the flexibility of the American freshman year of study. Just a thought! Of course, the British educational system boasts illustrious institutions such as the University of Oxford and the University of Cambridge, both of which excel in classics (and which, incidentally, provided Britain with a disproportionate number of prime ministers).

Training of a Persian monarch

The late Peter Drucker, (a man of genius and modesty and a believer in God) is considered by many, including this author, to be the greatest thinker in management and leadership of the 20th century. "Drucker's real contribution to managerial understanding lays not so much in the cash value of his ideas as in the rigorous activity of mind by which they are formulated. One can learn more —and more deeply—from watching him think than from studying the content of his thought", wrote Alan Kantrow in an article in Forbes in the Jan–Feb 1980 issue. (Kantrow,1980).

Leadership triumph (example: Cyrus the Great): Here is what Drucker had to say about books on leadership. "The first systematic book on leadership: the Kyropaidaia [Cyropaedia] of Xenophon — himself no mean leader of men — is still the best book on the subject.' And, "Despite all the books published on leadership by well-known academic researchers and successful CEOs, Drucker never altered his opinion. Xenophon was still the best" said William Cohen, a family friend of Peter and Doris Drucker. Drucker just leafed over leadership books and hardly read one from start to finish. (Cohen, 2010).

Cyropaedia has as its main theme the education of Cyrus of Persia as he was preparing to assume the Persian Monarchy. His training entailed a heavy dose of education and practice on how to become wiser. (Xenophon, trans. 2012).

Cyrus the Great. Now I will deal with the education of Cyprus concentrating on what he was taught and how this improved his leadership. I will present numerous excerpts from Xenophon's

Cyropaedia. It may interest the reader to know that Cyrus finally became one of the greatest leaders of all time and certainly of ancient times. [Cyrus's father] King Cambyses advised his son (the future Cyrus the Great circa 600–530 BC) to learn to differentiate between his own people and thus the people he would lead (Persians and allies), and the opposing army that he planned to defeat. Here is what the father taught the son:

Lesson number one: Know how to lead and how to be led, "Rule thou and be thou ruled." (Xenophon, trans. 2012: 28) and, "...the real incentive to obedience lies in the praise and honour that it wins against the discredit and the chastisement which fall on the disobedient" (Xenophon, trans. 2012: 28). Here is Cyrus's response to the above advice, "You would have me understand," said Cyrus, "that the best way to secure obedience is to be thought wiser than those we rule" (Xenophon, trans. 2012: 29). "Yes," said Cambyses, "that is my belief." (Xenophon, trans. 2012: 29). And then Cambyses told Cyrus how he can go about learning wisdom, "Well my son, it is plain that where learning is the road to wisdom, learn you must... when it comes to matters which are not to be learnt by mortal men, nor foreseen by mortal minds, there you can only become wiser than others by communicating with the gods through the art of divination. But always, wherever you know that a thing ought to be done, see that it is done, and done with care; for care, not carelessness, is the mark of the wise man" (Xenophon, trans. 2012: 29).

Lesson number two: Lead by example. Cambyses told Cyrus, "and so in war; if the campaign is in summer the general must show himself greedy for his share of the sun and the heat, and in winter for the cold and the frost, and in all labours for toil and fatigue. This will help to make him beloved of his followers" (Xenophon, trans. 2012: 29) and then Cambyses went on to tell Cyrus that the commander must be stouter-hearted in everything than those whom he commands. (Xenophon, trans. 2012: 29).

Lesson number three: Learn to be crafty with the enemy (at war). When Cyrus asked Cambyses how he could defeat the enemy he responded, "If your general is to succeed he must prove himself an arch-plotter, a king of craft, full of deceits and stratagems, a cheat, a thief, and a robber, defrauding and overreaching his opponent at every turn" (Xenophon, trans. 2012: 30). And Cambyses went on, "...you never meet the lion or the bear or the leopard in fair fight on equal terms, but were always trying to steal some advantage over them?" (Xenophon, trans. 2012: 30). Cambyses stressed that the general should not be careless if he wished to defeat the enemy.

Lesson number four: Respect the gods and be spiritual and do not think for a moment that man has all the answers. The greatest thing, perhaps, Cambyses wanted Cyrus to know entailed the spiritual, "Observe the sacrifices and pay heed to the omens; when they are against you, never risk your army or yourself." (Xenophon, trans. 2012: 33), and Cambyses continued, "But the gods, my son, who live for ever, they know all things, the things that have been and the things that are and the things that are to be, and all shall come from these; and to us mortals who ask their counsel..." (Xenophon, trans. 2012: 33) "How often have cities allowed themselves to be persuaded into war, and that by advisers who were thought the wisest of men, and then been utterly destroyed by those whom they attacked. How often have statesmen helped to raise a city or a leader to power, and then suffered the worst at the hands of those whom they exalted." (Xenophon, trans. 2012: 33).

(Note: for a full understanding of the catastrophic counsel advisers that are thought to be wise can sometimes give their leaders, read the story of Vietnam in: McNamara, 1995)

What Cambyses taught his son Cyrus about leadership:

1. Learn to be a follower as well as a leader.
2. Acquire wisdom through learning.
3. Lead by example.
4. Keep learning at all times.
5. Prepare and take care of everything and do not be careless.
6. Be stouter-hearted than your followers.
7. Operate cleverly/craftily and outfox your opponents in war.
8. Beware of advisers and their bad advice.
9. Do not fall into the trap of thinking that you know it all if you wish to avoid catastrophe.

Essay 2: Parents' influence

"...first, and perhaps the most destructive, was his widowed mother, a strong-willed, hysterical, brutal, bitterly frustrated woman who loved her son, and broke his spirit. She was a savage monster even by the none too exacting standards of humanity of the Russian landowners of those days.
(Turgenev, trans. 1975: 15).

A leader's relations with his parents are often brought up to partially explain leader behaviour in later years. In his monumental and seminal work on leadership MacGregor Burns raises the parent factor by making reference to major historic figures and how they were influenced by their parents. (Burns, 2010)

Hitler-Lenin-Ghandi. MacGregor Burns notes, "One could speculate that the common inclusive childhood experience for these [see below] monumental figures was intense positive attachment to one parent coupled with some intensely negative attachment to the other or an intensely traumatic and negative youthful experience." (Burns, 2010: 58). He then brings to the reader these examples: Lenin admired his father but Hitler loathed his father who was 23 years older than his mother. Hitler was unattractive and sickly making the contrast between him and his [more attractive] father painful. This and other things made Hitler insecure to the point of obsession. As it was discovered later in the autopsy the Russians carried out upon his death, Hitler had one undescended testicle making him a monarchist. Non-violent Ghandi feared his father.

Stalin. Stalin's father, Besarion Djugashvili was an alcoholic and abusive (including physical abuse) not only towards Stalin but also towards his mother Keke Djugashvili as well. He was also good for nothing as a cobbler. Stalin often tried to protect himself and his mother from abuse and violence and it is said that once he threw a knife at his father in self-defence and had to call for help when Besarion tried to strangle his mother. His mother was smart and took pains to support Joseph Stalin. She also disciplined Stalin, who was reckless and rebellious and very often out of control. To protect her unruly son she put him into seminary school and wanted him to become a priest. But, though for a while he joined the seminary, in the end he proved to be an atheist who believed in Marx more than God. He was expelled from school and then joined the Bolsheviks. The rest is history!

Though within the context of history generalisations are dangerous, one is permitted to do so provided common sense is applied. We grown-ups were all children at some time and most of us had close relations with our parents. Surely these relations must have left a mark on our behaviour in later life. The question therefore is not whether we were affected by our parents, but to what extent.

Alexander and his father, Philip.

Alexander. Alexander was [almost certainly] envious of his father's (Philip's) achievements and was unhappy with the fact that Philip had crossed into Asia in 334 BC, two years before him. Philip did so with his able and distinguished military chief, Marshal Parmenion and Parmenion's son-in-law Attalus. It was Parmenion who helped Philip lay the foundations for the Asia campaign. Alexander was strongly (obsessively perhaps) attached to his mother Olympias whose powerful personality, determination and beauty defied words. Philip was by all counts ugly and physically partly deformed; the result of injuries sustained in battle. Thus, his looks contrasted with those of Olympias. But, what Philip lacked in looks he more than made up for in strategic thinking, discipline and courage.

Fredricksmeyer distinguishes two sides of Alexander's relationship with his father Philip. The public side—Philip was the model general whom Alexander was to succeed; or perhaps his dynastic rival given the ethos of the times. The private side—Olympias (Alexander's mother) had a bad relationship with her husband Philip which got worse with time because of his extensive womanising (not unusual in those days). Philip married seven times, mostly for political reasons. Though Olympias was the premier wife and mother of Alexander, the heir apparent, her wounded pride and sexual jealousy caused her to feel, "… resentment at the possibility of that any one of Philip's women might produce a potential rival for Alexander's succession." (Fredricksmeyer, 1990).

Like his father, Alexander was a descendant of Heracles and as such had the air of a semi-god. Alexander's pedigree was a great influence on him. Their Argive (Spartan most would say) origin and half-god bloodline gave both Philip and Alexander an air of invincibility and greatness. Not that both were not great men in their own right. Philip created the League of Corinth and brought together all the Greek cities as a prelude to invading Asia and Persia. But fate played a cruel trick on him. He was assassinated in public view during the wedding procession of his daughter Cleopatra, Alexander's full sister. Philip was in his forties when he was felled by an assassin. As regards Philip's assassination, Cartledge tells us that, "Fingers of suspicion were pointed at Philip's estranged wife Olympias, Alexander's mother, and indeed at Alexander himself, perhaps with some reason." (Cartledge, n.d.:13)

Amongst other reasons Alexander's emotional antagonism to his father, caused him to kill Cleitus the Black who saved Alexander's life at the battle of the Granicus River in 334 BC (just as the Asian campaign had started). Cleitus was the brother of Alexander's wet nurse and a Philip general. This is what had happened, "...there was a massive flare-up between them... in autumn 328 during a wild drinking binge. Cleitus made the mistake of accusing Alexander of minimizing his father Philip's achievements in order to magnify his own, and Alexander, blind drunk and out of control, ran Cleitus through with a pike." (Cartledge, n.d.:72).

Undoubtedly mothers and fathers, and even grandparents perhaps, play a central role in most people's lives and in their later development and behaviour. It would be unreasonable perhaps to deny this. Cimon, the great Athenian general (died in Cyprus in 449 BC) was surely influenced by the fact that he was scion of an aristocratic family and was the son of the famous Athenian general Miltiades who was the first to do battle with, and win against, the

Persians. Cimon was the product of his upbringing. And this helped him achieve great things for Athens and the Greeks through his courage, dignity, kindness and generosity. Not only are most leaders influenced by their parents and their family backgrounds but undoubtedly they are also influenced by the great deeds and achievements of people they look up to (important others) in their lives. The great Themistocles, victor over Xerxis' navy at Salamis (480BC), could not find peace thinking of Miltiades' achievements at Marathon some ten years earlier (490 BC) and in which Themistocles took part. Themistocles obsessively wanted to surpass Miltiades, hence the, «οὐκ ἐά μέ καθεύδειν τό τοῦ Μιλτιάδου τρόπαιον." Freely translated, "Miltiades' glory does not allow me to rest."

> *The social environment in which the leader finds himself is particularly influential in shaping his value system and behaviour. The family is likely to be the most potent social environmental influence on the leader.*

Essay 3: Tenacity—dealing with failure

"I learned to survive very young", Lord Andrew Adonis

Lincoln-Nixon. People with a will to lead have a habit of coming back from failure and are not easily discouraged when things do not work out as planned. Some even overcome repeated failures, such as those Abraham Lincoln experienced before becoming US President. Richard Nixon was a great example of a man that was undaunted by failure. He lost a presidential election to Kennedy

Richard Nixon. Nixon achieved great things for his people but failed to tame some of his bad habits that finally got him into trouble. His social programmes benefited the poorer classes of American and his policies in foreign affairs gave the world hope, security and peace. He was forced to resign by the Watergate affair and by the vicious attacks against him coming from the establishment that disliked him immensely. No doubt in good time, and when all is viewed from a distance, he will regain his rightful place as a great American leader.

and then lost the vote for governor of California. Undaunted he came back to become the president of the USA by winning two presidential elections. It is my firm belief that after Watergate if Nixon had age on his side he would have probably rehabilitated himself nicely and made a comeback; though not in electoral politics maybe. Nixon was the historic president that ended the Vietnam War and placated the Soviets and the Chinese. Here is what The Atlantic had to say (correctly perhaps), "The life of no president says more about this country. Nixon's accomplishments sing of the finest American attributes—daring, audacity, resilience and grit. His fall is an incantation of the nation's flaws, of meanness, prejudice, avarice and corruption." (Farrell, 2013)

Nixon's character probably met most of Tolstoy's description of man (homo sapient). Tolstoy, who though an aristocrat championed the cause of the peasants, said that man is 'fluid' and his nature is full of antitheses: villain and angel, sage and idiot, strong and weakling and the list goes on. (Tolstoy, Wilks and Foote, 1977: 10)

But, both Lincoln and Nixon were unlucky in the end. The first fell victim to a fanatic that shot him and the second was a victim of his opponent's hatred and meanness and obviously his own failings. But, in certain ways Nixon was an angel compared to what we now read about presidents before him and their practices. Here is what The Atlantic wrote, "Franklin Roosevelt, Dwight Eisenhower and Harry Truman were as cold as Nixon when ordering US bombers to annihilate civilians in war. Ike and Jack and Lyndon had their own Oval Office taping systems, and imperturbably ordered the CIA and the Marines to overthrow the governments of foreign countries. The Kennedy Justice Department tapped phones and passed around tapes of Martin Luther King's sexual encounters. JFK slept with a gangster's moll, and reportedly ordered his intern mistress to fellate a friend in the White House swimming pool while he watched. As an act of dominance, his humiliated aides reported, LBJ made them watch as he defecated on the toilet. The Eisenhower and Kennedy administrations, when soliciting the services of the Mafia in the CIA plots against Fidel Castro, were 'running a damn Murder Inc.' in the Caribbean, as Johnson memorably put it." (Farrell, 2013). They were all lucky not to be caught!

Alexander the Great. One of the most serious misjudgements to have been made by a genius of war was made by Alexander the Great when he decided to cross the Gedrosian desert in 325 BC (two years before his early death). He decided on this disastrous route to take him back to Iran from India once the troops began to mutiny. Worse for Alexander's ego admiral Nearchus, who was vested with the responsibility of bringing the fleet back, did so successfully and with practically no losses. Nearchus commanded the newly built Greek navy in a voyage taking with him about a quarter of the army (around 20,000). The voyage lasted for about nine months (November 326 to July 325) and was anything but easy for Nearchus and his sailors. Another army unit (of the same size as that of Nearchus') under Craterus was also ordered to leave and go back to Macedonia. Alexander decided to go through the Gedrosian desert with most of the remaining army. This proved to be a disastrous decision with far too many losses in the crossing; particularly civilians such as accompanying women, merchants that followed the army and many animals (Arrian, The Anabasis of Alexander). Here is the tenacity part: this disaster did not stop Alexander from planning his next campaigns, to the west this time, and leaving his plans for the future with Perdicas.

Churchill. Dean Williams of the Harvard Kennedy School wrote on April 24, 2015 about Winston Churchill's terrible leadership failure at Gallipoli during WWI. He wrote that Churchill's leadership "was dreadful". Churchill was the secretary of the navy (First Lord of the Admiralty) when he decided to attack Turkey in the Dardanelles (Gallipoli.) The battle lasted for about eight and a half months. The result was half a million casualties (one million on both sides.) The campaign failed with disastrous consequences on the war effort and later on the Greeks, Armenians, Jews, and other minorities that were exterminated by the Turks. Had the Dardanelles fallen to the British the whole history of the area would probably have changed for the better. Dean Williams attributes this failure partly to Churchill's pigheadedness and stubborn defence of his viewpoint. He failed to evaluate data properly and adopted a "can-do attitude that verged on the hubristic". Poor listening skills and inability to see the other point of view, and particularly that of the head of the Royal Navy, then 74 years old Admiral John Fisher, who saw Churchill's plan as spelling disaster and doom. Worse still, Churchill tried to hide Fisher's view from the War Cabinet. Fisher resigned in the end, telling Churchill, "I know you so well." (Forbes.com, 2015). But, to Churchill's credit this disastrous and costly failure did not discourage him from leading Britain to great things later in WWII.

Stalin. Under the title, "Barbarossa Hitler Stalin: War Warnings Stalin Ignored" Patrick Jackson wrote on 21 June, 2011 that, "In an interview with Komsomolskaya Pravda newspaper, Russian military historian Arsen Martirosyan revealed that Soviet intelligence had named the exact, or almost exact, date of the invasion 47 times in the 10 days before Germany struck." And that, "Between 1 and 10 June, they captured 108 enemy spies and saboteurs, he told Komsomolskaya Pravda, and a further 200 or so in the final twelve days before the invasion. On 14 June, guards on the Belarusian section of the border relayed back to Moscow the correct date of the planned invasion, learnt from two captured saboteurs. The same date was revealed by saboteurs captured on 18 June." Air Major-General Georgy Zakharov, Soviet reconnaissance pilot reported days before Barbarossa that, "Frontier regions west of the state border packed with troops... tanks, armoured cars and guns poorly concealed or not concealed at all..." The BBC itself ends with this note, "The old debate about whether the USSR prevailed against Hitler because of the dictator's leadership, or in spite of it, refuses to go away. (Jackson, 2011). Here we see a disaster of gigantic proportions that cost the lives of hundreds of thousands of soldiers, put the country at risk and nearly brought defeat to the Soviets. This disaster was caused by a man who unjustly blamed others, including General Dmitry Pavlov who was put to death and then exonerated in 1956. This great failure of Stalin's, and many other failures that followed, did not discourage him from leading the WWII effort and in the end defeating the Nazis.

Using the Navy Seal creed of, "If knocked down, I will get back up every time. I am never out of the fight", Brent Gleeson wrote in Forbes on 2 June, 2016 under the title, "Great Leaders Learn to Fail Without Becoming a Failure". He wrote, "There are no perfect leaders, which means failures and mistakes are inevitable. Mistakes don't define us. How we learn from them does." Talking of his Navy Seal training he said, "I often exhibited the traits you find on those lists of 'what not to do' as a leader. Transparent feedback from the team became a crucial part of my personal and professional development. And trust me, it has not always been easy to digest." (Gleeson, 2016)

Writing in the Huffington Post on 23 January, 2016 under the title, "10 of the Greatest Leadership Mistakes in History" Bill Fawcett gives us hope that in today's world we can avoid many leadership mistakes thanks to new communication advances that provide a continuous flow of information, "With modern communications and an active press, no leader can today be as out of touch as were Louis XVI and Marie Antoinette." And, "The world has progressed, technology has grown, and the human race has reached the moon, despite all of the errors and stupidities of the past." Despite the many and drastic mistakes that leaders commit, humanity continues to progress. The will to lead and capacity to remain undaunted by failure are the two most essential requirements to making a comeback. (Fawcett, 2014)

Writing in the Business News Daily on 9 December, 2016 under the title, "How Successful Leaders Recover from Failure" Karina Fabian advises us on how to deal with failure:

1. Adopt a good attitude about failure. After all, failure is part of the learning process and in fact it is part of life. "... failure can be just as valuable as success." And "Instead of decreasing your confidence and your feeling of your abilities, it should boost those. Those experiences make you a better entrepreneur,"

2. "Apologize quickly and own up." Don't blame others and do not look for excuses,

3. Take action to fix the problem and stand by your people. Carry out a damage control exercise, apologise and move on,

4. Carry out diagnoses on what happened and do not repeat the same mistakes and

5. Do not throw in the towel. Get up and try again. (Martins, 2019)

Lord Andrew Adonis. I have always been fascinated by the astonishing life of Lord Andrew Adonis. Here is a short review of his unbelievable fight-and-win attitude. Andrew is the son of Nikos, a Cypriot migrant to the UK who worked as a waiter, and his English mother. His mother left the family when he was just three and has never communicated with her son since. He and his sister were placed in care seeing their father's long hours of work did not allow him to be with them when they needed him. Lord Adonis lived in a council children's home until the age of eleven, with his sister. Then his life took a miraculous turn for the better when he was awarded a grant to attend Kingham Hill School in Oxfordshire, as a boarder. Following secondary school he was admitted to Keble College, Oxford where he gained a first-class Bachelor of Arts degree and later a doctorate at Christ Church. He later became a Fellow, History and Politics, at Nuffield College. Here is his career after Oxford: journalist at the Financial Times and later at The Observer, advisor and then Head of the Policy Unit on appointment by Prime Minister Blair, Minister of State for Education, Minister of State for Transport, then Secretary of State for Transport and so on. Not surprisingly, when interviewed by Aida Edemariam of The Guardian on 10 May, 2013, he told her, 'I learned to survive very young'. (Edemariam, 2013).

I am moved whenever I read about Lord Adonis' life just thinking of a frightened little boy of three whose mother left him, mapping out in his child's head the next steps for survival, rather than decrying the bad fortune that befell him and his sister.

> *As human beings true leaders obviously get disheartened at times. But they never submit. They come back and start again from where they fell the last time around.*

Essay 4: Personal adversity

Not long ago a mother approached me to ask whether I could help her son with his education because he was not doing well at school and showed no signs of wanting to improve. He was in his last year at high school. She told me that the boy had little guidance from his father, who had divorced her, and that they had little money. I volunteered to help and called the young man on the telephone to set up a meeting in my office. We agreed on a time and date. He never showed up. I left it at that, with the hope that he would call me to explain what had happened. He called me three days later to tell me, "I forgot all about our meeting. Can we meet soon?" I suspected that he was avoiding our meeting because he knew that I would advise him to exert himself more, to get organised, become methodical, make a fresh start and generally set education as his top priority at this stage of his life. I readied myself with patience and started planning to find a job for him in the event I was successful with the counselling. I was hoping that he would end up as a tertiary education student. He never showed up to our second prearranged meeting. He called me days later to tell me that he had overslept. I felt sorry for this young teenager because what lay behind his behaviour was basically his inability to cope with adversity and initiate a new start in his life. He had been abandoned by his father, his mother was working flat out doing menial tasks to make ends meet, he was poor, not doing well at school, had lost his confidence, and worst of all, had lost the desire to bring about a reversal of his fortunes. I have not given up on him.

Many are the great leaders who were galvanised by the adversity they suffered [particularly] at a young age to reach great heights later. Equally, others were demolished by adversity that caused them to lose their desire to live. Great leaders have the capacity to take adversity in their stride, learn from their experiences and even turn adversity into an opportunity. David L. Dotlich, writing in the January/February 2005 issue of Ivey Business Journal, notes that strong leaders view adverse events as 'passages' that take them from one place to another. The emotional events that the person goes through helps him to see self and events differently. These experiences have the following three elements in common:

- While they are inevitable, they are random and unpredictable. Adding to the confusion is the fact that you can't predict how you will respond or where you will end up after you go through the passage. And the more significant the event, the more unpredictable

> your response and the results. The only certainty is that the way you respond will define your present and future career.
>
> - These passages are emotionally and cognitively intense. They test and push you. You will have to call on resources you didn't know you possessed, rely on skill sets you previously ignored, assess your priorities and re-evaluate your basic values.
> - As a result, your sense of yourself will change in some fundamental way. Who you are, what you're capable of doing and your place in the world will all shift." (Dotlich, 2005).

Napoleon. These people are not out of the ordinary in terms of their emotions. They typically have the emotions of normal people, but are endowed with a very strong will and are tough by most standards. They view bad circumstances differently from most other people. They do not easily collapse under the pressure of adversity. Though Napoleon is lauded as a great leader, one must not forget that when things were not going well in the Russian campaign, he abandoned the field to deal with a health problem. "... Napoleon left what remained of his army to return to Paris with a few followers. Six days later, the Grande Armée finally escaped Russia, having suffered a loss of more than 400,000 men during the disastrous invasion." (History.com, 2010).

Napoleon reappeared in Paris with his secretary Caulaincourt at his side while his troops perished in Russia. The question of whether Napoleon buckled under pressure or not will continue to haunt his legacy for ever.

William Moulton Marston, originally writing in 1928, identified four constructs of emotions which are: Dominance, Compliance, Inducement and Submission. As regards the construct of Dominance, Marston introduces these two notions: a) control over others and b) prevailing over adversity. (Marston, 1928: 108).

He itemises the following characteristics as compatible with the constructs of Dominance, "forcible removal of opposition (barriers to forward movement): ego-emotion, aggressiveness, rage, self-assertion, will, determination, high spirits, courage, nerve, boldness, purposeness, persistency, power, pioneer spirit, strength of character, doggedness, egocentricity." But these characteristics are not necessarily found together (Marston, 1928: xxii-xxiii).

Without being courageous, one may be aggressive; and without being either aggressive or courageous, one could be purposeful. Marston notes, "...the common denominator of emotional meaning is always dominance emotion, consisting of increase of the self to overcome an opponent." (Adversity in our case.) (Marston, 1928: 140) Marston continues, "...a feeling of an outrush of energy to remove oppositions. This feeling, with an admixture of unpleasantness accompanying the obstruction of the outrushing energy in so far as it is obstructed, and an admixture of pleasantness accompanying the increase of energy outrush in so far as it is increased, constitutes dominance emotion." (Marston, 1928: 140)

(For more on dominance and other constructs as applied to performance management read: Petasis, 1993)

Leaders of different personalities who overcame adversity

Thomas Jefferson. Thomas Jefferson was a very private man that few fully understood. Before his death he asked that an epitaph be written on his monument which read as follows, "Thomas Jefferson, author of the Declaration of American Independence, of the Statute of Virginia for Religious Freedom, and Father of the

University of Virginia." No reference was made to his eight-year presidency of America. (McCullough, 2001: 649)

This man of great deeds who left his mark on the world lost his father when he was only 14 years old (1757). His wife died when he was thirty-nine, and only two of his five children lived to adulthood.

Robert E. Lee. Robert E. Lee, (1807–1870) the great aristocrat and noble general, saw his father (Henry Lee III) go to the debtors' prison when he was just two years old, after his father had an unsuccessful venture with his plantation in the Panic of 1796/7. In 1809 Henry Lee became bankrupt and was jailed in the debtors' prison in Montross, Virginia. His father was a great General ("Light-Horse" Lee III) (1756–1818), a great American patriot, former ninth governor of Virginia and also Virginia Representative to the United States Congress. Yet he suffered the humiliation of a jail sentence, leaving Robert E. Lee in near destitution.

Richard Nixon. Richard Nixon (1913–1994), 37th president of the USA, member of the House of Representatives and Vice-President under Dwight Eisenhower, was forced to resign whilst in his second term in office, for fear of being impeached and maybe even imprisoned. His father had an unsuccessful and failed venture as a lemon farmer and then became a grocer (just as was Margaret Thatcher's father). He had an unhappy and troubled childhood, as he was raised by a father who was often abusive and a mother who was domineering and controlling. Two of Nixon's siblings died at birth. Some attribute Nixon's mania with success to his unlucky childhood. "Tricky Dicky" was an achiever from early life; at Whittier College he excelled both as a student and as a debater, was president of his class (when a freshman) and president of the student body (when a senior); he graduated 2nd in class, won a scholarship to Duke University Law School, and was a member of the national scholastic law fraternity. Most people would have buckled under the pressures Nixon had to endure. Read more: (Notablebiographies.com, n.d.).

John Adams. John Adams, second president of the USA, wrote in a letter to Jefferson Adams, "Had you read the papers enclosed they might have given you a moment of melancholy or at least of sympathy with a mourning father. They relate wholly to the funeral of a son who was once the delight of my eyes and a darling of my heart, cut off in the flower of his days, amidst very flattering prospects by causes which have been the greatest grief of my heart and the deepest affliction of my life" (McCullough, 2001: 569).

Joseph Stalin. Joseph Stalin (December 1878 – 5 March 1953) rose from obscure origins in Georgia to rule the Soviet Union from the mid-1920s until his death in 1953. It is said that when his simple and pious mother, Ketevan Gheladze Dzhugashvili (1858–1937) came to visit him in the Kremlin (the first and only time apparently), she asked him: "what work exactly do you do"? His response was: "I do the things the Tsar used to do before." Not realising exactly what Stalin was doing and whether he had a real job or not, she told him, "better had you stayed in the seminary."

His mother was a housewife, seamstress, and laundress. Stalin's father, Besarion Vanovis Dzhugashvili (1849/1850–1909), an alcoholic cobbler, very often used violence against his mother, and also against young Joseph. Mother and son sought the protection of a local kind and pious priest until Stalin joined the seminary.

References

Cartledge, P. (n.d.). Alexander the Great.

Cohen, W. (2010). Peter Drucker's Favorite Leadership Book. [online] Process Excellence Network. Available at: https://www.processexcellencenetwork.com/lean-six-sigma-business-performance/columns/peter-drucker-s-favorite-leadership-book [Accessed 1 Oct. 2018].

Burns, J. (2010). Leadership. New York, NY: Open Road Integrated Media.

Dotlich, D. (2005). Adversity: What Makes A Leader The Most. [online] Iveybusinessjournal.com. Available at: https://iveybusinessjournal.com/publication/adversity-what-makes-a-leader-the-most/ [Accessed 11 Oct. 2018].

Edemariam, A. (2013). Andrew Adonis interview: 'I learned to survive very young'. [online] the Guardian. Available at: https://www.theguardian.com/politics/2013/may/10/andrew-adonis-learned-survive-interview [Accessed 31 Jan. 2019].

Farrell, J. (2013). The Operatic Life of Richard Nixon. [online] The Atlantic. Available at: https://www.theatlantic.com/politics/archive/2013/01/the-operatic-life-of-richard-nixon/266963/ [Accessed 12 Dec. 2018].

Fawcett, B. (2014). 10 Biggest Leadership Mistakes In History. [online] HuffPost.com. Available at: https://www.huffpost.com/entry/10-of-the-greatest-leader_b_2057685 [Accessed 26 Oct. 2018].

Forbes Leadership Forum. (2015). Winston Churchill's Terrible Leadership Failure. [online] Forbes.com. Available at: https://www.forbes.com/sites/forbesleadershipforum/2015/04/2

4/winston-churchills-terrible-leadership-failure [Accessed 17 Oct. 2017].

Fredricksmeyer, E. (1990). Alexander and Philip: Emulation and Resentment. The Classical Journal, [online] 85(4), pp.300–315. Available at: https://www.jstor.org/stable/3297677 [Accessed 17 Apr. 2019].

Gleeson, B. (2016). Great Leaders Learn To Fail Without Becoming A Failure. [online] Forbes.com. Available at: https://www.forbes.com/sites/brentgleeson/2016/06/02/great-leaders-learn-to-fail-but-not-be-a-failure [Accessed 26 Oct. 2018].

History.com. (2010). Napoleon retreats from Moscow. [online] Available at: https://www.history.com/this-day-in-history/napoleon-retreats-from-moscow [Accessed 11 Oct. 2018].

Kantrow, A. (1980). Why Read Peter Drucker?. [online] Harvard Business Review. Available at: https://hbr.org/2009/11/why-read-peter-drucker [Accessed 1 Oct. 2018].

Jackson, P. (2011). The war warnings Stalin ignored. [online] BBC News. Available at: https://www.bbc.com/news/world-europe-13862135 [Accessed 26 Oct. 2018].

Martins, A. (2019). Bouncing Back: How to Recover from Failure. [online] Business News Daily. Available at: https://www.businessnewsdaily.com/9619-recover-from-failure.html [Accessed 26 Oct. 2018].

Marston, W. (1928). Emotions of normal people. London: Kegan Paul Trench Trubner & Co. Ltd.

McCullough, D. (2001). John Adams. New York: Touchstone.

Mcnamara, R. (1995). In retrospect: The Tragedy and Lessons of Vietnam. New York: Times Books.

Notablebiographies.com. (n.d.). Richard Nixon Biography. [online] Available at: http://www.notablebiographies.com/Ni-Pe/Nixon-Richard.html [Accessed 16 Jun. 2018].

Petasis, A. (1993). Managing Human Potential: a guide to assessing and improving performance. Nicosia: The Philips College.

Tan, M. (2014). Plato's Ideal Ruler Today. [online] Philosophy Now. Available at: https://philosophynow.org/issues/101/Platos_Ideal_Ruler_Toda y [Accessed 22 Oct. 2017].

Tolstoy, L., Wilks, R. and Foote, I. (1977). Master and man and other stories. London: Penguin.

Turgenev, I. (1975). Fathers and Sons. Translated by Rosemary Edmonds. London: Penguin Books.

Xenophon. (2012). Cyropaedia: The Education of Cyrus. Translated by Henry Graham Dakyns. Edited by F.M. Stawell. CreateSpace Independent Publishing Platform.

Book 8

Leader assessment

The following quote from Glenn Llopis writing in Forbes on 25 November, 2013 summarises well the subject of this book. Here is what he had to say about leadership and changing times, "Many leaders today don't belong in leadership positions anymore. The success factors for leadership have changed drastically because of the demands of a new global marketplace. It's not only about evaluating the charts, graphs and the numbers – it's much more than that now. Leadership has become more instinctual and requires broadened observation to connect the dots and understand the patterns of performance probability about the business, its people, its clients and the marketplace it competes in — simultaneously." (Llopis, 2013)

If there is a leadership position over which most writers on the subject would agree it is that there is no single leadership approach that works every time because: a) times and situations define leader effectiveness. It is said that the war of 1812 between Napoleon and Russia was the war of horses; who ever had a superior cavalry stood a better chance of winning. Though any idea of using horses in WWII was viewed as ludicrous, this did not stop some in Russia from suggesting it, b) an approach that worked in one era may not necessarily work in another. Would a [supposed] new Alexander succeed if he tried the approaches of his namesake who lived some two and a half thousand years ago? c) an approach that worked well in one setting may not necessarily work in another. Leadership in a school setting differs from leadership in the army and d) even in the same organisation leadership may differ from function to function. In the same mining company a leadership style may work in shaft mining but not necessarily in the marketing and sales function of the same company.

The question to be answered therefore is, "can leadership be packaged"? Obviously some of the fundamentals of leadership can be packaged and maybe marketed but even here one has to be careful. King Cambyses advised his son Cyrus to be cunning in war. But, would this leadership quality work in today's wars? Most military commanders would probably respond with a "yes". Маскировка (or masking/deceiving) is as central to the Russian military (and to all other armies one suspects) now as cunningness was to King Cyrus' strategy thousands of years ago. But on the other hand, would a general in the secular Swedish army of today go to war with his troops led by a Christian banner, just as his predecessors did some 800 years ago? Perhaps not.

To demonstrate what I wrote above I submit below relevant essays on:

Presentism

Trying to assign current meanings to events that happened hundreds and even thousands of years before makes no sense. Actions and ideas can only be evaluated within the prism of the times they take place. To say that ancient Athens was not a democracy because there was no universal suffrage is to miss the point because in the world outside Greece there wasn't even a modicum of democratic polity. In fact, universal suffrage is a very recent phenomenon within the context of man's long history. Athens planted the seed millennia ago. Without Athens maybe democracy would have been delayed by hundreds if not thousands of years. By the measures of the times Athens was the beacon that summoned the world to the cause of democracy. The Western world basically had its first experiment with universal suffrage in the early 19th century when it started focusing on removing the property requirement for voting. America practised slavery up until the mid 19th century.

Emulating past leadership styles

Leadership styles should be designed to reflect the needs of the times, considering that problems and issues exist in real time and affect real people in real environments. As such, the leaders ought first to weigh the risks before emulating a leadership style that worked well in the past, but under circumstances that differ to today's; even if on the surface the two sets of circumstances may look confusingly similar. Zhukov excelled during WWII and was the paragon of military leadership at the time. But, WWII entailed no nuclear weapons except for the limited attack America waged against Japan at the tail end of the war. After the Soviets developed the bomb the Soviet army was turned into a totally different army to that of WWII Zhukov knew. When Zhukov came back after "rehabilitation" and was offered the portfolio of Minister of Defence, he was in some ways out of his depth considering the advent of nuclear weapons and their monumental role in the defence of Soviet space. Considering that Zhukov was in disfavour for some time, unavoidably important events passed him by whilst he was in a form of "hiatus". Seeing how brilliant Zhukov was on military matters, he would in due course have caught up to developments of course.

Work setting and leadership

Leadership is exercised within defined work settings that call for approaches that are appropriate to the specific setting, but also to the prevailing ethos. In my consulting work I had occasion to study tens of work settings which amongst others included: industry and manufacturing, education, health, agriculture, travel, telecommunications, and so on. I can say with some confidence that each sector of activity requires its own particular leadership style. School systems are a totally different world to that of industrial production. A bottling plant is totally different to a software house as regards leadership approach even if the fundamentals of leadership may be similar. Equally, each major geographic area calls for its own particular leadership style. Anyone who has worked in different countries understands that working in Europe is not exactly the same as working in the Middle East or Africa or Russia or Central Asia or America even. Not to mention that the work settings of Arabic Egypt and Arabic Lebanon may differ.

Leaders seem to come in clusters

Working on the subject of leadership for so long I have come to the conclusion that great leaders very often come in clusters. Certain eras are more fruitful than others in the production of leaders.

Equally, great leaders seem to influence the emergence of other great leaders around the same generation. All the great thinkers of Greece came within a period of 150–200 years. After this period and as if by magical intervention the river on which so many great Hellenes sailed to greatness turned into a stream and then dried up almost totally and stayed like that for centuries. The same happened to Scotland that gave the world the Scottish greats of the 18th century (all came within a period of 100–150 years).

Leadership for different epochs and periods

Churchill-Attlee. Each epoch and time brings with it its own leadership requirements. Issues and problems most often vary with times. Each period has its own problems that need to be solved. Churchill learned this the hard way when he was beaten to the premiership by Attlee soon after the end of WWII. Churchill simply tried to apply the same style of leadership to two different epochs that were separated by only a few years. Here I am talking about the WWII epoch and the period just after WWII. Clearly the two periods were a world apart even if they were separated by one or two years only. The leadership styles required by each period were vastly different. The WWII period called for toughness, self-sacrifice, emphasis on physical security and so on. The period of peace that followed called for stability, schemes to put people's lives back to normality, social programs, etc. Churchill continued to use the same leadership style and narrative in peace as in war. In the end he paid for it.

Essay 1: Presentism

"In imposing Today's meanings on Yesterday, we run the risk of distorting it — whether wilfully, to suit our own purposes, or unintentionally, by unwarranted assumptions and because of meagre information." Douglas L. Wilson

Douglas Wilson wrote, "As the two hundred and fiftieth anniversary of Thomas Jefferson's birth approaches, a Jefferson scholar reflects on Jefferson 's life — and in particular on the enigma at its core: that a slave holder should be the nation's most eloquent champion of equality. To understand how this could be so, the author explains, is to appreciate the perils of 'presentism' and the difficulties that may impede the historical assessment of motive and character" (Wilson, 1992).

(For a better understanding of the impact of the generation gap, with all its attendant issues, on our understanding of the needs of each generation read Mead, 1972; Brands, 2016; Bew, 2017).

It's in the interest of a leader to understand how inter-generational differences affect the formation of people's world views and opinions.

"Presentism" and Medicising

In ancient Sparta 'Medicising' (meaning a Greek supporting or collaborating with the Persians) was something no Greek leader was supposed to do. Though absolutely forbidden, many Greeks of standing had medicised, including Hippias (in Greek, Ἱππίας' ὁ Ἀθηναῖος" son of the tyrant Peisistratus), who fled to Persia after the Spartans invaded Athens and forced tyrant Hippias to leave Athens. He then accompanied the Persian army to fight his Greek brothers at Marathon. Not only did he accompany the Persian fleet, but he also suggested Marathon to the Persians as the place to defeat the Greeks. He advised them where to land to invade Attica. Other Greek notables who medicised were Themistocles, who ran for his life not long after beating the Persians at Salamis, and Alcibiades who fell out with the Spartans during the Peloponnesian war as he kept changing sides, first betraying Athens, his city, to Sparta then back to Athens, then Sparta, and then Persia. He was finally executed on the instructions of the Spartan Lysander, who had orders from the Spartan magistrates (Ephors) to dispatch him. (Plutarch, trans. n.d.: 262)

In the 5th century BC, Spartan Regent, General Pausanias, the victor of Plataea against the Persians, was "suspected" by the Spartan Ephors who had an axe to grind, of "planning" to collaborate with the Persians whom he had destroyed a few years earlier. Here is what Herodotus had to say about Plataea and Pausanias, "...the most glorious victory ever known was secured by Pausanias, son of Cleombrotus, son of Anaxandridas." (Herodotus, The Histories: IX.64)

Grote, not a particular fan of Pausanias, wrote that. "After his great victory, Pausanias clothed himself in Persian attire, something the Macedonian army could not tolerate more than a century later in the behaviour of their leader Alexander the Great. Pausanias walked with Median and Egyptian guards and copied the behaviour of the Persian chiefs, both as regards eating and banqueting, and his conduct towards the free women of Byzantium".

(Grote, 1864: 255).

On a mere suspicion and on account of his dress and social habits he was put to death by the Ephors through extrajudicial killing. Of course the real reason the Ephors hated Pausanias was the fact that he wished to liberate the helots who fought alongside him at Plataea. Had this happened today Pausanias would have been raised to the level of martyr who was crucified for his antislavery position and support for human rights and equality. But two thousand five hundred years earlier this act of Pausanias was seen as a "betrayal" of the Spartans who benefited from having helots serve them as near-slaves. Thankfully, the Spartan leadership later repented for what they had done to Pausanias, but not before they had a curse placed upon them.

Less than fifty years after accusing Pausanias of adopting Persian attire and for collaborating to do harm, the Spartan leadership entered into an agreement with the Persians to unashamedly start a detestable collaboration against fellow Greeks; the Athenians. Of course Athens had tried the same trick before the Spartans but the Persians rebuffed them. In the end, with the help of Persia, Sparta won and Athens was defeated, starting the road to the demise of the Athenian civilization. At this juncture, the Spartan Ephors saw collaboration with the Persians as a legitimate action. They saw nothing wrong in this collaboration with the arch enemy of the Greeks who Pausanias had defeated at Plataea. The reality of course is that the Spartans were engaging in big-time debauchery and treachery against fellow Greeks. Times had changed, and Sparta was suffering from tunnel vision which made the Spartan Ephors see the defeat of Athens as the only thing that mattered. This act of treachery was even applauded by many Spartan people because of the feelings that the Peloponnesian war had generated. (Thucydides, History of the Peloponnesian War: 1.95.3–5, 1.128.3, 1.131.2). What the Ephors "suspected" Pausanias of planning to do (at some undefined future date) against the Greeks became totally legitimate behaviour fifty years later as a result of the needs of the Peloponnesian war and the fanaticism it had generated.

Interestingly, in later years the same Pausanias who was put to death was reinstated in the [guilty] conscience of the Spartans, and in his honour (and that of his uncle, King Leonidas) the Spartans inaugurated the Leonidia celebrations that were meant to bring to the people glorious memories of both these two great leaders.

Eras define issues

Each era brings with it its own definitions to suit the needs of the times as well as the needs of the leaders. Even "democracy" is subject to varying interpretations depending on the needs and objectives of the powerful and the political elite. Democracy takes different meanings in the Middle East, Africa, Central-South America, the EU and the USA. In countries friendly to America, for example, the definition is made to suit and accommodate all sorts of undemocratic practices by the US-friendly country. In countries that are antagonistic to the powerful the definition applied is strict and inflexible, bringing up in this way all the democratic deficiencies in these antagonistic countries. In the process these countries become targets for regime change, ostensibly for the benefit of democracy.

When in 1967 the Colonels abolished democracy in Greece countries such as America, Britain, and many others turned a blind eye because the colonels that carried out the coup were "their colonels". Apart from the expected "standard" commentary of rebuke not much was said to lambast the usurpers of democracy in the country that gave the world the institution of democracy. The same happened in the case of the many coups in Turkey that at the time was very close to America and a stalwart of NATO. Worse, in the case of the Colonels in Greece, America is suspected of giving them the nod to carry out a coup in Cyprus which was then used as an excuse by America-friendly Turkey to invade the country. The Colonels needed America's veneer of legitimacy and so they acted as American lackeys. We therefore see definitions change according to the plans of the strong. Coming from a tiny and weak country I got the shock of my life when I first realised that even the most iconic and "holy" word in the universe, that is the word democracy, can sometimes be turned into a tool in the hands of powerful leaders that wish to control the country from outside.

Let us now take three of the pillars on which the EU rests to a large extent to see how this institution defines and redefines these pillars based on expediency and the interests of individual member countries. These pillars are: a) Greco-Roman philosophy and culture, b) Judeo/Christian ethic and c) Enlightenment. The platform on which each of these three pillars rests is generally thought to be the following: a) Greco-Roman philosophy rests primarily on objective inquiry, unbiased questioning that is meant to find the truth rather than to favour any particular outcome, b) Judeo/Christian ethic rests on the fundamental belief that everyone is created equal. In this way the Judeo/Christian ethic strengthens the belief in democratic rule. Most importantly the rules of the Judeo/Christian ethic are laid down externally and as such are not subject to human bias depending on events and times and self-interest and c) Enlightenment rests on equality (democracy) and human dignity. Though enlightenment (a historically recent phenomenon) challenges religious views it agrees whole-heartedly with the fundamentals of the other two pillars (democracy and human dignity). Let us see below how all of these concepts are used in practice and how definitions are twisted to fit objectives.

The leadership of the EU knows full well that the invasion of EU member Cyprus is a gross violation of the democratic foundations of the EU. Yet, the leadership of the EU finds it difficult to castigate

Turkey's invasion of fellow EU member Cyprus. The truth is that the economics of major member states favour good relations with aggressor Turkey. But while EU countries keep silent on Cyprus some decry the absence of democracy outside the EU and are more than happy to join America in wars that are supposedly meant to bring democracy to countries such as Iraq and Libya. EU members and America supported the "Arab Spring" that was supposedly to spearhead the move towards democratic polity in many Arab countries. This ended in disaster. Egypt briefly ended up with an Islamist government that was a far cry from democracy. Yet some EU countries and America pretended not to notice the harshness of an Islamist regime in Egypt because they thought that the Islamists would prevail in the end and as such, why antagonise them? Fortuitously for Egypt, Marshal Sisi stepped in and restored stability and security.

At the time of writing Venezuela was threatened by invasion under the guise of the need to "restore democracy" to the country, yet, "…in 1973 General Augusto Pinochet staged a military coup… against Salvador Allende in Chile…The coup was hatched in Chile. But it was backed by Richard Nixon…It was one of the more notorious of many interventions by the United States in Latin America, starting with a war against Mexico in 1846, including other coups…" (Smilde, 2018: 55). The Economist makes reference to meetings organised by the Americans to overthrow the current President of Venezuela, "…Marco Rubio, a Republican senator, said recently that there was a case for military action to topple Mr Maduro." (Smilde, 2018: 55). So we now see practices of the past (that have no place in today's times) reinvented and re-engineered by the powerful for a cause. Most interestingly The Economist bemoans the absence of democracy in Venezuela but forgets to do the same with countries that trade heavily with Britain and are from being democratic. As expected the world listens mostly to 'standard' and 'benign' commentary coming from the West against friendly countries with huge democratic shortcomings.

What I am trying to highlight in the above paragraphs is that leaders of strong countries have the facility to change definitions to make these suit their purposes and that in practice there is little room for idealism. Also, I am trying to demonstrate that: a) the way leaders see things differ from era to era. Behaviours that were acceptable in one era may not be acceptable in another. Colonisation was acceptable in the 19th century but is not acceptable now and b) what is an acceptable definition is often defined by the strong in the way the strong wish to see the term or behaviour applied at a given time. But there is nothing new in this, considering that double standards have always been a feature of the history of nations. We are seeing the term 'democracy' used in vain. Take for example, Gaddafi's "Socialist People's Libya Jamahiriya" which Gaddafi claimed to be democracy minus political parties! Libyan and western secret agents worked closely together when despot Gaddafi was in good terms with the West. The same applies to the misuse of terms such as "liberal values" which is often twisted to fit specific objectives and to promote certain agendas that are sometimes stenchful. So, it's not just about presentism but also about double standards and hypocrisy.

Balancing two opposing ideas

I was talking with a well-natured and affable American intellectual recently over dinner. When I told him that I respect Jefferson as a great leader, his stance on equality and his Lockean views of governance, my guest reminded me that Jefferson kept slaves. I told him that he kept slaves because at the time people were not enlightened enough on the issue of slavery and as such he was a victim of his times rather than an evil-doer. I then remind him of the follies of presentism. The interesting thing was that although my interlocutor held anti-slavery views, at the same time he supported military intervention by the strong in the affairs of the weak, and often poor, countries. As such he simultaneously supported antithetical views. When I asked him how he managed to justify holding two opposing positions he tried to explain to me the difference between slavery and "dictating to others what to do" and that these two are in no way identical acts. I agreed that they were not identical but added that when people experience the dropping of bombs over their heads and destruction of their infrastructure they find it difficult to appreciate philosophically the difference between slavery and subjugation. I also tried to explain to him that in the case of intervention to bring about regime change, what the victims are forced to accept through violence is a government that is not of their own choice but is the choice of the invader-bomber. I continued by saying that no one should have the right to invade another country or to intervene militarily in internal affairs. In this debate I saw clearly two opposing ideas being held by the same person: a) opposition to domination and slavery using presentism and b) support of subjugation using sophistry such as, "the need to bring about democracy" or ostensibly "the need to stop the proliferation of weapons of mass destruction".

I continued saying that Jefferson was for peace and against alliances where a number of countries gang up against another country and reminded him of Jefferson's inaugural pledge "Peace, commerce, and honest friendship with all nations, entangling alliances with none." If these words had been heeded today, America would not have ended up in the Vietnam catastrophe, nor would the American taxpayers have to pay nearly a trillion dollars annually to keep American troops in half of the countries of the world. "Was Jefferson then ahead of his time as leader?" I asked.

Writing in Foreign Affairs, David Frimkin said that Jefferson's pledge became, "...more than a policy; it became an expression of a national point of view about ourselves and our place in the world, a view which contrasted the simple virtues of our Republic with the subtle and complex qualities (some said corruptions) of Europe. From 1789 until the Second World War, excepting only our relationship with Panama, the United States refused to enter into treaties of alliance with anyone. In the 25 years since the end of the war, however, in a dramatic reversal of national policy, we have allied ourselves with half the world." (Fromkin, 1970)

As regards presentism one wonders how the more puritanical amongst the readers would have taken Max Weber's following statement today, "The Puritan and the hygienic sex-rationalist generally tread very different paths...In a lecture, a zealous adherent of hygienic prostitution...defended the moral legitimacy of extra-marital intercourse (which was looked upon as hygienically useful) by referring to its poetic justification in the case of Faust and Margaret."

(Weber, Trans. 1976: 263).

Presentism on the verge of absurdity

Under the title of, "The growing threat of historical presentism" Paul Bartow wrote on 10 December, 2015, "The outrage began with the calls for removal of the Confederate flag and exploded to assaults on John Calhoun, Woodrow Wilson, and most recently on Thomas Jefferson. My purpose here is not necessarily to defend the merits of these individuals, as I find some more deserving of recognition than others. Rather I argue that the protests calling for the removal of affiliations with these historical characters or movements very closely resembles mob rule, and that these protests are founded on the snare of 'historical presentism' whereby one applies contemporary moral judgments and worldviews to those of the past." (Bartow, 2015)

Presentism, hypocritical presentism, pastism and selective pastism

According to Bartow historical presentism is the application of "... contemporary moral judgment and world views to those of the past". I will now introduce a new term which I call "hypocritical presentism" which is "The use of contemporary moral judgement to attack behaviours of the past whilst hypocritically holding on to the benefits these past behaviours bestow on beneficiaries to this day." And here I refer to the attack on Cecil John Rhodes by those that enjoy the benefits of the endowment he left to Oxford. And finally, I introduce "pastism" which I define as "The use of moral judgement and world views of the past to attack behaviours of the present". A good example would be the justification to attack other countries on the excuse that "aggression was used in the past and as such this provides a precedence". This means using a bad precedent to justify an unacceptable current behaviour. As this piece was being written Turkey had sent out to the Mediterranean a flotilla of some one hundred or more ships of its navy under the code name, "Blue Fatherland" employing "pastism" of Ottoman times to intimidate and threaten (with a view to subduing) the Greeks and others. If such action was acceptable during Ottoman times why not employ it now?, the logic of the Turkish leadership goes. "Selective pastism" is "The selective use of moral judgement and world views of the past to the present." For example, using the time-tested logic of "might is right" to justify current actions against an adversary but reversing the logic when it comes to a friend or supporter. Using the historic world view of the need for economic and political stability in the region, America invaded neighbouring Haiti in 1915 and occupied it until 1934, and then used the reverse logic in 1961 to carry out the Bay of Pigs invasion of Cuba to destabilise and overthrow the government of Cuba.

The mark of a great leader

> *Great leaders act under the guidance of a moral rudder that is unerring at all times and in all eras, present and past.*

Emulating leadership styles of the past

History provides us with plenty of examples of attempts at copying leadership practices of the past and applying these scrupulously in circumstances that have changed considerably. Copying a successful leadership style of the past under different circumstances is, to say the least, unwise and fraught with dangers. What is required is a clear understanding of the differences between the two sets of circumstances and the demands each places on leadership. Heraclitus reminded us long ago of the impossibility of stepping in the same river twice.

> *Effective leaders are careful not to blindly adopt past successful leadership models. Instead they develop their own model to serve the needs of their time.*

Essay 2: Work setting and leadership

The path to leadership is clearly not confined to one specific route. But, as Bower tells us, the sphere in which one operates defines to a large extent the requirements for successful leadership. He incisively gives us the contrast between business leadership and political leadership that require different traits and qualities. For one, system-managed businesses do not depend much on personal leadership and charisma but rather, depend more on structures, policies, procedures and systems that act as guides to managers, "… the requirements of business leadership are less demanding than those of great political leadership. The statesman must arouse people to do the unusual; the business leader need only stimulate them to do well in the task of earning their livelihood." (Bower, 1966: 252)

This means that one could conceivably excel as leader in one particular setting but fail in another. This basically tells us that leadership is situational and that certain leadership properties that prove useful in one situation may not work in a different setting. So, it is a matter for the leader to weigh up his strengths and limitations and to use these as appropriate for best results. But, Bower tells us that irrespective of the type of situation and prevailing conditions, every leader ought to be guided by integrity. "Every basic analysis of leadership emphasizes the importance of integrity." (Bower, 1966: 253). This is an overarching requirement which when absent is likely to render the leader ineffective. Bower then puts forward what is perhaps obvious to most of us. That is: people will not follow a person they do not trust.

Bower's observations are not entirely valid considering that we often see unscrupulous politicians win elections repeatedly whilst [knowingly] making [false] promises which they never intended to honour. Or giving out handouts the economy cannot afford in an effort to buy voter favour. Sadly, the reality is that many people follow leaders that promise to give them some benefit in a largely transactional relationship: "you give me what I need and I will give you my vote". Unprincipled leaders know full well how transactional relations work and how they can turn these to their benefit. In certain politically-developing countries with a lot of economically challenged people, elections can be won by a promise of just a few extra euros per month or an extra increment for a public sector employee. Take as an example what the supposedly socialist Greek government was doing just before the last European and municipal elections which took place at the time of writing. The government basically tried to buy favour by giving to the nearly three million retired citizens a 13th salary the debt-laden economy of Greece (€0.350 trillion debt) could ill afford. More such ill-conceived promises were made in readiness for the national elections.

Leadership is clearly influenced by the nature of the circumstances under which the leader is required to operate. Just as the fighter pilot's leadership skills differ from those of the passenger aeroplane pilot's so do the leadership requirements of a business leader differ from those of the political leader. Equally, church leaders need to have faith in God and must be demonstrably compassionate (to show demonstrable love) if they are to be effective. Business leaders need compliance to systems and processes and focus on efficiency and goal achievement. Professional hospital managers need managerial and administrative skills but also a degree of compassion for the sick if they are to perform well. Sports leaders have to win matches; otherwise they will not keep their position.

Why business CEOs don't often make effective political leaders

Bertrand Russell described the qualities of a business executive as follows, "The typical 'executive' impresses others as a man of rapid decisions, quick insight into character, and iron will; he must have a firm jaw, tightly closed lips, and a habit of brief and incisive speech. He must able to inspire respect in equals, and confidence in subordinates who are by no means nonentities. He must combine the qualities of a great general and a great diplomat: ruthlessness in battle, but a capacity for skilful concession in negotiation. It is by such qualities that men acquire control of important economic organisations." (Russell, 1960: 32).

He also described the politician's approach to power as, "A politician, if he is to succeed, must be able to win the confidence of his party machine, and then to arouse some degree of enthusiasm in a majority of the electorate. The qualities required for these two stages on the road to power are by no means identical, and many men possess the one without the other." (Russell, 1960: 32)

Writing in Forbes on June 22, 2016, David Davenport said that 21 of the US presidents were both lawyers and politicians and most were either one or the other. Two recent Presidents, Jimmy Carter and G.W. Bush were businessmen by profession. Both left little behind that would qualify them as great leaders. Harry Truman, considered by many Americans as a successful leader, was a failed businessman. Lincoln was not any better in business. Mitt Romney, a big-time businessman, ran for presidency and failed. Crossing the line from business to politics has not been a particularly successful crossing in many cases. It remains to be seen how President Donald Trump does and whether he can disprove the trend. Davenport brings the analogy of Michael Jordan, the legendary basketball player who failed as a baseball athlete despite his immense sporting prowess. (Davenport, 2016)

More recently we are reminded of the great Manchester United fan, world record holder in the sprint and Olympic champion Usain Bolt who gave up on his new career in football.

Politicians are typically products of the democratic process which does not necessarily provide the world with ideal leadership. The selection process in politics is in the hands of the 'average' voter rather than in the hands of those that might know better. "Democratic laws generally tend to promote the welfare of the greatest possible number; for they emanate from the majority of the citizens, who are subject to error, but who cannot have an interest opposed to their own advantage." (Tocqueville and Heffner, 1963: 101)

Alexis de Tocqueville argues that the [democratic] political system lacks the sound selection mechanisms of the business world where the candidate's CV goes through the most rigorous process and is evaluated by experts and professionals to determine whether the candidate meets the requirements of the job. But unlike the task sheet of the politician the business leader has set objectives that are specific and measurable and centre exclusively on two narrow and well-defined requirements: a) ability to achieve a healthy return on capital invested and its twin, b) shareholder value. No business leader can last for long if share value steadily drops. Unlike politics, business does not have fixed terms which leaders are to serve before they go. His popularity in the neighbourhood is unlikely to provide the business leader with job security! But in the broader philosophical view one would need to ask whether manager dedication to profit making and more money are the worthiest of objectives for great leaders to strive for!

Alexis de Tocqueville brings us down to earth once more and causes us to think again, "The men who are entrusted with the direction of public affairs in the United States are frequently inferior, both in capacity and morality, to those whom an aristocracy would raise to power. But their interest is identified and confounded with that of the majority of their fellow citizens. They may frequently be faithless, and frequently mistaken; but they will never systematically adopt a line of conduct hostile to the majority; and they cannot give a dangerous or exclusive tendency to the government." (Tocqueville and Heffner, 1963: 102)

Politicians are chosen by 'average citizens' who use their own selection criteria, whatever these might be, but "...who are subject to error, but who cannot have an interest opposed to their own advantage" we are reminded by Alexis de Tocqueville. But does the common-man-voter act rationally when selecting leaders? I guess some do and others do not but in the end all balances out with each society getting the leadership it deserves.

Leader mentality once set

From my experience as consultant and having worked with many senior executives in numerous countries and environments I would say that once the leader's ethos and mentality are set these are unlikely to change and will follow him in every future appointment he undertakes. A prospective school leader with long service in the business world is likely to bring to the school the business mentality and ethos which may not necessarily be exactly what the school needs. Certainly at the beginning of the appointment the new manager is likely to experience a culture shock. The ethos and philosophy of educational institutions are in many ways dissimilar to those of business. I have seen how difficult it is for people with long tenure in the civil service to transition into the business world. I found such transitions to be difficult because of the cultural differences of the two sectors. For example, a manager in the public sector with thirty years service is unlikely (but not impossibly) to change his definition of time and his understanding of the importance of cash flow which are so important in business. The same goes to setting priorities. Political expediency plays little role in business whereas in the public sector politicking is central to decision-making. Civil servants are nowhere experienced in the generation of revenues from sales; nor do they have to spend sleepless nights worrying about profits and return on capital and paying corporate bills that are due.

Public sector leaders enjoy the security of the taxpayer's money; businessmen do not have this luxury. I would go as far as to say that in the hundreds of selection committees for senior business management posts that I participated in during my career, I hardly remember more than a few cases of former civil service leaders making it to the next round of interviews in business. Competent though many were, they failed to convince that a successful transition could be made. Many of them found it difficult to appreciate the hard realities of business, the ambiguity inherent in business roles and the bare-knuckles nature of business. Maybe other colleagues have had different experiences on this matter.

I had similar experiences with former senior military officers that took up roles as HR managers in some economically developing countries. Those who employed them assumed that as leaders of men, senior military officers would find it easy to transition into a HR Director's role. They soon discovered that: a) in practice HR managers are not required to lead [many] people because it is the line managers that oversee their teams and not HR. HR managers deal only with their own immediate team members and not with the employees of other departments, b) HR teams are typically small, c) negotiating and influencing skills are critical in business considering that staff need to be convinced of the rightness of decisions. In the army the officer typically gives an order and this is hardly challenged; otherwise a case of insubordination is opened and d) employees in business are free to change jobs and as such management needs to be careful how staff are managed, lest good employees resign from their posts. Soldiers, and conscripts in particular, do not have the benefit of job mobility and as such are obliged to stay until discharge time arrives.

In summary, transitioning leadership skills from one sector to another is fraught with difficulties. As such great care should be taken to avoid unwanted consequences. Here is a list of considerations:

1. The culture which the leader is to leave should not be drastically different from the culture he will be entering into.

2. The skills set required by the new appointment should not be significantly different to the skills set the leader possesses at the time of taking up the new appointment.

3. The degree of ambiguity in the new job should not be drastically different to the ambiguity levels the manager had to face in his previous job.

4. To ensure a good match, the new task description should be carefully prepared to make sure the job is well defined and that it compares well with the qualifications of the leader.

5. The leader should carry out a good self-examination asking serious questions about whether he is totally committed to meeting the many and different challenges of the new job he is transitioning into.

6. In most cases change unavoidably means abandoning one's comfort zone.

> *Leaders transitioning from one role to a drastically different one ought to exercise vigilance, lest the new challenges in organizational culture and approach differ greatly from what they were used to. Most often change entails abandonment of one's comfort zone.*

Essay 3: Leadership for different epochs and periods

Churchill and Attlee. Winston Churchill steps down and Clement Attlee steps up. Winston Churchill was the leader of the British during WWII, which ended in August 1945. But was the hero Churchill and his leadership style needed or valued in post-war Britain? Was it maybe the turn of someone that was the opposite of Churchill in style and approach? Subsequent events tell us that Britain wished to have a new leadership paradigm. On 26 July, 1945, Churchill resigned and was replaced by Clement Attlee. Thus, a Conservative gave his place to a Labourite. Apparently, with the war's end Britain was ready for drastic social reforms and not for more belligerence. Churchill and his leadership style were not what Britain needed at the war's end. Churchill had been a good wartime prime minister who rallied people around Britain's cause, led people in their darkest hour and galvanised opposition to the Nazis and the Japanese. He did this brilliantly starting in 1939, when he replaced Neville Chamberlain, and up to 1945. He had done a splendid job as head of a coalition government and had in fact invited Attlee to join as his deputy.

At election time in July 1945 Churchill still held the view that his ideology and style would carry the day and felt very confident about this. But he was wrong because the British people had changed their mental state and their expectations were not those Churchill thought they were. They no longer had a war to think about; nor did they have an enemy. Their enemy now was low income, unemployment and all the accumulated social problems. The world had new and great expectations and all appeared to move into a new era of prosperity in which all were expected to benefit. Above all, people were looking for peace and economic security; they had had enough of war and its travails.

Here is what Attlee did and which the Conservative Churchill could not deliver. Attlee: a) nationalised public utilities such as coal, electricity and the railways; b) improved social services; c) introduced the National Health Service Act of 1946 which gave free access to all citizens; d) introduced the National Security Act, which now seems so natural to have, giving people a host of benefits in exchange for weekly contributions made by the members of the scheme; e) expanded the public sector; f) understood that the time was ripe for decolonization. The Indian sub-continent was decolonized, along with Burma and Ceylon. Attlee was the right man for the time when Britain was in need of major social changes. The Labour government was better suited to offer what the British wanted. Churchill failed to understand this, and continued with war rhetoric against the Soviets. This in the end frightened the war-weary British. (McCallum and Readman, 1947)

Paul Addison notes on 17 February, 2011, "In the event, he [Churchill] led them to one of their greatest ever defeats. It was also one for which he was partly responsible, because the very qualities that had made him a great leader in war were ill-suited to domestic politics in peacetime." He notes incisively that "Churchill lost the general election in 1945 because he had succeeded in completing the almost superhuman task he had taken on in 1940, and in a way this made him redundant." (Addison, 2011)

Attlee had the advantage of having worked in the East End of London, and this helped him change into a socialist appreciating the problems of the working class; he was voted MP for Stepney in 1922. Margaret Thatcher characteristically said of Attlee that "he was all substance and no show." Churchill said other things about Attlee,

"A modest man with much to be modest about." And, on Attlee as Prime Minister, "an empty taxi drew up to 10 Downing Street and Attlee got out." (Gopnik, 2018)

Yet the man who was a source of mirth for some won a landslide victory and brought so much good to the British people. In the end, even Churchill admired Attlee in the same way that Attlee admired Churchill. Attlee even took part in one of Churchill's blunders, namely the Gallipoli expedition during WWI. Attlee was a man of integrity, and this portrayed him to the people as a non-threatening figure. He was a great leader for his time, but would probably be out of his depth in today's Britain. His leadership style post-WWII would have probably made him a failure today, though Corbyn is not doing entirely badly in today's British politics.

Good leadership can assume one meaning at a given moment in history, and a different one at another, depending on what is socially, morally and practically acceptable at the time. The prevailing ethos and culture at a given time shapes our views and push us, often unwittingly, to take positions that are politically correct at a given time and wrong at another. Some things are simply not acceptable at given times, even if they are true. The intellectual climate of the time plays a major role in defining effective leadership. The same thing can be seen at two different times and interpreted differently each time, even if the time between the two periods is short. (read also: Bew, 2017)

> *There is a time and place even for leadership.*

In this book I tried to warn the reader about the difficulties: a) leaders face when trying to lead in one time whilst considering the successful leadership practices of another period, b) the consequences of failing to adjust to the new demands of the times and c) the difficulty we face when assessing leaders of the past with current measures and current leaders with past measures. Time and circumstances play a pivotal role in the success and failure of leadership.

References

Addison, D. (2011). BBC — History — World Wars: Why Churchill Lost in 1945. [online] Bbc.co.uk. Available at: http://www.bbc.co.uk/history/worldwars/wwtwo/election_01.sh tml [Accessed 26 Oct. 2018].

Bartow, P. (2015). The growing threat of historical presentism — AEI. [online] AEI. Available at: http://www.aei.org/publication/the-growing-threat-of-historical-presentism/ [Accessed 20 Feb. 2019].

Bew, J. (2017). Clement Attlee: The Man Who Made Modern Britain. Oxford: Oxford University Press.

Bower, M. (1966). The will to manage. New York: McGraw-Hill.

Brands, H. (2016). The General vs. the President: MacArthur and Truman at the Brink of Nuclear War. New York: Doubleday.

Brownworth, L. (2009). Lost to the West. New York: Three Rivers Press.

Davenport, D. (2016). Why Business CEOs Don't Make Effective Political Leaders. [online] Forbes.com. Available at: https://www.forbes.com/sites/daviddavenport/2016/06/22/why-business-ceos-dont-make-effective-political-leaders [Accessed 26 Dec. 2018].

Llopis, G. (2013). Eight Clear Signs It's Time To Make A Leadership Change. [online] Forbes.com. Available at: https://www.forbes.com/sites/glennllopis/2013/11/25/8-clear-signs-its-time-to-make-a-leadership-change [Accessed 20 Feb. 2019].

Forbes Technology Council. (2016). Council Post: The Nine Most Influential Technology Leaders Of Our Time. [online] Forbes.com. Available at:

https://www.forbes.com/sites/forbestechcouncil/2016/08/05/the
-nine-most-influential-technology-leaders-of-our-time
[Accessed 17 Feb. 2019].

Fromkin, D. (1970). Entangling Alliances. [online] Foreign Affairs. Available at: https://www.foreignaffairs.com/articles/1970-07-01/entangling-alliances [Accessed 10 Oct. 2018].

Gopnik, A. (2018). Never Mind Churchill, Clement Attlee Is a Model for These Times. [online] The New Yorker. Available at: https://www.newyorker.com/news/daily-comment/never-mind-churchill-clement-attlee-is-a-model-for-these-times [Accessed 7 Jul. 2018].

Grote, G. (1864). History of Greece, Volume V. Harper Brothers.

Herotodus. (2013). The Histories. A new translation by Tom Holland. Introduction by Paul Cartledge. New London: Penguin Classics.

Mead, M. (1972). Culture and Commitment A study of the Generation Gap. London: Panther Books Limited.

Pettinger, T. (2018). Famous People of the Enlightenment. [online] Biography Online. Available at: https://www.biographyonline.net/people/famous/enlightenment.html [Accessed 25 Nov. 2018].

Plutarch. Translated by Clough, A. (n.d.). Plutarch: Lives of the Noble Grecians and Romans. New York: Random House.

Russell, B. (1960). Power. London: Unwin Books.

Smilde, D. (2018). Why backing coups in Latin America is a bad idea. The Economist, 428(9109).

Strassler, R. (ed.) (1998). The Landmark Thucydides: A Comprehensive Guide to the Peloponnesian War. Translation by Richard Crawley. Introduction by Victor Davis Hanson. New York: Free Press.

Sutherland, S. (n.d.). Scottish Enlightenment | British history. [online] Encyclopedia Britannica. Available at: https://www.britannica.com/topic/Scottish-Enlightenment [Accessed 3 Aug. 2018].

Tocqueville, A. and Heffner, R. (1963). Democracy in America. New York: New American Library.

The Guardian. (2018). 10 of the best words in the world (that don't translate into English). [online] Available at: https://www.theguardian.com/world/2018/jul/27/10-of-the-best-words-in-the-world-that-dont-translate-into-english [Accessed 23 Nov. 2018].

Tolstoy, L. (1977). Master and Man and other stories. London: Penguin.

McCallum, R. and Readman, A. (1947). The British general elections 1945–1992. Oxford University Press.

Weber, M. (1976). Protestant ethic and the spirit of capitalism. London.

Wilson, D. (1992). Thomas Jefferson and the Character Issue. [online] Theatlantic.com. Available at: https://www.theatlantic.com/past/docs/issues/96oct/obrien/charactr.htm [Accessed 10 Oct. 2018].

Book 9

Leadership failures: some examples

"Each new generation is reared by its predecessor, the latter must therefore improve in order to improve its successor" Emile Durkheim

Puzzling as it may seem, the leaders of many countries fail to identify their country's single most burning problem (the problem). And, even if they identify this they fail to address it correctly. As a result the country's development is thwarted and its potential remains unfulfilled. If however the problem is finally identified correctly and solved the country quickly moves to a path of development and growth in all areas. This leadership failing could be the result of fear of the reactions of the establishment, or vested interests that want the problem to remain unresolved because they benefit from the situation.

Robert Mugabe. Zimbabwe under Mugabe suffered from corrupt leadership for nearly four decades and provides an excellent example of how the problem (corruption and autocracy in this case) can destroy a country and inflict great hardship on the population. As a result millions left Zimbabwe for South Africa, looking for a better life outside their own country. Unemployment inside the country is still running wild. When Mugabe took over from the government of Ian Smith, president Julius Nierere of Tanzania reminded him that he was taking over a jewel of a country, which he ought to care for and nurture. It did not take long before Mugabe started eating off the fat of the economy he inherited from Ian Smith, destroying the country brick by brick. The single problem that the leadership of Zimbabwe (including the current one) has failed to address in the last forty years is corruption and autocracy. Instead, the leadership of the country continues to blame the past administrations for its never ending ills. Typically it is [the now dead] Ian Smith, Britain and colonialism that are to blame, forgetting that the Mugabe government ran the affairs of the country for roughly the last forty years! Of course rampant corruption is not unique to Zimbabwe, considering what happens in many countries around the world.

Political leadership in particular is prone to committing grave errors of judgement because of the pressures and divergent demands placed on them and especially because of the consuming desire to get re-elected. Sometimes bad decisions are the result of selfishness, politicians' self-interest, or low concern for the welfare of the general public. Leaders sometimes fail to address major problems because they do not wish to antagonise strong vested interests (many found in government) that benefit from the problem. The dependence and control of some politicians on powerful sponsors is well documented. Politicians simply do not wish to antagonize super-strong power centres even if they know that this is wrong.

In certain cases leaders fail to see the problem altogether because of the brainwashing they suffered at some point in their life. For example, a leader that is brought up on a diet of communist ideology is unlikely to oppose damaging subsidies which ultimately render the economy uncompetitive. Worryingly, the decision makers behind much calamitous behaviour are often highly intelligent leaders who are driven more by preconceived ideas (or manias in some cases) than by rationality and intelligent thought. More disturbingly, some leaders lack wisdom though [academically] intelligent. This makes them act below par and sometimes even foolishly. Tunnel vision often causes leaders to make catastrophic decisions. "National consensus" is sometimes the reason behind bad decisions because the pressure to reach consensus sometimes blocks saner voices from being heard. Some people find it difficult to go against the views of an overwhelming majority even if their opinion is intrinsically superior to that of the group. Group-think and fear of being considered a heteroclite inside the political party or the group causes leaders not to focus on real issues but rather to adopt what the group wishes them to do, in order to be in their good books. What all these things mean is that good judgement, that is so essential for good leadership, is often absent from the decision-making process.

Turkey. At a regional level, we see the leadership of Turkey, for example, continuing to operate under the obsession of becoming the dominant power in the Eastern Mediterranean (EM) just as in Ottoman times. As such she demands obedience from the countries in the region and even has territorial demands. It does not matter that other countries do not wish to accept Turkish hegemony. Nor does it matter that the Ottoman Empire died at the close of WWI. Her default position whenever she does not get her way is to employ intimidation and the threat of violence to force her will over others. Under this kind of mindset the option of advantageous cooperation with neighbours, based on respect of international law ceases to exist, but Turkey's decision makers do not mind. Dreams of revival of past regional dominance take precedence over good judgement. In the end Turkey misses out on the fruits of cooperation with her neighbours and exerts itself in major military expenditures gradually endangering her long term prospects. Though some in the leadership of the country see, one would assume, the option of cooperation and respect for international law as a better option than intimidation and violence, Turkey refuses to consider such an alternative. Trying to make reality the unrealisable dream of regaining control over the countries in the region she formerly ruled in Ottoman Empire times does not make sense. The leadership of Turkey is oblivious to the dangers. .

This single-minded concentration on one catastrophic route while there are other more beneficial routes to follow, and failing to reverse a catastrophic course is not limited to one or few countries, or to one or few decision makers. Greece. Take successive Greek governments, for example, and their obsession with big government and bureaucracy, apparently to satisfy the need for reelection.. Political parties know that this is detrimental to the competitiveness and economic health of the country. They also know that the kind of "socialism" [mostly] the left but also the right tried to implement for the last two hundred years has not led the country to its promised land. Most, if not all, Greek governments of the last circa two hundred years supported a bloated civil service with layers of bureaucracy that frighten away investors and ruin productivity. Deep in their minds, most of the Greek leaders probably know that what they are doing is wrong and harmful to the nation. Yet they continue these destructive practices for no reason other than winning the massive number of state employee votes. No compunction or sense of guilt is shown by many of these politicians that would make them stop such untoward and catastrophic practices! Worse still, this populist approach carries with it a contagious effect that infects everyone in Greek political life and spills over to Cyprus. The nation has been in a race for more and more handouts and giveaways that ended up corrupting the system, bringing the country's economy to its knees and making the country unproductive.

Now take the sin of corruption that we highlighted before in Zimbabwe. The leaderships of corrupt countries of the world know full well that corruption is a terrible and catastrophic practice. Yet, leaders allow this to happen.

Through the use of examples I intend to demonstrate the pervasiveness of leadership failures that have bad judgement as the root cause. I chose the example of America and the American decision makers' inability to address America's most serious problem, which is its insistence on maintaining one-country world hegemony to perpetuity. In other words, these decision makers wish to have a unipolar world in which America is the only world leader. This infatuation with world hegemony brings the American administrations of the last eighty or so years in opposition to what America's founding fathers had in mind. The founding fathers wished for an America that would not meddle in other countries' affairs and that would not get involved in permanent alliances.

Some reasons why leaders fail to use good judgement:

- Need to be popular.
- Fear of vested interests.
- Brainwashing.
- Preconceived ideas.
- Lack of wisdom.
- Tunnel vision.
- Need for "national consensus".
- Group-think and fear of being seen as aberrant.
- Obsession with unrealistic targets.

Leadership In Practice

Oftentimes elected leaders know what needs to be done but are unable to do it because of varied barriers emanating from:
a.) the leader, such as the need to maintain control in his hands
b.) the group, such as the loss of advantages by certain group members from the leader's actions and
c.) outside, such as the interference of a powerful country in affairs of a nation
Examples from running the affairs of:
The United States
Egypt
Israel
Iran
Syria
Greece
Turkey
Lebanon
Cyprus

Essay 1: Leadership failure: The case of America's search for continued world hegemony

"In any case you mustn't confuse a single failure with a final defeat." F. Scott Fitzgerald

As said earlier, the central problem of America which decision makers fail to address is the country's obsession with world hegemony, maintenance of the existing world order (that favours America) and as a consequence her frenzy with global reach. In other words, American decision makers wish to keep America at the top of the world as the single world power to perpetuity. The aforementioned has been decided in the full knowledge that the project is unattainable. History bears testimony to the elusiveness of this American venture. Interestingly the leadership of America includes a very smart and well-educated cadre who surely ought to understand that unending world hegemony and maintenance of the status quo are impossible. All major powers that tried this in the past failed. Yet, America's leadership continues with its tunnel vision and clouded judgment which blocks their ability to discern and take the right action in good time. Under the title, "The End of Our World Order Is Imminent" Alfred McCoy wrote on February 28, 2019 that, "At least 200 empires have risen and fallen over the course of history, and the United States will be no exception." (McCoy, 2019). All America needs to do is look at economically paralysed Greece that is now up to its neck in debt and remember that the Greeks ruled he world in the late 4th century BC. They simply overstretched themselves and paid the price.

America knows that history is littered with futile attempts to rule the world and yet her leadership continues to behave, and invest/spend, as if America is destined to defy this inescapable historic rule. If one were to ask the average American person to say what America's severest problems today are, they would probably give the standard and oft-repeated response of: healthcare, education, employment, improved lifestyle, and so on. The more sophisticated may add to the list of problems America's largely stagnant productivity and its effect on the US economy. As regards American productivity Greg Satell wrote on 29 October, 2016 in Forbes under the title, "Wake up America! This Is The Real Problem

With The US Economy", "As economist Robert Gordon explains in The Rise and Fall of American Growth, productivity growth soared between 1920 and 1970, but has sputtered since then. What's more, he predicts that the productivity picture will get even worse in the decades to come, making it even harder to raise living standards." (Satell, 2016). Rightly, few if any respondents to the above question are likely to mention security threats to the USA coming from abroad. Equally, for the common American citizen US hegemony is unlikely to come up as a major objective or concern.

After all, the average American is not involved in war (and war is a necessary ingredient for hegemony) considering that America's army is now professional and as such the worry of being conscripted and sent to some faraway country to fight (and die) does not enter the average person's mind. That was not the case, of course, when America had the draft during the Vietnam War. At that time most people had war high up in their worries list, considering that they or their children or relatives were liable to be called up to do service in the jungles of Vietnam and Cambodia, thousands of kilometres away from home, risking death and injury. But, people forgot quickly about the draft and the tussle with the military draft authorities that many young men experienced.

The average American is now hardly aware that the country's leadership spends more than two trillion dollars (in today's values) every three years on "defence". The American leadership of course knows these facts in detail and also knows what the defence budget can buy if most of it could be spent on non-military purchases and on the needs of the American people. In rough figures America spends more than eleven times the amount [its supposed adversary] Russia spends on defence, and some five or more times that of [its other supposed adversary] China. Russia has to defend a territory of roughly seventeen million square kilometres and China has to defend a population that is over one billion. In addition, America pressurises NATO members into spending inordinate amounts of money on their own defence, irrespective of whether they have a need for such expenditures or not. And, by the looks of it, this pressure on NATO members is likely to intensify. Yet, and despite such dizzying levels of expenditure, "Unfolding events in Washington and Beijing raise the disturbing spectre of a global passing of the torch from the United States to China..." wrote Lawrence J. Hass in the US News and World Report on 6 March, 2018. (Haas, 2018)

If we were to agree with Hass' assessment, how then can China achieve global leadership with a fraction of what America spends on the military? The answer is that just like Russia, China is not concerned about having a global military presence around the entire world. Both are more interested in their own neighbourhood. This makes sense. Had America spent on defence what China spends the country would have had more than half a trillion dollars to spare annually and invest in the needs of people inside America. Not to mention the immense goodwill America would create as a country that would be exercising moral rather than military leadership. Considering the generous nature of the America people and the strengths of the country I have no doubt that America can quickly assume the moral leadership of the world once it abandons her hegemonic ways. America has great potential as a moral leader. First, though, it would need to drop its obsession with world hegemony and global reach and start investing its money wisely.

But where does some of this wasted American money go? David Vine comes to our aid through his July/August 2015 article in Politico, "Despite recently closing hundreds of bases in Iraq and Afghanistan, the United States still maintains nearly 800 military bases in more than 70 countries and territories abroad—from giant "Little Americas" to small radar facilities. Britain, France and Russia, by contrast, have about 30 foreign bases combined." Vine continues, "By my calculation, maintaining bases and troops overseas cost \$85 to \$100 billion in fiscal year 2014; the total with bases and troops in warzones is \$160 to \$200 billion." (Shafer, 2015)

Global reach and America's unfulfilled promise

Time magazine reported the following unsettling statistics about America's domestic needs which successive administrations failed to address, largely because their priorities are global hegemony and maintenance of the current world order (that is, American monopoly on power). The gist of the Time article is that America's infrastructure is in urgent need of repair and yet its leaders continue to ignore the problem. One would assume that the needs of the military do not allow the leadership of the country to address such pressing problems as the repair of the electricity grid, for example. The reality of course, is that no country would dare attack America even if America spent a fraction of what it now spends on defence and invested the balance in much-needed infrastructure repair. Here are the statistics from Time magazine:

1. On transportation and water projects the US is now spending 2.7% of GDP whilst in 1965 it spent 6%.
2. A whopping 53% of rubbish is discarded, only 34% is recycled and 13% combusted for energy, thus putting a great pressure on the environment.
3. On levee repairs America would need to spend about \$100billion (more than Russia's defence budget).
4. On maintenance of its airports the country would need to spend about \$32 billion.
5. On drinking water alone the US needs to spend a massive \$400 billion just to maintain or replace pipelines, treatment plants, storage facilities and other projects.

6. To bring its highways up to standard America would need to spend some $170 billion; that is China's total defence budget for a year!

7. A massive amount, circa $1 trillion, would be required to repair and upgrade the country's electricity grid.

8. On bridges alone the country would require $106 billion and on rail and related matters another $10 billion.

9. Solid waste projects now require $56 billion. (Barone, 2016)

The urgent needs of all US public projects would require many times the annual military spend of the USA. America has other grave needs outside those reported by Time. Here is what Elizabeth Dias wrote in the same edition of Time under the title of, "The terrible, horrible, no good, very bad child-care problem". In her article Dias highlights the plight of America as regards day care that affects future generations of Americans (Dias, 2019). This makes one wonder about the judgment of the country's leadership over the past say, sixty years and the priorities they set. Many are now asking whether it would be better for America to spend its money on domestic needs rather than on maintaining a global reach and trying to bring "democracy" to Iraq and in the process leaving behind circa one million casualties.

Chasm between the leadership of Thomas Jefferson and G.W. Bush

"We will succeed in the Gulf. And when we do, the world community will have sent an enduring warning to any dictator or despot, present or future, who contemplates outlaw aggression. The world can therefore seize this opportunity to fulfil the long-held promise of a new world order — where brutality will go unrewarded, and aggression will meet collective

resistance."—President George H.W. Bush, State of the Union Address 1991.

How come Jefferson saw clearly, and rightly in my view, that America should not get involved in foreign wars, permanent alliances and adventurism and instead should concentrate on its domestic affairs, its education system and economy, spending only what is required for its own defence? And how come G.W. Bush thought in exactly the opposite way and never took heed of Jefferson's wise counsel, and in the process squandered the county's treasure and [most importantly] the country's goodwill in meaningless and useless wars that have little to do with America's defence. Were Washington and Jefferson leaders of better judgment than Bush or have domestic and international pressures changed so much since Jefferson's time? Or is it perhaps that there was no military-industrial complex to speak of in Jefferson's time and no pro-war lobbyists and no Neoconservatives? Or is it maybe that the leadership qualities America found in abundance in its founding fathers gradually dried up and are now a scarcity?

In an article in Politico on 17 January, 2019 Andrew Glass quoted excerpts from Eisenhower's farewell speech as president and his warning about the emergence and power of the military-industrial complex. Here are parts of Eisenhower's speech: "Until the latest of our world conflicts, the United States had no armaments industry... But we can no longer risk emergency improvisation of national defense." And, "... to this [permanent armaments industry] three-and-a-half million men and women are directly engaged in the defense establishment. We annually spend on military security alone more than the net income of all United States corporations... Now this conjunction of an immense military establishment and a large arms industry is new in the American experience. The total influence — economic, political, even spiritual — is felt in every city, every statehouse, every office of the federal government." And,

"In the councils of government, we must guard against the acquisition of unwarranted influence, whether sought or unsought, by the military-industrial complex. The potential for the disastrous rise of misplaced power exists and will persist." (Glass, 2019).

As I was about to write in this piece that presidents Obama and Trump did better than their predecessors of the last seventy years in that they were more restrained in starting wars and getting involved in adventurism, the following baffling piece appeared in Time, "Under White House direction, the administration [of Donald Trump] is drawing up demands that Germany, Japan and eventually any other country hosting US troops pay the full price of American soldiers deployed on their soil — plus 50 percent or more for the privilege of hosting them, according to a dozen administration officials and people briefed on the matter...In some cases, nations hosting American forces could be asked to pay five to six times as much as they do now under the "Cost Plus 50" formula." And, "One of the first US allies to confront the Trump administration's hardball tactics was South Korea, which last month agreed to pay $925 million for hosting 28,500 American troops. That was an 8.2 percent increase from the previous year's payment and about half the total costs." "Trump is correct in wanting US allies to bear more responsibility for collective defence, but demanding protection money from them is the wrong way to do it," said Stephen Walt, a scholar of international relations. Trump invokes new demands for extracting billions of dollars from US allies. "Our armed forces are not mercenaries, and we shouldn't send US troops into harm's way just because another country is paying us." (Wadhams and Jacops, 2019)

The Time piece puzzled me in that it now looks that the USA is getting into the business of providing protection for pay whilst at the same time projecting Global Reach at host countries' expense. It seems that Jefferson's worse fears are about to materialise. One would hope that this extra money would go on infrastructure improvements and welfare.

Worse news was to come soon after I had read the above disturbing piece, "US issues warning to Italy on China economic initiative" wrote Daniel Jativa on 9 March, 2019 in the Washington Examiner under the title, "The US issued an indirect warning to Italy on Saturday for its coziness with China." In other words America, the champion of globalization, is now threatening a fellow NATO member telling her what she is allowed to do and not do to save her economy; basically warning her against joining China's global Belt and Road Initiative. Here again we see the obsession with global hegemony going one step further and in fact crossing the line and damaging the interests of an ally, while spoiling America's good name. Does it make ethical sense for America to try and stop free countries from exercising their economic options and joining an economic expansion plan that will connect Hong Kong and Shanghai with the Middle East, Africa and the UK? The "new Silk Road" as the Chinese call their new initiative cannot be stopped and all those that see benefits from joining will join, sooner or later. Worse still for American hegemony is the Chinese initiative that aims to create the Asian Infrastructure Investment Bank to rival the International Monetary Fund and the World Bank. These last two institutions were behind most major international development projects, providing funding to the recipients and power to America! All of the above are about American global leadership, using methods that in different times would have been characterized as un-American, considering America's insistence on free trade, globalization and competition. America's attempt to curb Chinese economic power is the non-military equivalent of global reach. Curbing economic activity on a binary logic in the end will harm the world economy and reduce American moral influence. Most importantly such attempts will prove to be futile in that they will not stop China's drive for globalisation and economic resurgence. (Jativa, 2019)

Essay 2: Leadership failure: the case of Eastern Mediterranean (EM) leaders' inability to reinvent the region's greatness

"Great civilisations are not murdered. Instead, they take their own lives."
Arnold Toynbee in "A Study of History"

The disappearance over time of great leaders that had demonstrated their capacity for greatness, e.g. taking the EM to great heights, is an interesting leadership subject. Equally fascinating is the study of the epochs that follow the disappearance of great leaders and the dearth of achievement in the times that follow great epochs. It is a historic fact that at some point countries descend from the heights of greatness to insignificance. Just think of Britain at the start of the 20th century and compare it with the Britain of today. As such it is easy for me to understand why the EM that was once the cradle of civilization is no longer a serious player and only features in the news in times of trouble.

Let us take Greece as an example. How come Cimon and Pericles managed to be paragons of leadership, raising Athens to the pinnacle of greatness while Greece's leadership of the last two hundred years (with one or two rare exceptions maybe) got Greece to languish near the bottom of the European rankings? How come the Athens of old was the city to be in whilst the Athens of today is the place to emigrate from to escape either unemployment or crippling taxes? The majority of one's income in present day Greece is now returned to the government in the form of taxes, leaving one in poverty and unable even to benefit from the country's grossly inefficient public services. With little hope for a promising future child births have plummeted to dangerous levels and threaten Greece's very future. With the exception perhaps of Israel the formerly great countries of the EM are now a shadow of what they used to be in antiquity.

I chose the EM to include in our discussion because the differences between past and present are striking. The past reminds us of great achievements under great leaders while the present is about catastrophic decisions, conflict, insecurity, low/middle per capita income, and with a potential for disaster and major conflagration. This former powerhouse of a region is now basically a conflict zone. When relative comparisons are to be applied between the two epochs (separated by thousands of years) the current fails to match the past on most counts. The countries of the EM were the centre of learning in ancient times and during Byzantine times, with Constantinople as the capital. Now they are the centre of conflict and simmering war. The region was the centre of art and now hardly produces any major works of art. At the time of writing there was a war raging in Syria that formerly was the jewel of Anatolia. Syria boasts one of the world's oldest civilizations with a heritage in culture and art that most countries cannot hope to match. This great country is now shrinking and can hardly stand on its own feet. But is this the result of bad leadership, or of ceaseless external destructive interferences and internal incompetence?

Admittedly, all the countries of the region experienced the inequities of Ottoman occupation that kept people back and made them second class citizens, especially if they were Christian or Jewish. Three of the region's large islands, Cyprus, Crete and Malta also suffered atrocious sieges by the Ottoman Turks as prelude to occupation that set them back by centuries. Malta was lucky to survive the siege and consequent subjugation. Or, is it maybe a cocktail of events that brought the EM countries up to their knees in trouble? But, can the poor performance of the EM be blamed totally on centuries of Ottoman Turk occupation and subsequent decades of British (mostly) colonization and influence? Considering that the region borders three continents and is blessed with a temperate climate, one would have expected that the leadership of this part of the world would have taken advantage of the region's geography and climate. But alas, the region failed to meet expectations. (for an excellent review of the history of the region the reader is encouraged to read: Norwich, 2006)

The EM gave the world three of the greatest civilizations the world has ever had: Egypt, Greece and Rome (though Rome is a little to the west of the region). The EM also gave the world three of the greatest religions: Judaism, Christianity and Islam. The seven wonders of the world had their home in the broader EM region: Great Pyramid of Giza (still survives), the Hanging Gardens of Babylon, the Temple of Artemis at Ephesus, the Statue of Zeus at Olympia, the Mausoleum at Halicarnassus, the Colossus of Rhodes and the Lighthouse of Alexandria.

Lebanon boasts Byblos (modern Jbeil near Beirut) that, "... settled in paleolithic times...it may well be the oldest continuously inhabited site in the world." (Norwich, 2006: 2). Ebla in Syria is considered to have existed since the time of Byblos, around 3,000 BC, and as such is considered to be one of the oldest settlements in history. The Phoenicians (Tyre, Sidon, etc) were among the ancient world's greatest seafarers. They remained great until about the 8th century BC when they were overtaken gradually by other forces and later surpassed by the Greeks who fought and beat them after the Phoenicians chose to side with the Persians against the Greeks. It is the Phoenicians that first evolved the alphabet of the region with the Greeks adding the vowels to make it into a proper functioning tool for writing. Earlier writing, using consonants only, were found in Byblos and other nearby places but this can only be considered primitive writing. Egypt was a dominant civilization for centuries and stayed like that, with a few interruptions such as when the country was invaded by the Persians before Alexander the Great. The country was held by Ptolemy (323 BC) and the Greeks for about three hundred years until the death in 30 BC of Cleopatra, a descendant of Alexander.

The Greeks gave the western world its very soul and spirit and helped the west acquire and solidify its most precious institutions: education, democracy, justice, military, arts, and much more. The Greeks gave Russia and most other Slavs their alphabet and the Eastern Orthodox religion. Sparta gave Russia much of the military thought that makes the Russian army formidable. King Minos of Crete taught the world what it means to have an organized navy. Minos built an extraordinary civilization that continues to be the standard reference to this day. This included fashion, a liberal lifestyle that also allowed liberal practices including toplessness, which even today is frowned upon in some countries in the region. King Minos also brought luxury to the fore at a time it was unimaginable outside the Greek world.

At or near the time of the Trojan War that was ostensibly fought over Helen ("the face that launched a thousand ships") the great march of the Hebrews out of Egypt commenced. This lasted for forty years, covering a distance of some 400 miles, thus telling us how tortuous the trip must have been. The Hebrews were led by Moses who took them from Egypt to the land of Canaan (or Palestine as it was better known). This marked the beginning of another set of travails for them (following those in Egypt) considering that primarily the Philistines but also others in the area resented the presence of Hebrews. Under pressure the twelve tribes united under their first king, Saul. Later under King David they managed to create a kingdom of greatness having first subdued the Philistines. This did not last long, for after the reign of Solomon (David's son), the kingdom split into the Kingdoms of Israel (north) and Judah (south). As expected the split created troubles between the two which weakened them to the point of falling prey to the Assyrians some three centuries later (8th century BC). The kingdom of Judah survived but only just. The Assyrians spelled the end of the kingdom of Israel. A new and terrible tragedy struck a century later when the Hebrews of Judah were carried off to captivity (598/7) by the King of Babylon Nebuchadnezzar. Captivity lasted for about sixty years until the Persians (under Cyrus the Great who we cover in this treatise) allowed their return to Palestine in 538 BC. Israel gave the world Judaism and in many ways Christianity as well, considering that Christ was a Jew, though not accepted by the Jews in the way Christians accept Him. Judaism has been an influential force on the west, both from its theological contribution but also for its contribution to the work ethic. Judeo-Christianity brought the groups Judaism and Christianity together, in the sense that Christianity is in some/many ways derived from Judaism. Both have shared values, common reference points and other commonalities that now form one of the pillars of western culture and thought. The Judeo-Christian ethic continues to guide the West as regards proper behaviour, integrity, family values and common decency. George Orwell is credited with coining the term "the Judaeo-Christian scheme of morals" in 1939, which was accepted by the West.

The EM region was under Ottoman Turkish rule for some 400 years and as such had to suffer the expected setbacks characteristic of occupied regions. Turkey is new to the region and in fact is the only country in the EM that has no roots or origins in the EM. Amazingly, Turkey managed to this day not to be considered a colonial power even though it colonized a big part of the EM region. The Turks came to the region through the sword as recently as eight hundred years ago. Because of Ottoman tyranny the region was unable to develop authentic leadership outside the constraints the Ottoman Turks set for them. This situation continued until the end of WWI when the Ottoman Empire was destroyed largely by the British, the Russians and the French, "... the war that ended Ottoman rule also destroyed many of the institutions that had sustained it." (Mazower, 2015)

This break-up of the institutions of the region by the Ottomans made things worse for budding leaders, considering that new institutions had to be set up and developed. Then came the meddling of Britain and France (and later of America on account of the Cold War), largely for geopolitical reasons but importantly due to the importance of the region's oil after WWI and the West's insatiable thirst for oil. This led Britain and co to look for puppet governments to serve Western interests. Basically all the countries in the region, including Greece which officially became independent more than a hundred years before other countries in the region, suffered heavily from outside meddling, as did the Arabs, "...the growing popularity of geopolitical thinking as well as the strategic anxieties of the rivalrous great powers, and its spread was a sign of growing European meddling in the destiny of the Arab-speaking peoples."

(Mazower, 2015)

Worst of all for the nurturing of leadership, Britain initiated a campaign to install kingdoms in the area to ensure its political influence via local palaces rather than relying on the "whim" of the masses and popular vote. So, we saw in Iraq a line of kings such as Faisal I, Ghazi and Faisal II. In Egypt, after Britain had occupied the country in the late 19th century, we saw Husayn Kamil installed by the British as sultan, pretending that Egypt was still Ottoman. In Libya we saw king Idris who was overthrown by Gaddafi, who in turn was overthrown by the Americans, British and French. Iran had the Pahlavi dynasty (Reza and then Mohamed Reza) plus several revolutions. Jordan saw the installation of the Hashemite kingdom. Even Syria had its self-proclaimed and short-lived Arab Kingdom. Cyprus was annexed by Britain late in the 19th century and controlled directly until 1960. A small part of Cyprus is still under the control of the British as a Sovereign Base Area and outside the control of the Republic of Cyprus.

So, considering foreign influence and puppet rule in certain countries of the region, a great opportunity to create and nurture leadership was lost. Even in Greece, that was the first to free itself from Ottoman tyranny, the country's politics were split soon after independence into pro-British, pro-French and pro-Russian.

Turkey continues to create trouble for its neighbours and worse still allowed her borders to be used by armed Islamists. Ahmet S. Yayla and Colin P. Clarke explain in their article in Foreign Policy of April 12, 2018, "Beginning in late 2013 and early 2014, Turkish border cities became the chief logistical hubs for foreign fighters seeking to enter Syria and Iraq to join the Islamic State and other rebel groups" and continues, "Nevertheless, contraband Islamic State oil was consistently sold at points along the Turkish border throughout 2014 and into 2015." (Yayla and Clarke, 2018)

When belatedly the region began to grow its own leadership, free to a great extent from direct foreign influence, the experiment did not go exactly according to plan, as populism began to take its toll leading most of the countries in the region to impaired rule. Turkey continues to dream of reviving Ottoman rule in the region, never coming to terms with the fact that the Ottoman Empire is gone and will never return, no matter how much aggression Turkey exercises. The unresolved Palestinian problem adds to the divisions in the region.

References

Barone, E. (2016). Rebuilding our foundations. Time Magazine, 188(16–17), pp.46–47.

Dias, E. (2019). The terrible, horrible, no good, very bad child-care problem. Time Magazine, 188(16–17), pp.38–43.

Glass, A. (2019). Eisenhower warns of 'military-industrial complex,' Jan. 17, 1961. [online] POLITICO. Available at: https://www.politico.com/story/2019/01/17/eisenhower-warns-of-military-industrial-complex-jan-17-1961-1099265 [Accessed 10 Mar. 2019].

Haas, L. (2018). Passing the Torch to China?. [online] US News. Available at: https://www.usnews.com/opinion/world-report/articles/2018-03-06/global-power-is-shifting-from-the-us-to-china [Accessed 8 Mar. 2019].

Jativa, D. (2019). US issues warning to Italy on China economic initiative. [online] Washington Examiner. Available at: https://www.washingtonexaminer.com/news/us-issues-warning-to-italy-on-china-economic-initiative [Accessed 11 Mar. 2019].

Mazower, M. (2015). End of the Ottoman empire | Financial Times. [online] ft.com. Available at: https://www.ft.com/content/af218024-b2bf-11e4-a058-00144feab7de [Accessed 18 Mar. 2019].

McCoy, A. (2019). The End of Our World Order Is Imminent. [online] The Nation. Available at: https://www.thenation.com/article/end-of-world-order-empire-climate-change [Accessed 4 Mar. 2019].

Norwich, J. J. (2006). The Middle Sea. London: Vintage.

Satell, G. (2016). Wake up America! This Is The Real Problem With The US Economy. [online] Forbes.com. Available at: https://www.forbes.com/sites/gregsatell/2016/10/29/wake-up-

america-this-is-the-real-problem-with-the-us-economy
[Accessed 8 Mar. 2019].

Shafer, J. (2015). Where in the World Is the US Military?. [online]
POLITICO Magazine. Available at:
https://www.politico.com/magazine/story/2015/06/us-military-
bases-around-the-world-119321 [Accessed 18 Mar. 2019].

Wadhams, N. and Jacops, J. (2019). http://time.com. [online] Time.
Available at: http://time.com/5548013/trump-allies-pay-cost-
plus-50-troops [Accessed 10 Mar. 2019].

Yayla, A. and Clarke, C. (2018). Turkey's Double ISIS Standard.
[online] Foreign Policy. Available at:
https://foreignpolicy.com/2018/04/12/turkeys-double-isis-
standard [Accessed 18 Mar. 2019].

Book 10

Leader triumphs and failures: the Eastern Mediterranean (EM) case

*"Hillary Clinton's support for violent regime change in Syria has thrown
the country into one of the bloodiest civil wars anyone has ever seen…"*
Donald Trump. (Trump, 2016)

What Donald Trump said about interference in the EM and
ensuing violence reflects correctly the history of the region and
explains adequately the present state of leadership in the region. It
also tells us how some of the leaders in the region are used (and
often exploited) by big powers to create their own world. There is
hardly a country in the region that can map out its foreign policy
independently.

Though Aaron David Miller fails to mention the occupation by
Turkey of Cyprus and the economic devastation of Greece he
nevertheless manages to give us a pretty good picture of the
failures of the area. Aaron David Miller wrote this about the region
on 26 June, 2013, "Nevertheless, much of the region looks bad:
violence in Iraq; civil war in Syria and violent spillover into

Lebanon; growing popular despair in Egypt; repression in Bahrain; lack of central authority in Libya; and an impasse in the Israeli-Palestinian peace process. Even in Turkey, the wonder state, things have become unhinged." And, "What's going on here? Why, when much of the world seems to be moving forward, is the Middle East being left behind?" Then Miller continued with the following, "To be sure, outsiders still influence the Middle East in very negative ways. But that's no excuse for believing its people can't shape their own destiny." (Miller, 2013)

Anyone that knows the area well can add an endless list of other ailments of the region that are a function of: a) foreign interference and b) less than capable leadership in some countries of the region. Foreigners interfere to support their own interests with little concern for the people in the region; a generally deficient leadership does the rest. Here are just some highlights on how the two worked in the past to give us the situation we have today: a) innumerable coups in "democratic" Turkey that is also a stalwart of NATO, with foreign powers sitting on the sidelines and watching, if not applauding. Turkish invasion of Cyprus, Iraq, Syria and a host of other adventures, sometimes encouraged from abroad, b) a revolution in Egypt in 1952 removed the Commander in Chief of the Armed Forces of Egypt, General Haidar. His place was taken by the leader of the revolution General Mohammed Naqib, ultimately unseating King Farouk, tenth ruler of Egypt from the Mohammad Ali dynasty. This was followed by another mini coup two years later which unseated the head of the 1952 revolution General Mohammed Naqib. By the end of this tumultuous few years Egypt ended up with a few wars and a misconceived version of communism under the charismatic Gamal Abdel Nasser. After Nasser's death Egypt experienced a presidential assassination, autocracy with relative stability, a short-lived Islamist state and extremism, followed by today's relatively stable government that is threatened by terrorism coming from religious fanatics, c) Greece saw a coup in 1967 that lasted for seven years and which was tacitly supported by some Western powers with the US in the lead. Then, and as a result of the destruction of Cyprus by Turkey, a series of Greek governments, mostly of an incompetent nature ruled the country and in the end brought Greece to its knees economically and forced the young to voluntary exile, d) Cyprus suffered British colonialism, fettered independence, mostly immature administrations post-independence, a mini coup, an invasion by Turkey, forced break-up of the country and continued occupation to this day, e) The situation in Syria was well described by President Donald Trump above, f) Lebanon suffered a couple of devastating civil wars with the last one literally tearing the country asunder, foreign army invasion of the south of the country and for a time foreign military presence by two foreign armies, no president for a couple of years, no government and cabinet for some time, uncollected trash that threatened peoples' health, electricity and water shortages, system breakdown and political paralysis, g) Israel had a few wars, one of which threatened the very existence of the country followed by asymmetric war coming mostly from outside, Israeli retaliatory bombings of Gaza and South Lebanon, low-key military involvement in the Syrian civil war and so on. Despite her problems, Israel continuous to be the most stable, most economically vibrant and richest country in the region.

So, what do all the above say about foreign interference and a generally poor leadership that has created the combustible situation we are experiencing today in the region? What does it also tell us about the inability of leaders to work things out amongst themselves rather than seeking the assistance of self-serving foreigners to help them undo their neighbours or to defend themselves from their neighbour in the case of the Greeks?

The economies of the EM region

The leadership of the countries would do well to look at their economies considering that the economy of a country tends to mirror to a large extent how well a country's leadership is performing. Then to ask how these economies would have performed had there been regional cooperation. The data below shows clearly that, with the exception of Israel's economy the countries in the region could do much better if only all the countries in the region respected international law and engaged in inter-country cooperation. Despite its high expenditures on defence, Israel continues to invest relentlessly in technology, realising that in this day in age technology is a prerequisite to economic development and the survival of Israel.

What I did was to gather some key statistical markers on the region's economic performance from the Global Competitive Index report of 2018, published by the World Economic Forum. The data below shows how each of the countries in the region compares against a sample of 140 countries that participated in the World Economic Forum's study. In reading the data below the reader will need to remember that the lower the number the better the performance of the country except for GDP per capita In bold the worst performing country of the six on the particular performance indicator. Notice Israel's performance on innovation.

Performance of EM countries in select areas: 2018 World Economic Forum Report

(Schwab, 2018)

Egypt

Pay and productivity: 75

Soundness of banks: 32
Cost of starting a business: 71
Growth of innovative companies: 53
Innovation capability: 50
Overall rank: 94
GDP per capita in USD: 2,500

Israel

Pay and productivity: 22
Soundness of banks: 12
Cost of starting a business: 50
Growth of innovative companies: 9
Innovation capability: 1
Overall rank: 20
GDP per capita in USD: 40,200

Turkey

Pay and productivity: 95
Soundness of banks: 84
Cost of starting a business: 87
Growth of innovative companies: 49
Innovation capability: 38
Overall rank: 61
GDP per capita in USD: 10,500

Lebanon

Pay and productivity: 62
Soundness of banks: 59
Cost of starting a business: 124
Growth of innovative companies: 66
Innovation capability: n/a
Overall rank: 80
GDP per capita in USD: 11,400

Greece

Pay and productivity: 111
Soundness of banks: 137
Cost of starting a business: 45
Growth of innovative companies: 120
Innovation capability: 40
Overall rank: 57
GDP per capita in USD: 18,637

Cyprus

Pay and productivity: 73
Soundness of banks: 126
Cost of starting a business: 86
Growth of innovative companies: 105
Innovation capability: 68
Overall rank: 44
GDP per capita in USD: 25,000

- No data was available on Syria due to the situation there.
- Cyprus's relatively high per capita GDP also reflects large transient windfalls. Cyprus' banking system is still in a shaky condition and the economy is sitting on a very narrow base.
- All countries in the region, including Israel are blighted by high employee numbers in the public sector that stifle economic growth. Indicatively, at the time of writing Cyprus employed circa 68,000 staff in the broader public sector, from a total of circa 420,000 persons eligible for employment (Cyprus Statistical Service). This means that circa one in six is employed in the public sector.
- Again, with the exception of Israel, pay and productivity in the region is at disturbingly low levels showing once more the importance of technology.

Essay 1: An overview of the EM leadership, threats to the region, and foreign interference

"I cannot give you the formula for success, but I can give you the formula for failure — which is: Try to please everyone" Herbert Bayard Swope

The present state of affairs pays scant compliment to the leadership of most countries in the EM and also to the countries that interfere in the region. Much blame can justifiably be placed on the shoulders of colonisers and more particularly the Ottoman Turks, that kept the region back institutionally for nearly four centuries and blunted any efforts to set up proper structures and government. The same holds for foreign interference. It should be remembered that self-government for the luckier countries in the region came not long ago, and even that was fettered. The demise of the Ottoman Empire after WWI liberated most of the countries in the region from the yoke of the Turks but then some of these countries fell under British or French mandates that started a new round of control from foreign powers.

Cyprus got its fettered independence in 1960 and fourteen years later was half-occupied by the Turks who still have their occupation troops in place. Three percent of the island's territory is still under colonization in the form of British Sovereign Bases on the territory, that Britain refused to decolonize and hand over to the Republic of Cyprus as she ought to have done. Britain and France are also guilty of taking sides in domestic conflicts and even fomenting strife in some cases. America cannot be absolved of blame either, considering that Britain bequeathed to the USA its "protector" role of the area after the calamitous and humiliating (for the French and British) war for control of the Suez Canal. All these calamities did not allow proper leadership in the area to grow and be nurtured, since many of the needed big decisions required the approval of "neo-protector" powerful countries. It goes without saying that countries that fall under "protectors" fail to grow copious leadership, seeing all major decisions are taken by outsiders who make sure that such decisions are aligned with the "protector's" interests.

Some leaders in the EM area are their own worst enemies

With the reality of centuries-long occupation by foreigners and the divisions that exist within their own countries, leaders of countries in the region ought to have rallied to each other's help to create a better future. Instead of cooperating with each other these leaders played into the hands of outsiders whose only aim was the promotion of their own (outsider's) interests; be these access to cheap oil and gas or geostrategic advantage. Thus, the emphasis shifted away from improving the unity of the countries in the region to reducing internal rivals and/or antagonising neighbouring countries with the support of foreigners. We are now used to seeing neighbour against neighbour with foreigners supporting one or the other belligerent. Israel did better than most other countries in this competition for big power support, largely because of the steady support the country receives from the USA since the end of the Suez Canal crisis. Syria has Russia helping her. But, help arrived a bit late and not before the country started unravelling on account of civil war that was largely fomented from outside. The situation looks more promising now.

Israel: Whilst Israel can confidently depend on the USA no other country in the region can say the same, except maybe for

Turkey. Turkey has had American support starting with the advent of the Marshall Plan which was primarily designed to help countries find their feet after the catastrophe of WWII. Some of this help went to Turkey, that hadn't participated in the war and did not have a single victim. By default, America would go to war to support two countries in the world: the British with whom Americans have a "special relationship" and Israel. American support for Israel is largely the result of work done by the powerful Jewish lobby in the US, but also from the dedication and commitment to Israel's survival of the leadership of Israel since the days of Ben-Gurion. The Jews of the diaspora feel Jewish first, no matter where they live and for how long they have been living there. Yet, all this has not improved Israel's soft power in the region considering that a large majority of its Arab neighbours continue to consider Israel and America (in that order) as their biggest threat. "About 82 percent of survey participants in 12 Arab countries said they believed the US poses a threat to stability in the region, according to a poll unveiled in Washington, D.C. on Tuesday. The 2016 Arab Opinion Index, conducted by the Arab Center for Research and Policy Studies in Doha, Qatar, found that among foreign powers, only Israel was perceived to be a bigger threat. About 90 percent of survey respondents reported that Israel is a threat to the region's stability." USNews reported on 11 April, 2017 (Haynie, 2017). Knowing the feelings of most of its neighbours and the hostility of organizations such as Hamas and Hezbollah, Israel unsurprisingly feels uncomfortable and unsafe. So, even the leadership of militarily strong Israel has much ground to cover in terms of living in peace.

The leaders of the other countries in the region have not managed to find a corresponding America (or Russia) to fully guarantee their future integrity. Syria cannot claim that its relationship with Russia is at the level of Israel's with America, but is strong enough to make the country feel relatively secure. The fact is that no leadership in the region can claim to be able to map out an independent foreign policy for its country. The jewels of ancient times are now either fully or partly client states resting their hopes on others and praying that their protectors will prove loyal when the need arises. But as the Greeks know full well such prayers remain largely unanswered. "Protector" America and "guarantor" England both sat on the touchlines when Cyprus was attacked by Turkey in 1974; not to say that both these countries gave their tacit support to Turkey and to this day remain largely silent.

So, we see countries in the region in an unrelenting search for a reliable "protector" that rarely proves reliable except in the case of Israel and and to an extend Turkey. Protection is sought to save them either from their own brothers (see internal conflicts in Syria and Lebanon) or from their neighbours (see Turkish aggression against its neighbours). In the Lebanese internal strife the Lebanese Christians first threw their lot in with the French and later with the Americans. They were disappointed in both cases and in the end lost (certainly did not win!) They now find themselves with an existentially uncertain future just as the Greeks of Cyprus find themselves in this situation. Call this bad decision making or/and bad luck if you wish! Lebanon's "perfect storm" is developing in the form of a perfect split along sectarian lines, even if ephemeral alliances camouflage the breadth and depth of these divisions. Hezbollah is the dominant military force in Lebanon and constitutes Israel's biggest threat because of the asymmetrical war it can wage, and also because of Hezbollah's determination and ability to fight and accept losses.

Considering that the threat to Israel from the armies of its neighbours has waned, Israel is now focusing on the Shia arc that starts from Iran and stretches through Iraq, Syria and southern Lebanon. When the leadership of Israel decided to invade southern Lebanon in 1982, little did the Israeli leadership know that they would be opening the road for Hezbollah's emergence and dominance in the Lebanon. The decision of the Israeli leadership to invade southern Lebanon proved to be disastrous. Was it bad judgment or over-confidence on the part of the Israeli leadership?

Egypt. After its long experience with Ottoman domination (direct or indirect) Egypt had Britain (and France in many ways) thrust on her as "protector", then America, then Russia, then America once more. Now the leadership of the country is searching yet again for a "protector", most often tilting towards America which is, paradoxically, Israel's staunchest and most dedicated supporter. Of course the EM is full of such paradoxes so what is happening in Egypt comes as no surprise.

Greece has been the most consistent client state, first of Britain and later (after the end of WWII) of America, despite public anti-American rhetoric by politicians to conceal the truth. At the time of writing the government of Greece calls itself "socialist" and made its name through rhetoric that was supposedly antagonistic to the USA but which was just for show. Now these politicians that were formerly known for their "America out of Greece" rhetoric have come full circle and are employing the exact policies of the party they accused as sell-outs over their support of American policy. The "socialist" government in Greece is now America's docile representative in Greece with their antagonists sitting on the wings to replace them. Basically, the major Greek parties were and still are on the side of America, no matter what they claim in public and the coded language they use publicly. The actions of the political elite often go contrary to public feeling that is consistently pro-Russian on account of historical ties, Russia's support in the war of independence in 1827, and above all the cultural ties between the two peoples considering that the Greeks gave Russia her alphabet and Eastern Orthodoxy. The Russian government has little or no trust in the present "socialist" government of the Siriza party.

When America intervened behind the scenes to "solve" the Imia crisis with the Turks (the crisis was over two Greek islets) the "socialist" Greek Prime Minister at the time thanked America publicly for its "helpful and constructive role". All America did with her intervention was to take away from Greece the sovereignty of the two islets and place them in a grey zone! To this day America declares publicly that the two islets do not belong to Greece (nor to Turkey that opportunistically laid claim over them). Thus, the "helpful" intervention of America got the Turks to consider the islets theirs as per the position of the Turkish foreign ministry, "'The Kardak (Imia) Rocks and their territorial waters and airspace above them are exclusively under Turkish sovereignty...'" (Greek City Times, 2018). For all practical purposes these islets are occupied territory in the sense that the Greeks cannot even visit them without Turkey's permission.

Paradox galore! So, here we see once more the farcical and difficult-to-explain decisions of some of the leaders of countries in the EM explaining in some ways the predicament of the region. While former American Secretary of State Kissinger was apparently the man to give Turkey the nod to invade Cyprus in 1974, the Cyprus leadership agreed to have America and Britain lead the political process for the freeing of Cyprus from occupation by Turkey! This of course is music to the ears of NATO member Turkey, that is in no hurry to take out of Cyprus even one of her 40,000 troops, hundreds of thousands of settlers/occupiers or hundreds of tanks and armaments. So, "negotiations" continue just as they have done for the last forty odd years, under the guidance and chaperoning of America and Britain. Of course, this allows Turkey freedom to consolidate her position on the island.

Syria. What happened to Syria in the last circa seven or more years will certainly be the subject of many articles and books on resilience and defiance. These books will probably attempt to answer how a leader (President Assad of Syria in this case) that the world considered to be dead and buried at the start of the conflict managed to come back from the dead to keep his country together. Needless to say the odds against him were overwhelming considering that the pressures from inside and outside were formidable. I am sure that objective observers on the subject of leadership will have much to write about this extraordinary escape (and survival) no matter what one thinks of President Assad and his life. Some thirty years from now the confidential archives will almost certainly reveal some fascinating goings-on that allowed him to survive the onslaught. .

Everything but the proverbial kitchen sink was literally thrown at him: a) Syria was bombed to smithereens, b) armed Islamists and other fanatical groups from a host of countries attacked Syria from all sides, c) local opposition militias were organised against him along with all those that had an axe to grind, d) American arms to Assad's opponents flew in, including some military personnel, e) Turkish troops and armaments invaded his country, all sorts of shady groups also joined in the fray as is usual in such cases and f) some Syrian military personnel changed sides and went against Assad with a few acting as foreign agents and tasked with defaming the Syrian government; hoping to break the country's morale and benefit from those they wrongly thought would be the eventual winners. And the list goes on.

At one point the country was in shreds with minimal territory in the hands of the government forces. Yet, and most incredibly, the vast majority of the Syrian army remained loyal to Assad, as did the majority of the Syrian people. At one point it looked as if the government was minutes away from falling but miraculously found its feet again. At the most crucial point, and as the government was about to fall due to colossal pressure, Assad managed to get Russia to throw its mighty weight on the side of Syria after the government invited Russia to come in. Iran and Hezbollah stood by the Syrian government, as well as lending support with personnel and materiel. It will be interesting to see what future books on leadership will write about this phenomenal escape. Assad's great challenge of course still lies ahead of him. The challenge of uniting the country may prove to be a more difficult mountain to climb, however. Reform is probably Syria's biggest single challenge and this must come sooner rather than later. Equally, advancing a "no winners no losers" culture will be a make or break action for Assad. Rebuilding the nation and helping create the conditions for people to express freely their views and choices after their harrowing experiences are massive challenges that lie ahead. Syria cannot yet declare victory.

The EM continues to be threatened and the region will continue to be a cauldron full of burning charcoal and other combustible materials even after Syria finds its feet and peace hopefully reigns in the country. Two major issues that have been the affliction of the region continue unresolved, however. Both these issues call for extraordinary leadership if they are to be solved amicably and fairly for all: a) as long as the Israel-Palestinian problem remains unresolved a big sore will continue to remain unhealed leading to continued strife, conflict and instability of one or another form and b) as long as Turkey continues to dream of domination of the region and assumption of the role of regional Hegemon the region will continue with conflict which will not allow countries to meet their potential. Turkey threatens everyone, literally, of her neighbours. The freeing of Cyprus from the Turkish army and Turkish colonisers is an absolute must. Turkey continues to employ intimidation and force almost daily even against EU member countries in the EM. This is dangerous stuff for everyone in the region and for the EU in particular, considering that Turkey wishes to put at least two EU member states (Greece and Cyprus) under her Ottomanesque and Islamist orbit. But, it is not just the Greeks that are under threat from Turkey, Syria is as well and so are Bulgaria and Iraq. Not to mention the occasional Turkish threats against Israel and even Egypt for that matter. Not so distant (from the region) Armenia is also under continued threat from Turkey which to this day continues not to own up to the Armenian genocide it committed when it exterminated the Armenian population in Anatolia in the first two decades of the 20th century.

At the time of writing Turkey had put to sea nearly all of its navy, laying claim to a self-assessed and invented Turkish Exclusive Economic Zone (EEZ) whilst vehemently refusing to abide by international law. In a recent speech the Turkish Minister of Defence laid claim to 462,000 square kilometres of what he called Blue Fatherland; a euphemism for the planned usurpation of the sea of the Greeks and other countries. More particularly Turkey lays claim to parts of: the Aegean Sea, Eastern Mediterranean, Cyprus, and part of the Black Sea and Armenia. To this effect Turkey is prepared to employ violence and smash and grab tactics to take from her neighbours what international law has given them. Here again, Turkey is encouraged by the silence of those powerful countries that ought not to keep silent. As a result of these and other actions the region continues to be an epicentre of instability with daily violations of international law.

In summing up the many leadership failures of the EM region one could equally say that it is a miracle how all these countries avoided total catastrophe in the face of never-ending destructive interference and meddling, coercion and violence sometimes.

Essay 2: In search of EM leader-heroes in the six militarily powerful EM countries

"Ye shall know them by their fruits. Do men gather grapes of thorns, or figs of thistles?" (Matthew 7:16, King James Version)

We have already noted that the EM has given the world three outstanding civilizations and three major religions. The populations of all countries in the area trace their origins to the ancient past of the region, except for the Turks that are historically newcomers from the wider region of Central Asia. They came to colonise the region as conquerors through the sword less than a thousand years ago. As such it would be interesting to show how the leadership of the area managed things and whether the leaders of the last hundred years or so years are worthy sons and daughters of their illustrious ancestors of ancient times. All we need do is examine the state of the region today and then judge how well its leadership has done. We have already said a few things about the history of the region.

To start with all the leaders in the region claim to be products of democratic processes; no matter how faulty these processes are in some countries. Below I discuss the leadership situation in the six militarily powerful countries in the region.. Because military power gives a country a say in the development of events I am limiting my analysis to the following six countries: .

a) Egypt: The country is headed by retired marshal Abdel Fattah el-Sisi who was voted in as the country's president when Egypt was on the precipice of disaster on account of the religious fanaticism the former short-lived Islamist government employed. Many see Egypt's current leadership as saviours of a country that was just about to move into the dark ages. But one wonders how in the first place it was possible for Egypt to have elected an Islamist radical as president and then to have him replaced by a former marshal soon after. But, these things happen in Egypt and most Egyptians are happy, one would think, that things turned out the way they did and the country returned to relative stability under Sisi and his team. The Middle East Forum had this to say about Marshal Sisi, current President of Egypt, "...he has turned out to be the most moderate president in Egypt's modern history, and among the most enlightened of Muslim politicians anywhere" wrote Cynthia Farahat in the Middle East Quarterly of Spring 2019. (Farahat, 2019)

b) Greece: The Prime Minister of Greece Alexis Tsipras is a former student and labour agitator. He was an activist known for his anti-everything antics and expert at organising street demonstrations. He is known for having led protests against education reform, which he continues to oppose to this day, irrespective of the merits of such reforms. He is particularly opposed to private tertiary education and as such will not listen to arguments. He has the habit of signalling left and turning right. He is known for his readiness to do anything to stay in power. But, he is not known for his total commitment to democratic principles, seeing he does not mind trashing the expressed wishes of the [vast] majority of the Greeks on national and other major issues. He learned most of his trade as member of the Communist Youth of Greece in the 1980s and 1990s. He is seen by independent analysts as a very divisive figure with great flair for populism. As regards democratic polity he once arranged a referendum the results of which told him clearly what to do regarding the Memoranda on the Greek economy. Immediately after he trashed and totally ignored the results, even though he himself initiated the referendum. Equally, he went against the vast majority of Greeks on the issue of Macedonia which he dealt with autocratically; fearing the results of a referendum he did everything in his power to thwart all efforts to have one. He was ready to adopt the wishes of outsiders, (those of the Americans surprisingly), but not those of the Greeks. It is said that some senior international figures considered him and his team to be light-weight floundering novices.

c) Syria: Syria is run by a still embattled head of state with doubtful, by western standards, democratic credentials but with phenomenal ability to survive and keep his country together. Bashar Assad entered the military academy and soon after oversaw the Syrian military presence in Lebanon. He is a trained medical specialist who served as a medical doctor in the Syrian Army. He specialised in ophthalmology (with post-graduate studies at the Western Eye Hospital in London). Very tenacious, shrewd, and able to dodge attacks from outside and inside, "Bashar al-Assad promised much but delivered little on the economic and social problems endured by the Syrian people" wrote Adam Coutts in the Guardian on 18 May, 2011 and then continued, "Most had accepted a decades-long trade-off: stability, security and a decent standard of living in return for not openly criticising the government. All this in a region plagued by rampant insecurity, sectarian polarisation, foreign intervention and inadequate social welfare..." (Coutts, 2011)

d) Iran Though not in the immediate vicinity of the EM, Iran plays a significant role in the region. Ancient Persia ruled over the region for centuries starting from the 6th century AD. The country is presided over by Supreme Leader Ali Hosseini Khameini, who in his life suffered six arrests and a three-year-long exile. Also, he was the target of an assassination attempt that paralysed his right arm. The US and Britain call Iran a theocratic state that is far from democratic polity, even if elections of sorts are held regularly as per the Iranian constitution. Overall he is considered to have the wilfulness and tenacity to stand up to outsiders and in this way keep Iran's position as regional leader.

e) Israel: The Prime Minster of Israel has just been re-elected. He is an MIT graduate with BSc and MSc degrees. He formerly was with the Boston Consulting Group. Prime Minister Benjamin Netanyahu is democratically and cleanly elected, able and smart. "When asked recently by a London think tank how he would want to be remembered, he said as 'the protector of Israel. The one who created the means to be sure of the country's future.'" (BBC News, 2019)

f) Turkey: Turkey's president Tayyip Erdogan was mayor for four years, prime minister for ten years, president since 2014 with an Islamist political background. He was once banned from political office and imprisoned for a period of four months. Here is what Human Rights Watch said about the country he runs, "Turkey is the world leader in jailing journalists and media workers as they face criminal investigations and trials, with around 150 behind bars at time of writing. Most newspapers and television channels lack independence and promote the government's political line." (Human Rights Watch, 2019)

Daniel Pipes wrote this about Erdogan, "He has ruled as a near-absolute dictator for about six years…He controls the military, the police, the parliament, judiciary, the banks, the media, and the educational system. He does whatever he wants." (Pipes, 2019)

Summary of leader backgrounds in the six militarily powerful countries of the EM

—Sisi: A former marshal that wrested control from the hands of radical Islamists.

—Tsipras: A trained engineer and former labour and student agitator. Disregards the results of referenda and blocks referenda if he suspects that these will go against his wishes. .

—Assad: A specialist ophthalmologist with close connections to the army. A survivor of great enormity who runs a country in need of more democracy.

—Khameini: An Ayatollah who suffered arrests and exile and an assassination attempt for his political involvement. Seen as undemocratic by the US and Britain and many others in the West and fighter-leader by his supporters..

—Erdogan: A professional politician that has been at the top of the power hierarchy for fifteen yeas. Islamist roots. Briefly in prison for political reasons. Runs a country that is known for its coups and toppling of elected governments by the army.

—Netanyahu: A highly educated Prime Minter who rose to the rank of captain in the elite corps of the army. Democratically elected, capable and smart.

Essay 3: Big and small countries in the EM

A few words about the two largest countries in the EM region, that is Turkey and Egypt.

"From a European standpoint, Ankara's political choices at home and on the international stage amount to a near-total dismantlement of the rule of law and the use of the judiciary as an instrument of political power. Turkey's foreign policy is more attuned to domestic political necessities than to Western alliance objectives. And the country's public diplomacy consists of verbal aggression, attempts at electoral interference, and the propagation of doctored news." 15 March, 2018 (Pierini, 2019)

Turkey. Of the countries in the region Turkey is a NATO stalwart and aspiring EU member, even if its wings were clipped on account of umpteen coups and for reasons of non-compliance with EU democratic principles. Greece is also in NATO but relatively weak, at least for now. Turkey boasts the region's largest economy and army as well as the largest number of coups. Coup champion in the last fifty years: one coup every ten years on average (1960, 1971, 1980, 1993, and 2016). In one such coup dictator Evren had circa half a million people imprisoned. In the last coup attempt against the current president both America and the EU delayed their reaction and this angered the government that was the target of the coup. To calm down Turkey's anger, America then dispatched to Turkey no lesser figure than the US Vice President. The EU tried to patch things up as quickly as possible and almost asked Turkey for forgiveness considering that the EU needs Turkey's cooperation on a number of issues, including the EU economy. Turkey is also a conduit for the flow of refugees to Europe. Russia acted smartly and expressed its dissatisfaction with the coup attempt immediately after it was made known. It is interesting to see that for economic and geostrategic reasons both America and Russia cosy up to Turkey. Russia's relationship with Turkey looks rather ephemeral considering that Turkey has been a NATO stalwart for the last circa seventy years. As regards peace in the EM it is interesting to note that at the time of writing Turkey had its invasion troops in three different countries: Cyprus, Syria and Iraq. In addition, at the time of writing Turkey is involved in a civil war with the Kurds in the eastern part of Turkey and is in attack mode in Syria. Furthermore she continues to threaten Armenia, that receives protection from Russia. Very knotty stuff as far as Turkey is concerned!

Egypt. "Bureaucracy is a huge problem in Egypt. An estimated 5.6 million civil servants (24 percent of the total labour force) are infamous for obstruction." Fanack.com 14 September, 2014. Add to bureaucracy the legacy of bad management, inefficiency, nepotism and unemployment, and you get a full picture of Egypt's greatest problem: bad economy, poverty and over population.

Egypt is in the throes of economic problems just as she has been for most of the last sixty years. But the government is holding the country together even if society looks somehow divided, considering that the Islamists and some peripheral groups never stop agitating. At the time of writing Egypt is also suffering from low-level violence coming from the forces of the Islamists, and mostly concentrated in the Sinai Peninsula. Egypt's Ahram newspaper of 18 October, 2016 wrote, "Egypt's army said one soldier and nineteen militants were killed in the third day of its recent air and ground operation against insurgents in the restive North Sinai region. Military air forces pounded thirty-one militant hideouts and arms caches while ground and special troops raided a number of other targets, killing nineteen militants..." (Ahram Online, 2016). But overall the current government has brought security to the country and is trying hard to deal with economic problems.

Though Egypt is relatively peaceful the area around Egypt is not and this means that Egypt continues to maintain an army of roughly half a million, with about 800,000 reservists. About 1.5 million young men reach military age every year. The government is trying hard to balance things and to establish relations with all factions to improve security and the economy. While security issues continue to take priority the government has its eye steadily on the economy, considering that roughly half of the population of the country are on the poverty datum line or just above, creating a combustible situation that is of concern to this great and ancient country. High unemployment, particularly among the young, is another major concern that for decades defied solution. Living standards are low with the majority of the nearly one hundred million citizens of Egypt experiencing economic hardship. (FocusEconomics, 2019)

The smaller population countries of the region

Syria

For more than seven years Syria has been blighted by a proxy war which has cost this ancient country dearly, and almost totally destroyed its economy and infrastructure. UN and Arab League envoys to Syria reported that between 15 March, 2011 and 23 April, 2016 alone 400,000 people were killed with double that number injured; plus millions of refugees. Many millions more are living in squalor inside the country. "About 560,000 people have been killed since the Syrian war began March 2011..." (Haaretz.com, 2018). Russia is probably the biggest winner out of the senseless war in Syria because it entrenched its position in the EM particularly through its air and naval presence. But it was not Russia that started the conflagration.

Lebanon

"Lebanon's political system leads to paralysis and corruption" The Economist 19 April, 2018 (The Economist, 2019)

The Lebanon is in perennial political chaos as a result of its undemocratic constitution of a sectarian nature that defies the rules of representative democracy and forbids people from uniting around common national objectives. Here is what James Haines-Young wrote on 16 August, 2018 about Lebanese politics, "On the surface, Lebanese politics can appear static. The same men who led militias through the 15-year civil war still lead many of the largest parties in parliament and, some waxing and waning of influence aside, a small group of people still hold most influence in the country. While those in power have on most counts governed poorly — the economy is stagnant, unemployment is high, crumbling infrastructure fails to provide even basic services and anything but the most straightforward decisions can be bogged down for years in bickering and back and forth — they have largely managed to preserve a semblance of stability." (Haines-Young, 2018)

Consequently the country is divided in one hundred ways and with shifting alliances that make the minds of reasonable people boggle. Private militias are the rule even if there is a nominal national army which again is structured on factionalism. This makes one wonder how a country full of private militias can qualify as a normal country. Though no one knows which side the army will take in the event of a major upheaval most expect it to splinter into opposing factions. For almost two years the country was without a president as the various factions refused to agree on a common candidate. The economy of Lebanon operates below par and is known to operate at times through shadowy corridors. "... 0.3% or approximately 8,000 people of the estimated workforce... own about half [of GDP] (48% to be exact)..." The remaining 99.7% of Lebanese own slightly more than half of GDP. And, "The story doesn't end there. Even among those 0.3%, there are disparities... who actually owns most of the country?" The answer is, two families." (Fares, 2015). Lebanon operates a clan system which allows members of certain families and their relatives to hold power every time there are elections. A look at the wealth of Lebanese politicians makes very interesting reading.

The outside observer finds it difficult to believe that a country that hosts some of the region's most celebrated academic institutions is clannish. The country is flush with weapons and a multitude of militias ready to strike at short notice. There are umpteen militias with Hezbollah the strongest. Hezbollah earned its stripes against the Israeli army and as such is admired by many in Lebanon as a worthy fighting force. Hezbollah fought in Syria on the side of the government and as such gained added experience in the field. Lebanon is a tinder box and this explains the high emigration rate and the staggering number of people holding dual passports, allowing them to settle in other countries in the event of armageddon materialising. In the meantime, the leaders of the country live under heavy guard with roads closed to protect their homes and lives from direct hits. Lebanon's roadblocks outside politicians' homes make an interesting spectacle!

Israel

"I am against Israel's occupation of Palestine in the West Bank, Gaza and East Jerusalem. I understand and empathize with the existence of and right for a Jewish national state. I cannot overlook the terrifyingly vast amount of anti-Semitism that exists worldwide and I recognize the Holocaust's impact on making the establishment of a Jewish state a literal life-or-death necessity." Story by Caroline Rothstein, self-defined 'Liberal American Jew' as told on 10 April, 2016 (Rothstein, 2016)

On record Israel stands out amongst the countries of the EM in many and varied ways. Though Israel applies democratic standards internally, some accuse the Israeli leadership of not giving a fair deal to the Israeli Arabs that make up circa twenty percent of Israel's population. The way to deal with the Arab minority in Israel is of concern to the Jewish State of Israel judging from the heated debates over the matter inside the country. Here is what the BBC wrote on 19 July, 2018. "Israel's parliament has passed a controversial law characterising the country as principally a Jewish state, fuelling anger among its Arab minority. The "nation state" law says Jews have a unique right to national self-determination there and puts Hebrew above Arabic as the official language. Arab MPs reacted furiously in parliament, with one waving a black flag and others ripping up the bill." (BBC News, 2018)

A country of less than ten million boasts a military that punches way above its weight. The total area of Israel is 22,145 square km of which 21,671 square km is land. At its widest point Israel is only 115 km across, even if its length is some 420 km. The country is bordered by the Arab countries of: Lebanon (north), Syria (north-east), Jordan (east), Egypt (south-west), and the Mediterranean Sea to the west. At one point the country can be traversed by a military jet in less than four minutes. No country in the area can challenge the Israeli military machine; not even Turkey that is many times the size of Israel and has a huge army. The Israelis' dedication and military technology will not allow a defeat. Also, the Israelis know that all it will take for them to be dismembered as a nation is just one irreversible military defeat.

The Israeli economy is way ahead of all other economies in the region on all major performance measures. In terms of per capita GDP Israel comfortably leads the EM pack. The Israeli economy and the country's technological prowess serve as benchmarks for other countries in the area. Israel rates as the most technologically advanced country in the region, and is up there with the best of the world as regards innovation and information technology. Technology provides the country with substantial income as well. But when all is considered Israel's Achilles' heel continues to be the unresolved Palestinian problem that cannot be wished away and needs to be solved fairly. As long as the Palestinian problem remains unresolved Israel will be kept awake. Israel is trying to resolve the problem but some of the tactics she uses do not endear her to her Arab neighbours, whose goodwill Israel needs dearly. Containment is not the solution and Israel knows that. Some of Israel's approaches are seen as harsh and as such multiply rather than contain the problem. As things stand now Israel cannot be defeated militarily but it cannot find permanent peace either. The area stands to reap immense benefits from a satisfactory resolution of this problem and everyone in the area hopes that this may come to pass soon.

Jordan

Jordan used to be a protectorate of Britain but when the mandate was terminated, Jordan continued to be under some type of British suzerainty for many years. This relationship was then "transferred" by Britain to the USA. As an economically small and militarily weak country Jordan needed and still needs protection against the many dangers and risks it continuous to face as a strengthless country. Though a welcoming country which generously plays host to millions of Palestinian and Syrian refugees, Jordan finds itself in political conflict even with some Arab nations that do not fully agree with the course she follows at times. Many in the Arab world are not comfortable with the fact that Jordan is very close to the US seeing the latter is brotherly with Israel. But here again the EM is not without paradoxes! Though on a knife's edge for years Jordan managed to avoid destabilization. Her involvement in the 1967 war against Israel cost the country dearly including loss of territory. But Jordan put up a good fight. The Jordanian king is said to be the direct descendant of Prophet Muhammad and this gives prestige to the post. It is generally admitted that the monarchy provided the country with continuity and relative stability, though not all is as stable as it looks if one were to look at the risk profile of the country. Jordan gets a "C" rating on account of, "A very uncertain political and economic outlook..." (globalEDGE, 2018)

Essay 4: Greek leadership

After reading the below I hope the reader will appreciate why I turned Greek leadership into an essay

Greece

"Where is the recognition that when the Greeks recently elected an even more leftist and socialist government, it sped up the path to collapse?"
(Novak, 2015)

Greece filed for bankruptcy before it was even a sovereign country following the first loan she received on November 30, 1823. Greece became officially independent on February 3, 1830 when the major European powers recognized Greece's independence. Worse still some (or most) of the money from the first loan went towards financing the two civil wars of 1824–5. Sixty-three years after Greek independence was officially recognized the Greeks were in for a rude awaking when in 1893 they heard their then prime minister telling them that "regrettably we have gone bankrupt" (the well-known Greek phrase: Δυστυχώς επτωχεύσαμεν). Another bankruptcy was to follow in 1932.

In the 1940s British and American money pored into the country to finance the Greek civil war (rather than the two "benefactors" of Greece intervening to stop brother killing brother they financed the killing sprees of one of the two sides!). America's Marshall Plan (what former British diplomat and historian William Mallinson called "America's Business Plan") followed, with much money flowing into the country only for some of it to be siphoned off to support the high life of the upper class and the elite (some 5,000 families probably) forcing America to turn on the screws and apply more stringent checks on money to be spent. The situation remained unchanged in later years leading to the current financial crisis that hit the country. Mismanagement took different forms depending on the era. Money was handed to construction companies to build shoddy structures in the second half of the 1950s and the first half of the 1960s, the EU was tricked with fake financial data from Greece's foxy socialist leaders to allow Greece to gain entry into the Euro zone. How a nation with smart people and great reserves of patriotism ends up with such poor quality leadership defies logic! Though it ought to be said that not all political elites were incompetent and corrupt; some were reformist and as such helped the country achieve considerable convergence with more economically developed countries. Most others were catastrophic and self-serving.

Since gaining independence from Ottoman Turkish rule nearly two hundred years ago, Greece has seen more governments come and go than one would care to remember. The country was also in shaky economic condition for much of its recent history. At the time of writing Greece was run by a government which through the use of grandiloquent language, calls itself "progressive" rather than populist and a windmill. Many in the leadership are stowaways from the discredited and largely defunct PASOK party that ruled Greece for decades and left the country's economy in ruins. Some (perhaps most) in government are political novices who, by any independent measure have little understanding of where the country should be going. Some in the government strut around in suits but tieless carrying the air of revolutionaries that are in a vain search for one more cause! Operating as pseudo-revolutionaries, sometimes they manage to fool people into believing that they are true revolutionaries with a real cause. The distinctive characteristic of this government is obedience to foreign edicts on international affairs. But the current administration is lucky that the opposition is also not fully trusted, on account of past sins.

"Efforts to reform and rebuild Greece's economy in the future will be undermined because the country's government, businesses and civil servants not only fail to stop corruption but actively participate in it." (GlobalSecurity.org, n.d.)

Political mediocrity and corruption is not new to Greece (as is the case maybe for most of the countries in the region). This largely explains why the country (and most other countries in the area) has been blighted by an assortment of economic and other ailments for most of the region's modern history. Two of modern Greece's founding fathers, Ioannis Capodistrias and Demetrius Ypsilantis, were both paragons of honesty and exemplary personal behaviour. No amount of praise about the moral behaviour of these two Greek semi-gods would seem brazen or meretricious. It is a great pity that the behaviour of both these legends was not entrenched in the polity of Greece, the former jewel of the world whose history continues to be the beacon for all that is good. Though it ought to be said, the [controversial] Eleftherios Venizelos did much good for modern Greece and towers above the rest. Moratinos writes this about Venizelos, "The Hellenistic spirit regained momentum with the arrival of Eleftherios Venizelos. His leadership and political skills brought Greek influence to the decision-making process at the Paris Conference;" (Moratinos Cuyaube, 2016: 196)

Indicative of the situation in the modern history of Greece, the Greek government at the time of writing was headed by a leader that took far longer than required to complete his university studies, and not because he lacked in smartness. Simply, in his time at university he had better things to do such as organizing student demonstrations in the streets of Athens to fight education reform, of all things, and to take over public buildings. He loves to boast that he is an "internationalist" and is disrespectful to those that take a patriotic stance and put Greece first. Here is what the

Huffington Post of 27 January, 2015 had to say about him, "Born on July 28, 1974 in Athens, Tsipras stood out as a student at Ampelokipoi Academic High School, and was the face of the mobilizations against educational reforms promoted by the Ministry of Education." (Prifti, 2015)

He often talks about the merits of socialism and comes out verbally in support of the disadvantaged. But the country's communist party, that walks the walk of communism, laughs at him. Greece's financials are in a mess and the economy is paralysed by high and unmanageable sovereign debt and a killer tax regime that stifles every activity. This has led some of the most brilliant brains of Greece to emigrate or simply not to return to Greece after completing their studies abroad. Greece is now a financial and geostrategic dependency; the result of failed leadership over many decades, not to say for most of the last two centuries. Plus, the country is open to all sorts of security risks. The dilemma here is that the Greek people do not know which political party to support wholeheartedly, considering the third degree burns they had suffered in the past from the two big parties that mainly controlled Greek politics. So, for the voters it is a catch-22 situation, though a change in leadership cannot possibly worsen the current ineptitude. Not that the voters are absolved of blame, seeing that it is through their votes that ruinous political elites rose to power. Though difficult to detect accurately the lowest point of leadership behaviour in Greece, I would rate the following incident as a good sample of the lowest of the lows. After a catastrophic fire that killed some one hundred people and brought to the surface the utter incompetence of the current government to deal with such emergencies, the Prime Minister gave a speech in the midst of the catastrophe in which he said, "I will not deny that I am overcome by mixed feelings at this hour... I am anxious to know whether we (me and my government) did what we ought to have done, whether we reacted correctly in these critical hours or whether we committed the mistake that others (meaning the opposition) committed many times in the past." (freely translated by the author from Greek) (ERT 1, 2018)

In this one finds the lowest of leadership qualities a prime minister can display under pressure. He used the catastrophe that killed his brothers to make political capital by referencing what others supposedly failed to do in the past. Instead of standing squarely and irrevocably by his people, he turned devastation into a propaganda opportunity.

Cyprus

"...Cyprus' political machine that many voters — particularly younger ones — derisively view as...ineffectual." From the Independent of 3 February, 2018. (The Independent, 2018)

We already said that a good part of Cyprus, 37% of land and 54% of sea-shores, is under occupation by the armies of NATO stalwart, Turkey. This has been going on non-stop for the last forty-five years. The future of the country rests to a large degree on how the elected representatives of the country deal with the Turkish occupation and how firmly they stand by a solution that will rest one hundred percent on democratic principles and on the European acquis communautaire. Cyprus boasts a highly qualified cadre and in fact the country ranks 15th in the world on talent with some of its young university graduates coming from the world's elite universities. Yet when it comes to electoral politics the average voter shows an incomprehensible naïveté and a political immaturity that harms the standing of the country. Cyprus went under Troika strictures having borrowed as much as half of its GDP and was the only country in the EU to agree to a bail-in which saw many people's savings evaporate into thin air. Equally, the reserves of the Social Security Fund that in the past were borrowed by successive administrations were never returned, plunging the fund into despair and forcing people to pay increased contributions to sustain current benefits. Equally, Cyprus spends a large part of the annual defence tax it collects on maintaining a bloated civil service rather than on upgrading its defences.

To a very large extent the country's future depends on regional alliances and the leadership's ability to receive foreign support, considering how weak the country is militarily and how little is amazingly done in the area of defence. The offshore energy finds of Cyprus wetted the appetite of Turkey (that has no known offshore energy reserves of her own and is heavily dependent on oil imports) and caused her to threaten anyone that wishes to abide by the rule of international law. Although it is unlikely that any great power will lift a finger to save Cyprus from Turkish aggression, the Cyprus leadership is, as of late moving in the right direction, steadily building relations also with non-Greek neighbouring countries and more specifically with Egypt and Israel. Cyprus is working on securing international political support as well and is not doing badly considering its membership in the EU. Cyprus's single worry for the time being is the risk of its leadership yielding to demands from Turkey and its allies (America and Britain in particular) to sign a disastrous agreement that would spell the end of the Greeks in Cyprus, thus ending a four-thousand year presence of Hellenism in Cyprus. At the moment the situation is stable but worrying considering the heavy presence of Turkish troops on the island and the silence of some of the more powerful countries.

Essay 5: What the EM leaders failed to achieve

So, what do the previous analyses of the situation in most of the countries in the EM tell us about leadership?

a) Clearly the region is suffering from instability. In other words the leadership of the area as a whole failed in their most important task, which is to provide the preconditions for a peaceful life. Are they to be blamed totally considering the non-stop external meddling in the region? Maybe the leaders are not totally to blame, but surely they share much of the blame seeing the failure of the countries to cooperate for the good of the region.

b) The region failed to reach its economic potential due to a composite of factors which also include: a paralyzing bureaucracy, corruption, poor democratic polity and failure to bring to book corrupt politicians and others. Israel differs, maybe considerably, on this score. According to Haaretz, "Since 1996, a period of more than 20 years, every Israeli prime minister has been subject to a police investigation…" (Arlosoroff, 2018)

What Haaretz wrote is both good and bad. It's good that justice works and bad in that justice is forced to deal with behaviours of political malfeasance. Other countries in the region may have recently imprisoned some politicians for corruption but only Israel seems to apply the strictness of the law to such an extent. This was the heading of the Independent of 2 July, 2017 regarding Israel's former Prime Minister, "Israel releases former PM who was jailed for corruption after just 16 months." (Deitch, 2017)

c) The region is yet to produce a Jefferson; so there is hope that one day this may come to pass!

d) One of the countries in the region, Cyprus, is uncertain as to whether it can survive internal defeatism that for now is limited to a small but vociferous group and external threats, partial occupation and the apathy of big powers.

e) Greece is unlikely to come out of its current economic predicament anytime soon given its current less-than-competent (and in many ways amateur) leadership and worries about the country's ability to defend itself against outside (Turkish) threats. So, here again there is plenty of scope for a leader to show the extraordinary capabilities the country now needs and which would allow it to fulfil its potential.

f) Egypt is trying hard to resolve its intractable problems but is stuck in an economic and institutional quagmire that is worsened by the threats coming from Islamist and other extremist groups.

g) Turkey has grand, fanciful and bizarre plans to rule the region and to reinstate the Ottoman Empire under Turkey. This is dangerous and in fact could in the end bring about the breakup of Turkey itself if Turkish aggression leads to a major conflagration involving many countries in the region. Pipedreams have been known in history to be dangerous in that these get the country into prolonged and unwinnable conflicts. Typically, leaders that wish to dominate outsiders, start off by first dominating their own people and browbeating them into accepting their adventurist plans. In the end this often leads to autocracy inside the country and later to destabilisation as people begin to express insubordination to autocratic rule. The leadership of the country, therefore, would need to reconsider its current aggression, militarism and proneness to conflict and start respecting their neighbours, for their own good and that of the region. Much will depend on what America (and to an extent the EU) decide to do with Turkey. Without severe pressure from these two Turkey is unlikely to change its wayward ways. Powerful countries ought to force it to stop its aggression. The cocktail of politics, Islamism and militarism is clearly bad for Turkey and the region.

h) Lebanon is sitting on a powder keg. The country is in the same predicament it has always been since it gained independence and adopted an undemocratic constitution. As long as the current constitutional arrangements of Lebanon continue to apply the country is unlikely to experience normality because factionalism and sectarian antagonism will not allow normality and peace.

i) The ancient country of Syria is still in grave danger considering the horrors of the last seven years and what could go wrong in the future. The country has just gone through what seems like the greatest catastrophe of its history and now has open wounds. The need for unity and rebuilding would need to be at the centre of every effort.

j) And now a general comment about the overall leadership in the EM region. One would think that the people in the EM must be disgruntled with the quality of leadership the region has had, considering the situation in the region. And here I am talking about the leadership of the last seventy or so years. In judging the region's leadership one would need to take stock of the often destructive role of outside powers which in their quest to serve their own interests did great harm to many countries in the area and destroyed many lives. When all is considered one can, however, find glimpses of hope in most countries. But, overall the region has a long way to go in providing enlightened leadership that would be able to reverse the division and conflicts that bedevil the region. Voter apathy and voter recklessness is much to blame for the situation.

In the past, failure to vote in Cyprus' elections was considered a criminal offence with the "violator" running the risk of receiving a prison term for his choice. Unavoidably there was a high (almost total) voter turnover. Once this unacceptable and coercive constraint on freedom was lifted voter participation plummeted and now it is at an all-time low. The situation is not better in most of the countries of the region and is reflective of the disenchantment with the quality of leadership. Party propaganda to get voters back to the voting booths has proved to be in vain because only real change for the better can be the answer. Efforts to trick voters, such as bundling together a typically high-voter-turnout election (such as a municipal election) with a lower-turnover-election (such as European parliamentary elections) cannot possibly provide the answer to disenchantment. Voter turnout measures quite accurately how people view their country's leadership and how well the democratic process works.

Greatest challenges facing EM leaders

- Instability in the region.
- Generally poor regional economic performance.
- Gridlock of the Lernaean Hydra of bureaucracy.
- Unacceptable levels of corruption.
- Institutional challenges.
- Turkey's aggression and adventurism.
- After effects of the Syrian civil war.
- Voter apathy.
- Need to guarantee the long-term survival of countries such as EU member Cyprus.
- Level of political maturity.
- Outside interference.
- Outside dependency.

Essay 6: Four actions current EM leaders ought to take to redress the leadership failures of the past seventy years in their country

"The Eastern Med has a long history of dispute, and this is feeding off of that and adding new ones." and, "You bring in the existing problems, a Syrian war, a Lebanese civil war, and then add energy, which always brings the potential for dispute," Ahval News on 27 January, 2019. (Ahval News, 2019)

"The Eastern Mediterranean is getting more dangerous, and it's not because of Russia, Syria, or Iran" aei.org 18 September, 2018. (Rubin, 2018)

The leadership of the EM can only be judged on results. The essays on the region in this treatise are not fully complimentary about what has happened in the last seventy years considering that the EM continues to be in turmoil. I would therefore suggest that the current and future leaders of the region concentrate on solving the following core problems specific to their country if they are to go down in history as great. First, though, they would need to adopt a mindset that promotes: a) moral values, b) reconciliation based on equity, c) democratic values and d) respect for international law. Critically they would need to reject violence and aggressive behaviour as means for settling issues.

Required leader mindset to enable the EM countries reach their potential:

- ♦ Strong moral values.
- ♦ Spirit of reconciliation based on fairness and equity.
- ♦ Democratic values.
- ♦ Respect for international law.
- ♦ Rejection of violence and aggression.

The four core objectives leaders in the EM ought to focus on by country

Egypt

A great country with unrealized potential.

1. Put in place a successful plan to take Egypt out of the poverty cycle and give the poor hope.
2. Narrow the income and wealth gap between the rich and the poor and strengthen the middle class.
3. Establish Egypt to its rightful role as leader of the Arab world and make it less dependent on foreign powers.
4. Use Egypt's status as leader of the Arab world to solve the Palestinian problem fairly and permanently so that one of the two major problems of the region can be solved for good. The peace treaty would need to be comprehensive, covering all issues so that a new chapter free of potential conflict can be opened.

Israel

The high achiever of the EM but with unresolved [existential] problems.

1. Capture the conscience of the people living in countries with an adversarial relationship with Israel rather than just project strength.
2. Share the country's great achievements with others in the EM and engage in joint projects.
3. Address fairly the rights and interests of the Palestinians paying due attention to Israel's legitimate rights and interests. (Isseroff, n.d.)
4. Be generous with Israel's neighbours to help Israel gain more acceptability from its neighbours.

Turkey

Her policy of "Zero problems with neighbours" has been turned into the policy of "problems with all neighbours".

1. Accept that the region is not Turkish property and start creating goodwill with all neighbouring countries.
2. Appreciate that international law is there to ensure peaceful coexistence between countries and that the flouting of international law goes against the long-term interests of Turkey and the region.
3. Reject and denounce aggression as a tool for solving international problems and your neighbours will for sure reciprocate.
4. Concentrate on improving the lives of the Turkish people particularly in the east of the country rather than continue to spend the country's treasure on armaments against imaginary enemies in the neighbourhood and stop suppressing the Kurdish minority and others.

Syria

An ancient country rich in cultural heritage that has come back from the dead and deserves to build a bright future.

1. Take a leaf out of the book of Yakubu Gowon of Nigeria who, though he won the civil war, nevertheless offered an olive branch to the losers, turning his name GOWON into an acronym for Go On With One Nigeria. Syria should turn the name ASSAD into the acronym of A Stable Syria And Democratic.
2. Unite the country after the terrible devastation it has experienced. Apply the maxim, "no victor, no vanquished". Give people a bigger voice.
3. Set the rebuilding of the country's destroyed infrastructure as first priority to avoid long-term poverty.
4. Reduce income and wealth inequality in the country.

Lebanon

Blessed by nature and threatened by the Lernaean Hydra of sectarianism.

1. Tear up the current sectarian constitution speedily and replace it with a Western type democratic constitution based on "Citizen" rather than on "Religious Sect".
2. Unite the country around its Arab heritage but do not become insular.
3. Make the political system more inclusive and gradually bring in all those that can contribute on merit rather than on social class and religious grouping.
4. Close the income inequality as a matter of urgency. This will help give everyone a stake in the country.

Greece

From a bejewelled past to an impecunious present on major fronts.

1. Restore the lost political credibility to encourage decency in public life; stop the rot.
2. Treat every citizen fairly and stop pampering the self-serving party apparatchiks.

3. Develop an independent Greek foreign policy with fewer directives from the outside. Remember Greece's lustrous past and how the ancient Greeks dealt with external threats.

4. Understand that he who wishes to survive ought to depend on his own prowess rather than on outsiders, whilst maintaining alliances based on common interest and values.

Cyprus

Cursed by geography to be craved by major powers and every aggressor in the region.

1. Understand the monumental difference between negotiating over existential matters and negotiating over trivial issues.

2. Do not give away your birthright in the naïve belief that your conqueror will take pity on you and will return your rights.

3. Before asking for help make sure that you have convincing evidence that you have done your best for the defence of you country, otherwise no one will lift a finger to help you.

4. Build a properly run small country to provide small Cyprus with outsized soft power.

One advice to country leaders in the EM if they wish to achieve greatness

Egypt

"Restore Egypt to its rightful position as leader of the Arab world"

Lebanon

"Get everyone in the leadership of Lebanon to emulate the life and teaching of the great first prime minister of Lebanon Riad El Soloh"

Israel

"Power will assure Israel's life but winning the conscience of the people of neighbouring countries will guarantee Israel's peace and future prosperity"

Turkey

"Stop coveting your neighbours' land and riches and respect international law. Start cooperating with your neighbours for a peaceful and bright future"

Syria

"Put your faith in democracy and the country will be unified and ready to deliver a great future for all"

Greece

"Start honouring your illustrious and glorious ancestors by thinking less of self, party and the next election, and dedicate yourselves to the greatness of Greece"

Cyprus

"Commit yourselves to creating an advanced democracy, thus gaining much-needed soft power for your country. Make the citizen the centre, not the ethnic group"

All EM countries

"A peaceful region where respect for international law is paramount and undoubtedly serves every individual country's national interests"

References

Ahval News. (2019). Soon there is going to be trouble in East
Mediterranean. [online] Available at:
https://ahvalnews.com/east-mediterranean/soon-there-going-
be-trouble-east-mediterranean-analyst [Accessed 16 Mar. 2019].

Ahram Online. (2016). One solider, 19 militants killed in 3rd day of
military operations in north Sinai: Egypt Army. [online]
Available at:
http://english.ahram.org.eg/NewsContent/1/64/246022/Egypt/P
olitics-/One-solider,--militants-killed-in-rd-day-of-milita.aspx
[Accessed 19 Oct. 2016].

Arlosoroff, M. (2018). Four Israeli prime ministers, 20 years of
corruption. Why?. [online] haaretz.com. Available at:
https://www.haaretz.com/israel-news/business/.premium-four-
prime-ministers-20-years-of-corruption-why-1.5850409
[Accessed 20 Jan. 2019].

BBC News. (2018). Israel approves 'Jewish nation state' law. [online]
Available at: https://www.bbc.com/news/world-middle-east-
44881554 [Accessed 16 Mar. 2019].

BBC News. (2019). Israel's Benjamin Netanyahu: Commando
turned PM. [online] Available at:
https://www.bbc.com/news/world-middle-east-18008697
[Accessed 15 Mar. 2019].

Coutts, A. (2011). Syria's uprising could have been avoided through
reform. [online] The Guardian. Available at:
https://www.theguardian.com/commentisfree/2011/may/18/syri
a-uprising-reform-bashar-al-assad [Accessed 11 Mar. 2019].

Deitch, I. (2017). Former Israeli PM released from prison sentence
11 months early. [online] The Independent. Available at: https://
www.independent.co.uk/news/world/politics/israel-former-
pm-ehud-olmert-release-prison-a7819446.html [Accessed 20 Jan.
2019].

ERT 1 (2018). Τσίπρας: Αναλαμβάνω ακέραια την πολιτική ευθύνη για την τραγωδία. [video] Available at: https://www.youtube.com/watch?v=SNC7RvbqYsM&t [Accessed 11 Mar. 2019].

Fanack.com. (2018). Governance & Politics of Egypt. [online] Available at: https://fanack.com/egypt/governance-and-politics-of-egypt/ [Accessed 14 Mar. 2019].

Farahat, C. (2019). Who Is Sisi of Egypt? A Reformer.. [online] Middle East Forum. Available at: https://www.meforum.org/57907/egypt-sisi-reformer [Accessed 11 Mar. 2019].

Fares, E. (2015). 0.3% of Lebanese Own 50% of Lebanon. [online] A Separate State of Mind. Available at: https://stateofmind13.com/2015/02/18/0-3-of-lebanese-own-50-of-lebanon/ [Accessed 19 Jan. 2019].

FocusEconomics. (2019). Egypt Economy — GDP, Inflation, CPI and Interest Rate. [online] Available at: https://www.focus-economics.com/countries/egypt [Accessed 11 Mar. 2019].

globalEDGE. (2018). Jordan: Risk Assessment. [online] Available at: https://globaledge.msu.edu/countries/jordan/risk [Accessed 20 Jan. 2019].

GlobalSecurity.org. (n.d.). Greece — Corruption. [online] Available at: https://www.globalsecurity.org/military/world/europe/gr-corruption.htm [Accessed 14 Mar. 2019].

Haaretz.com. (2018). 560,000 killed in Syria's war according to updated death toll. [online] Available at: https://www.haaretz.com/middle-east-news/syria/560-000-killed-in-syria-s-war-according-to-updated-death-toll-1.6700244 [Accessed 11 Mar. 2019].

Haines-Young, J. (2018). The future of Lebanon's political dynasties. [online] The National. Available at: https://www.thenational.ae/world/mena/the-future-of-lebanon-s-political-dynasties-1.760691 [Accessed 19 Jan. 2019].

Haynie, D. (2017). Poll: Arabs See US as a Threat. [online] US News. Available at:

https://www.usnews.com/news/best-countries/articles/2017-04-11/poll-arabs-believe-israel-us-are-biggest-threat-to-the-region [Accessed 19 Mar. 2019].

Human Rights Watch. (2019). World Report 2018: Rights Trends in Turkey. [online] Available at: https://www.hrw.org/world-report/2018/country-chapters/turkey [Accessed 23 Jan. 2019].

Isseroff, A. (n.d.). How can Israeli-Palestinian peace be achieved?. [online] ZioNation. Available at: http://zionism-israel.com/issues/How_Can_Peace_be_Achieved.html [Accessed 13 Mar. 2019].

Moratinos Cuyaube, M. (2016). The challenges of the Eastern Mediterranean. In: A. Petasis, ed., Intractable Dilemmas in the Energy-Rich Eastern Mediterranean. Newcastle upon Tyne: Cambridge Scholars Publishing, pp.195–205.

Novak, J. (2015). Why are we ignoring this colossal socialist failure?. [online] CNBC. Available at: https://www.cnbc.com/2015/07/01/greek-disaster-is-all-about-socialism.html [Accessed 14 Mar. 2019].

Pierini, M. (2019). Can Europe maintain relations with 'autocratic' Turkey?. [online] EuroNews. Available at: https://www.euronews.com/2018/03/15/can-europe-maintain-relations-with-autocratic-turkey-view [Accessed 14 Mar. 2019].

Pipes, D. (2019). Istanbul mayoral election is an anomaly, Recep Tayyip Erdogan's tyrannical impulses may emerge. [online] Washing Times. Available at: https://www.washingtontimes.com/news/2019/jun/25/istanbul-mayoral-election-is-an-anomaly-recep-tayy/?utm_source=Middle+East+Forum&utm_campaign=acb9a97477 [Accessed 10.08.2019].

Prifti, K. (2015). What You Need To Know About Alexis Tsipras, The Greek Leader Who Wants To Change Europe. [online] Huffpost. Available at: https://www.huffpost.com/entry/alex-tsipras-profile_n_6547474 [Accessed 23 Jan. 2019].

Rothstein, C. (2016). Why I've Always Been Silent About Israel and Palestine. And Why I'm Speaking Out Now.. [online]

Narratively. Available at: https://narratively.com/why-ive-always-been-silent-about-israel-and-palestine-and-why-im-speaking-out-now/ [Accessed 14 Mar. 2019].

Rubin M. (2018). The Eastern Mediterranean is getting more dangerous, and it's not because of Russia, Syria, or Iran. [online] American Enterprise Institute (AEI). Available at: http://www.aei.org/publication/the-eastern-mediterranean-is-getting-more-dangerous-and-its-not-because-of-russia-syria-or-iran [Accessed 16 Mar. 2019].

Schwab, K. (2018). The Global Competitiveness Report 2018. Insight Report. [online] Geneva: World Economic Forum. Available at: http://www3.weforum.org/docs/GCR2018/05FullReport/TheGlo balCompetitivenessReport2018.pdf [Accessed 14 Mar. 2019].

The Economist. (2019). Lebanon's political system leads to paralysis and corruption. [online] Available at: https://www.economist.com/middle-east-and-africa/2018/04/19 /lebanons-political-system-leads-to-paralysis-and-corruption [Accessed 14 Mar. 2019].

The Independent. (2018). Inexperienced minister takes on career politician in Cyprus election. [online] Available at: https://www.independent.co.uk/news/world/europe/cyprus-election-preview-inexperienced-minister-goes-to-polls-against-career-politician-stavros-malas-a8192321.html [Accessed 4 Mar. 2019].

Trump D. (2016). Full transcript NYC speech on stakes of the election. [online] POLITICO. Available at: https://www.politico.com/story/2016/06/transcript-trump-speech-on-the-stakes-of-the-election-224654 [Accessed 19 Mar. 2019].

Book 11

Epilogue

We have come to the end of our sojourn on leadership and we are now ready for the final and concluding remarks on the subject. Below I discuss briefly some of the important points that were raised in this treatise, in this way giving the reader an opportunity to revisit most of the material covered already. I start by noting that leadership is a multifaceted concept that does not lend itself to simplification. No one definition can capture the complete essence of leadership and no list of traits can explain the full extent of the subject.

We already noted that leadership is neither a list of bullet points in power point format nor a set of attractive headings, titles and itemized traits. Clearly, leadership cannot be explained by in-vogue language or terminology that is popular at the time a treatise on leadership is written. Simplistic statements such as, "Leadership is all about 'emotional intelligence'" cannot explain leadership no matter how popular the subject of emotional intelligence happens to be and how valuable its contribution has been in helping us understand better the subject of "people and organisations". (Coleman, 2006)

> *Leadership is neither a list of bullet points in power point format nor a set of attractive headings, titles and itemized traits.*

We cannot understand leadership from statements that take the form of, "Leadership is all about getting the job done" for example, or from more fanciful statements such as, "Leadership is all about influencing people". This would be tantamount to saying that the worldwide conflicts of our time are the product of "The clash of civilisations", taking out of the equation economics, geostrategy, power politics and a host of other factors. (Huntington, 2003)

> *Leadership is vastly complicated and as such cannot be explained by simplistic language, aphorisms, dogmas, ideologies or fixations.*

The myth of the ideal leader. The ideal leader is more fiction and romanticism than reality. Leaders are known to be competent in certain areas and incompetent in others; strong and weak at the same time; polished and crude at times. Not many of his close associates thought much of Churchill's soul and some of his personal habits but almost all considered him to be a towering war leader; though not necessarily a great politician in times of peace.

Even the greatest leaders make terrible mistakes sometimes. The iconic leader of ancient times, Pericles, failed to understand how the Spartans felt about Athens' drive for supremacy and hegemony over the other Greek city states and islands. Sparta was not at all happy with the hegemonic Athenian strategy. Cimon, who was older than Pericles by some two decades, understood this and did all in his power to stay close to Sparta. He likened Athens and Sparta to a pair of oxen that together shared the yoke of Greece. Pericles, who succeeded Cimon, failed to fully understand Sparta's concerns. This cost the Greeks a terrible civil war that in the end proved to be the undoing of Athens itself as the leading nation. The outcome of the Peloponnesian war turned Athens from Hegemon to dependent city.

Walden explains for us the two sides that leaders have, saying this about Mandela, "...the autocratic incompetent Mandela..." and "... the noble and dauntless Mandela", summarising in this way both Mandela's incompetence and competencies. (Walden, 1998: 38) Mandela did some great things and is a world icon for that but failed terribly in other areas. Just look at South Africa that now swims in a pool of corruption and incompetence. The self-styled "Economic Freedom Fighters" faction, that ominously garners circa 10% of the vote, is free to wreak vengeance on anyone considered to be an enemy. Where has Mandela's "forgive and forget" proclamation gone?

Leader virtues and vices. Leaders have both virtues and vices as well; with great vices sometimes contradicting great virtues in the same person. As such we can hardly find a leader without blemish. That great leader of ancient times King David once sent the husband of a woman he lusted after to die in war to free her for him. "But there is no question that [John Kennedy] by nature was reckless. Take for instance, the endless liaisons with women" wrote Brian Walden. (Walden, 1998: 32–33) In the same breath Walden also says that Kennedy "...was a man of some dignity."

Physical characteristics do not make a leader. The popular view that leadership correlates with particular leader physical characteristics is simply not true, though some characteristics can improve a person's potential to emerge as leader. In today's world of propaganda, public relations and social media optics can play an important role in building a leader's image. History reminds us of some great tall leaders such as Charles de Gaulle as well as some shorter ones such as Napoleon Bonaparte; both coming from the same country. The same holds for slim (Field Marshal Bernard Montgomery during WWII) and stout (Winston Churchill),leaders. America had a handsome former president in the form of John

Kennedy but also a not so physically attractive, clumsy in gait, gangly and lanky Abraham Lincoln, just to name a few of his less than attractive physical characteristics.

Leaders born or made. The issue of whether leaders are born or made has always been at the forefront of the leadership debate. No definitive answers have been supplied to this day. Though the verdict is not out, a plurality of students of leadership, including the author of this treatise, tend to believe that both nature and nurture play a role. But few are willing to provide percentages of the influence of each factor. Adler summarised the issue well when he said that, "Heredity only endows him [man] with certain abilities. Environment only gives him certain impressions. These abilities and impressions, and the manner in which he 'experiences' them—that is to say, the interpretation he makes of these experiences—are the bricks, or in other words his attitude toward life, which determines this relationship to the outside world." (Adler, 1935)

Adler made a substantial contribution to our understanding of the impact of both nature and nurture on leadership. He clarified well the issue of experience (nurture) when saying that it all depends how one interprets his experiences and what he learns from these and what he makes of them. So basically, it's all about behaviour that stems from one's interpretations of his experiences. Two people may have the same experiences but perceive and interpret these experiences differently. I remember talking to an ex-rebel leader of the 1955–9 rebellion against the British in Cyprus who was arrested with his group of rebels. All of them were sentenced to long prison terms after being convicted for the crime of carrying weapons. They had not committed any violent acts. This particular group leader was subsequently sent to HM Prison Wormwood Scrubs and later transferred to Mason prison. I asked him what he had learned from his three-year incarceration, considering that he was pardoned when an agreement for decolonization was signed. He told me that he felt no malice against the judge who sentenced him because in his words "he was simply applying the law in line with his role as judge; after all I was captured carrying guns". He then went on, "But I never came to terms with the fact that they (the colonial authorities) kept me in the same prison with common law criminals. I was never a criminal and I never harmed anyone". He felt great offence for being "demoted" to the status of a common criminal which he obviously was not. When later I asked a second group leader who had almost the exact same experience as the first one for similar offences he told me, "Though life in prison was hard it gave me the opportunity to meet other people of different cultures and outlook to life. In the end I even made a few friends from amongst the lighter-sentenced prisoners". Here we see two leaders with identical experience but with different interpretations and feelings about their similar experiences.

Existential theorists support that man is free to become whatever he wishes, has a free will and as such is not constrained by heredity. Others believe in the influence of both heredity and environment. Some downplay the hereditary factor as determinant of behaviour because of reasons of political correctness. Others, however, take the opposite view.

Charisma. In popular literature on leadership, charisma often features high up on the ladder of leadership determinants. But, Peter Drucker reminded us earlier in the this book that three of the leaders that caused great harm to humanity were charismatic. He then went on to tell us that what counts is the leader's mission rather than his charisma. Though charisma is an attractive feature of leadership it can also be very dangerous in the hands of perfidious or deceitful leaders.

Extroversion. Some leaders are perceived as charismatic simply because they behave extrovertly. Yet, the three charismatic leaders that Drucker mentioned: Hitler, Stalin and Mao, were not flowing with extroversion and as such contradicted the myth that leaders are extrovert. Marston helps us understand why some people are influential but not necessarily extroverts, "Perhaps the most simple trap one could fall into here is to confuse charm and persuasion with extroversion or outgoing and stimulus-seeking social behaviour..." (Marston, 1989: xxiv). On charm Marston had this to say, "...a fair proportion of the most charming, seductive and captivating personalities in literature and in real life are perceived as shy, retiring and subtle in their ways." (Marston, 1989: xxiv)

Psychological environment. Few deny that the situation within which behaviour occurs and the circumstances under which this is manifested is central to our understanding of leader behaviour. Thus, it is important to understand the context within which leader behaviour occurs, including understanding of the socio-cultural context of the behaviour. Leader motivation is a function of multiple motivational variables, and as such cannot be limited to a few superficial interpretations.

Parents and home environment. It is now well known that Churchill's childhood was not exactly the childhood most children would have loved to have. Churchill's childhood experiences were unpleasant, considering the neglect he suffered from his mother and the behaviour of his father that verged on the tyrannical. Unsurprisingly he did not do well at school, was generally distrustful of others and maybe disloyal as well. Yet he did well during the war against the Nazis and in fact made his name through his performance during WWII. Margaret Thatcher, the longest-serving British prime minister of the 20th century and a Conservative like Churchill, was brought up by a grocer father that was also an alderman and a local Methodist preacher. Thatcher had a vastly different social background to that of Churchill. Equally, Alexander's father was a king and military head of the Macedonian army and was brought up in a disciplined (and militaristic) environment that was totally different to that of Churchill and

Thatcher. Thus, there was little similarity between the backgrounds of these three leaders. Kennedy's father pushed his son to the limits and in fact at one time Kennedy admitted that he ran for political office because his father wanted it. So, varied parent backgrounds and varied family circumstance can lie behind successful leader behaviour. As such, the idea that particular parent behaviours and home influences are a determining factor of leadership needs to be evaluated with scepticism. Most of us now accept the fact that parents have an influence on their children's future development. Most psychologists (and common sense) tell us that parents' influence on children's later behaviour can in fact be critical.

Personality. Does personality alone explain leadership? No, though it can be a significant factor. But, here again what is personality? Is it the ability of a leader to elicit positive reactions from different people under different circumstances? Is a leader's personality defined by his unique individual behavioural set that is so distinctive as to give him a unique position among the rest? Which personality is best for leadership: the "aggressive" or the "gentle" type? Or is the "abrasive" and "harsh" personality better under some circumstances? Again, even if we are to agree on the definition of personality we will soon notice that dissimilar personalities are sometimes as good (or bad) for leadership. Reagan (charismatic) did not have the personality of Lincoln (good natured and honest to a fault) nor did Lincoln have the personality of Nixon (able and cunning) nor did Nixon have the personality of Kennedy (charismatic) and so it goes. Scott McGregor wrote on 23 December, 2015, under the title, "Personality Profiles of Great American Presidents" that, "There is evidence indicating that at least some of the variation in presidential greatness can be linked to their individual personality traits." (McGreal, 2015)

Character. We need not try to define "character" because this can prove confusing, considering the multiplicity of definitions the literature provides us. For our purposes we will call character "that which others think of us after they assess our behavioural set". Here, we make an assumption that the sum total of the assessments the leader receives from a multitude of people must in the end be correct, considering that in the long-term a leader cannot fool all of the people all of the time. It's all about collective opinion and median scores. If others think that we are of "good" character then that's it. The same applies if others think of us to be of "bad" character. We will not try to define character against ideal standards because this would take us into the realm of philosophy. It's well known that if a leader is perceived as being of "good" character then he typically gains the sympathy of followers, thus making it more likely that they will listen to him. But does "good" character also mean able leader? Character does not suppose a good decision maker or good implementer of sound decisions. We have all seen how some good decision makers mess up on implementation. Nor does character assume leader creativity or innovation that is crucial to effective leadership. "Nevertheless, being of good character is the leadership quality that distinguishes great leadership. It is the quality that most people admire. Leaders of good character have integrity, courage and compassion. They are careful and prudent. Humble in their awareness of their own limitations, they seek out the knowledge and counsel of others. They constantly learn and others want to learn from them. Their decisions and actions inspire employees to think and act in a way that not only improves the bottom line, but that contributes to the well-being of the organization and society." wrote Carol Stephenson, in the January / February 2011 issue of Ivey Business Journal. (Stephenson, 2011)

Greed. We have already seen that some leaders bring with them a latent propensity for greed and love of wealth and money. This weakness sometimes manifests itself after the end of their tenure when they are free from the strict overseeing of the press, political competitors and the public. But does greed or propensity for greediness make a leader bad or ineffective? I guess, it all depends on when the passion for greed takes a person over and how strong this passion is. If the passion for greed conquers the leader while he is serving his tenure then this may even have catastrophic effects on the country, on people and the leader himself. We have seen plenty of examples of leaders siphoning off state treasure into personal offshore accounts out of greed. In 2018 Giulia Paravicini reported in Politico that, "A POLITICO investigation into €16 billion of the Libyan dictator's assets held in Belgium discovered big, regular outflows of stock dividends, bond income and interest payments." (Paravicini, 2018)

History tells us that some leaders, though exemplary in their behaviour towards money and wealth whilst in office ultimately, and after leaving office, fall victim to delayed greed. It is not the creation of wealth that is wrong, but the love of money for its own sake that makes a leader contemptible. Greed quickly besmirches the legacy of the leader because people generally despise greedy money-grubbing leaders. Even if the leader is not corrupt his love of money degrades him in the eyes of others. Worst still when the leader is greedy and parsimonious as well. Margaret Thatcher is credited with saying, "It is not the creation of wealth that is wrong, but the love of money for its own sake." (Hutchings, 2013). Greed is an all consuming passion that in the end destroys a leader's legacy and certainly his ability to act as role model.

Jose Mujica. In his report on 15 November, 2012 Vladimir Hernandez gave us the brighter side of how money and riches should be treated by those in public office. "It's a common grumble that politicians' lifestyles are far removed from those of their electorate. Not so in Uruguay. Meet the president — who lives on a ramshackle farm and gives away most of his pay. Laundry is strung outside the house. The water comes from a well in a yard, overgrown with weeds. Only two police officers and Manuela, a three-legged dog, keep watch outside. This is the residence of the

Mujica Jose: Former President of Uruguay. Mujica is a beacon of decency, humility and purity. As president he saw himself as just a humble civil servant in contrast to the often self-serving (stereotype) politician. Mujica should serve as a model for all in public office around the world. His life and attitude to public service should be studied carefully by all those that engage in unacceptable practices and those who squeeze every penny out of the office they are supposed to serve.

president of Uruguay, Jose Mujica, whose lifestyle clearly differs sharply from that of most other world leaders." (Hernandez, 2012). Mujica is a shining example of how those in public office should see themselves. After all they are civil servants paid by the taxes of the people they are supposed to serve. Rightly, Mujica went a step further and saw himself as a lowly civil servant who ought to live frugally if he were to set an example for others. The reader might now wish to compare the lifestyles of Mujica and Mobutu, whose behaviour in public office has also been described in this treatise, and draw conclusions.

Fear. Fear is that all-paralyzing character flaw, which in the extreme can paralyse a leader's judgement and cause him to panic. "I learned that courage was not the absence of fear, but the triumph over it. The brave man is not he who does not feel afraid, but he who conquers that fear" said Mandela. (Independent, 2013). The feeling of fear is natural and resides in all people including the most daring leaders. Leaders ought to manage fear without acting foolhardy. Here is what Dietrich Bonhoeffer said in one of his sermons, "Fear is, somehow or other, the archenemy itself. It crouches in people's hearts. It hollows out their insides, until their resistance and strength are spent and they suddenly break down." (Bonhoeffer, 2012)

Leaders that easily succumb to fear fail the test of true leadership. Had the Soviet leadership succumbed to fear in the battle of Stalingrad the outcome of WWII would have been different. Many free countries would have been turned into protectorates.

Circumstances. Circumstances are central to leadership successes and failures though on their own they do not define leadership. Had it not been for WWII Churchill would have probably gone down in history as an unremarkable person who had not done anything memorable and who loved a drink or two. He was nearly sixty-five at the start of WWII when circumstance gave him his chance to prove that he was daring and merciless, considering the pitiless bombing he ordered on Dresden in 1945, as the war was coming to a close. After the war was concluded he lost the general election (of 1945) because he failed to understand what the new circumstances demanded and what the British people wanted. During his new prime ministerial tenure, that started in 1951 and ended on his resignation in 1955, he again failed to achieve anything remarkable. In fact it was in this time that the gradual demise of the British Empire started; starting with the Suez Canal debacle. The Suez fiasco humiliated Britain in 1956 and started its fall as a world power. Due to circumstance and right decision making Churchill went down in history as a great war leader.

Luck. Luck is critical to leadership though not many successful leaders would admit to that. On the other side many who fail in leadership attribute their failure to bad luck. But does good luck alone make a leader? No, but bad luck can undo a leader, cut short his progress, and even destroy him. The two Kennedy brothers were assassinated and this meant the end of their lives both as human beings and as leaders. Michael J. Mauboussin wrote in the 7 February, 2011 Harvard Business Review edition, "When we enjoy a good outcome due to luck, we are naturally inclined to chalk up our success to skill. Similarly, if we suffer an adverse outcome because of poor skill, we blame our bad luck". (Mauboussin, 2011)

Here we are not of course talking about excusing some failure by attributing this to bad luck but rather we are talking about what I call "raw" luck that can either catapult a leader to great heights or cut short his progress and even his life. Had Khalkhin Gol not been there Zhukov would have probably been arrested and executed with no questions asked. Had the Japanese not been so foolhardy to attack Pearl Harbour in 1941 Britain would have been left without an American ally. Churchill would have probably achieved little had the Russians not fought an all out war, losing more than twenty million people in the process. Almost certainly Churchill would have had to accept surrender had Russia fallen. The British owe a lot to Russia but some of their leaders find it hard to acknowledge this.

Self-actualised leaders. As a student of leadership I owe much to Abraham Maslow for his momentous work on human motivation and for giving us a clear and simple classification of human needs: a) basic needs (or deficiency needs that are ordered in a hierarchy) such as hunger, affection, safety and security, self-esteem, and b) metaneeds (or growth needs that are not in any hierarchical order and in fact can be substituted for one another) and are inherent in man: goodness, order, justice, beauty, unity and others. Maslow helped us understand better how man (and leader) is driven into action. Maslow was not really the first to address such issues but he certainly popularised the matter. Aristotle in his Nicomachean Ethics expounded similar views thousands of years before. (Aristotle, trans. n.d.)

Self-actualised leaders are psychologically robust and as such can better deal with difficult issues. Mahatma Ghandi and other great leaders like him that risked their lives for a cause are good examples of self-actualised leaders. The move towards self-actualization requires time and typically ripens with age.

Striving for superiority. Austrian psychiatrist Alfred Adler postulated that all people have in common the goal of achieving superiority (self-actualization, to use Maslow's terminology). Adler tells us that in our own way we each try to achieve superiority. Some turn to intellectual activity, reading, studying, thinking, debating, painting, philosophising. Others strive for superiority by turning to sport and physical activity, to politics, or to farming and so on. As such we each take the first step by selecting the style of life we wish to have. We then take steps to serve our chosen lifestyle through which we can reach superiority. As such we enact the behaviours that are in congruence with our preferred lifestyle. Adler then adds that our striving for superiority is fundamentally driven by our sense of inferiority (commonly known as an 'inferiority complex'). Apparently, the Napoleonic complex is nothing more than Napoleon's attempt to compensate for his physical shortcomings and problematical height. Hitler almost certainly suffered from sexual impotence and was a monarchist, seeing as he had an undescended testicle (cryptorchidism). People with one testicle are typically able to have an active sex life but apparently this was not the case with Hitler. Taking Adler's view one step further we can maybe conclude legitimately that most leaders achieve superiority through the power they can exercise over others. But there are psychologists galore in the world with each giving us a different view of human motivation, so we can never be certain as to what is right and what is wrong. Hall and Lindzey make this incisive observation about psychologists and their varied and often divergent views on human behaviour, "One may indeed wonder at the apparently endless ingenuity of psychologists in devising new ways of viewing or ordering the phenomena of behaviour." (Lindzey and Hall, 1970: 599)

Lust for power. Lust for power is probably worse than lust for money and is a more despicable need in the needs structure of the leader. It can drive the leader to carry out contemptible acts to perpetuate power and dominate others. Lust for power often has no limits and no justification. As such the afflicted leader is almost certainly going to end up doing harm to his country or the group he leads. It is an insatiable desire that ultimately corrupts not only the afflicted person but also those around him. Quoting Friedrich Meinecke from Machiavellism: The Doctrine of Raison d'État and Its Place in Modern History, (English translation, 1957) George Smith wrote,

"The striving for power is an aboriginal human impulse, perhaps even an animal impulse, which blindly snatches at everything around until it comes up against some external barriers. And in the case of men at least, the impulse is not restricted solely to what is directly necessary for life and health. Man takes a wholehearted pleasure in power itself and, through it, in himself and his heightened personality. Next to hunger and love, pleonexia is the most powerful elemental and influential impulse in man." (Smith, 2014)

Lust for power (and for other things as well) is best described above by the Greek word pleonexia (Greek πλεονεξία). Pleonexia is about wanting more than one's fair share, thus depriving others of their rightful share. It is about greed and avarice; a characteristic of people that are selfish and arrogant and who assume that what exists is theirs and only theirs. One can only imagine what terrible things can happen under the leadership of someone that is consumed by pleonexia.

Murray's list of human needs. Murray offers us a list of human needs from which I selected the following four which I consider helpful to our understanding of leadership. Namely: 1) Achievement (similar to David McClelland's nAch). The need to increase one's worth by achieving something considered worthy and doing it as independently as possible 2) Affiliation (similar to David McClelland's nAff). Need to cooperate, associate, stay next to people, please and win over others, 3) Dominance (similar to McClelland's nPow). Need to control and influence the behaviour of others using seduction or command plus persuasion, 3) Aggression. Need to forcibly overcome opposition, to fight, to revenge, to attack and maybe even to kill. (Murray,1938). It is now generally accepted that most leaders have a pronounced need for achievement and dominance, and maybe aggression as well.

Traits. In this treatise we already discussed traits and their relative importance to leadership. Gordon Allport considers the need for a psychology of becoming; in other words a psychology of growth and development of personality. He classified traits into "common" (which place individuals into comparable categories) and "individual/personal" (which separate individuals). Individual traits, which he calls personal disposition (morphogenic) are of interest to our study of leadership. A personal disposition is a "unique patterned individuality" which has to be inferred from behaviour. Like all other human beings each leader has his own personal dispositions, which we can infer from his behaviour. For example, one leader could have a disposition for goodness and another leader a disposition for badness or for greed, and so on. (Allport, 1960)

Fortitude. Fortitude is a major requirement for leadership considering that no project is without imponderables, reverses and maybe serious losses. Strong leaders are not expected to give up easily. We saw earlier in this treatise examples of leaders that simply refused to give up even in the face of impending catastrophe. When Stalingrad was just about to fall, Zhukov and Vasilevsky came up with a new plan instead of capitulating. This saved the city and most importantly won the war. Instead of surrendering to the Persians Themistocles evacuated the city of Athens and moved all her population to the nearby island of Salamis ready to give one of history's most epic battles. In the end he won and became an icon of perseverance, courage, boldness, ingenuity, strategy, fortitude, and greatness.

A leader may understand and appreciate the importance of all that has been covered above and yet be unable to apply these in practice. Some in the American leadership must surely know that what has been happening with regards to the massive investment in the military is wrong and that global hegemony has to come to end one day. Yet, they fail to deal with this major issue that is bedevilling the prosperity of America because of internal opposition particularly from the military-industrial complex. The Egyptian leadership knows that it ought to tackle poverty in earnest yet it cannot. All attempts in the past to deal with this particular problem went nowhere. The Greek leadership knows full well that creating a bloated public sector is wrong and yet it did not manage to deal with it because maybe this practice serves the interests of many politicians. The leadership of Lebanon is comfortable with the current status quo because it serves them well. But, the people are unhappy and periodically protest clamouring for more democracy.

Concluding remarks

Achieving leadership potential

Maslow seems to have captured well what leaders ought to possess if they are to make their mark in the pantheon of great leaders such as Jefferson, the historic figure I admire immensely, largely because of his contribution to enduring democracy and his advice to America not to get involved in other people's affairs. Maslow includes many names in this elite group of self-actualized personalities whom he had occasion to study. Amongst such complete personalities stand the likes of: Beethoven, Albert Einstein, Martin Buber and others. I would suspect that had he included in his study great figures of antiquity he would have included giants such as Cimon, Aristides and Pericles of Athens. Maslow gives us numerous characteristics of the behaviours of self-actualized personalities which we will see below. I would certainly add a few more to Maslow's list such as generosity and temperance for example; behaviours that are an antidote to greed. Great leaders are generous to a fault, not only to their own but oftentimes to their adversaries as well. Despite his many faults General Pausanias refused to deal with the dead Mardonius in the same way the Persians dealt with the dead Leonidas (Pausanias's uncle) a year earlier. The Persians severed Leonidas' head and displayed it in public. Equally, he refused to listen to advice to kill the children of all Theban traitors, saying that the children were not to blame for their fathers' treachery against Greece. Equally, strong leaders are able to fight the two great human fragilities that afflict some leaders: fear and greed. Here is what Petasis and Kyprianou say about these two infirmities of spirit and mind, "Human nature (and its great iniquities, fear and greed) can make the difference to the workings of a social system..." (Petasis & Kyprianou, 2016: 236)

Here are some distinguishing characteristics of self-actualized people who succeeded in reaching their potential. I modified these to suit our discussion on leadership. As such below I share some key requirements leaders are advised to consider as they move along the path to successful leadership.

1. Realism. Great leaders need to show realism and plan their actions in a down-to-earth manner. They need to set objectives that are achievable and within their capabilities. When Alexander the Great was met by the opposition of his troops after the costly battle in India against King Porus, he fundamentally accepted their position even if he harangued them. In the end he turned back and in this way avoided the all-out rebellion that was brewing, and which he would have lost. He realised that his army was not inclined to go any further and that the troops wanted to return after ten years of tortuous fighting.

2. Acceptance. Great leaders are successful in accepting themselves, others and nature as well. In this way they remain in a harmonious relationship that minimises potential problems and conflicts. On achieving victory Lincoln's first objective was to bring the losers into the fold by genuinely accepting them back as brothers. He more or less gave them an alibi for what they had done by saying that they were born in a place that taught them the wrong things and gave them the wrong beliefs. As such, therefore,

the losers were victims of their own circumstances. He did not show any sign of superiority and went straight to work to rebuild the nation.

3. Spontaneity. Great leaders hate hidden agendas and behind the scenes [two-faced] dealings. After all, why hide things from colleagues when a leader serves the needs of the team? Leader responses are spontaneous rather than calculated or mischievous. Mandela employed spontaneity with his supporters as well as with his former adversaries. He was honest and forthright in his negotiations with the white leadership, with the Zulu representatives, and all others. This approach paid great dividends for peace and the future of South Africa.

4. Centre on problem rather than on self. Great leaders focus on the problem at hand rather than on themselves. They worry less about their image and how they will be perceived and more about making sound decisions and getting things right. As such they take difficult decisions even if these can make them unpopular. At the end of the civil war Lincoln had to solve the problem of reuniting the nation, and as such ignored calls for action that would have made him popular but which would have been divisive and wrong for America.

5. Need for privacy. This requirement refers to the need to maintain psychological distance between leader and led, which I think is proper for the leader to do. This protects the leader from too much familiarity and also gives him the opportunity to gather his thoughts away from pressures. Importantly this helps create a helpful minimum dose of mystique around the leader that is often necessary. Queen Elizabeth II of Great Britain hardly ever speaks in public and rightly so. Perhaps this is one of the many reasons why people have high regard for her.

6. Freshness rather than stereotype. Great leaders display imagination and think laterally. They see things in their own unique way rather than in the way these are stereotyped by others (including the group). Before independence the whites of South Africa were stereotyped as undemocratic and power-hungry. Mandela changed all that by embracing all South Africans as co-citizens, colleagues and associates that, like him, had the good of South Africa at heart. This helped heal the wounds of the past even though the deteriorating situation in the country today is not exactly what Mandela hoped for.

7. Spirituality. In the mostly secular age we now live in, it may come as a surprise to learn that most of the glorious leaders of the past had a strong faith and many claimed to have had at least one strong spiritual experience. And here I am referring not only to religious experiences. Strong and even life-changing spiritual experiences can take varied forms. Alexander the Great personified the leader that, in his view, benefited from spiritual experiences. He was relentless in his search for spirituality, spiritual meaning and divine experiences. He had an obsession with Zeus and believed that he was his son because his mother drilled this into his head. This explains why in the year 332 BC he visited the oasis of Siwah in the desert of Libya, seeking the advice of the oracle of Zeus-Ammon.

8. Identification with mankind and own people. Most of the great inventors and other leaders in varied fields dedicated themselves to serving humanity first, and not self-interest. Otherwise they would not have found the patience and commitment to work long hours in research, study and experimentation. Great leaders defy Machiavelli's view that mankind is fickle, hypocritical and in search of gain. Great leaders are positive, believe in the human race and

the welfare of the environment, and transmit these beliefs to others.

Andrey Nikolayevich Tupolev, the great Soviet military and civilian aircraft designer, who designed the world's first supersonic passenger plane, was arrested in 1937 under trumped-up charges and accused of carrying out activities that were against the state. In prison, rather than holding a grudge he designed, with his team, military aircraft such as the Tu-2 that played a central role during WWII and gave great honour to the government. He was freed in 1943. Tupolev is a great example of a leader who put the defence of his people first, even though the state imprisoned him.

9. Close relationships with people they love. Though Alexander did not live long enough to gain self-actualization in his relationship with Hephaestion, and some of the other generals and advisors, he serves as a good example of strong relationships. Sound and healthy relationships build loyalty and camaraderie that is critical to leader success.

10. Democratic outlook. In our day democracy is enjoying a revival considering what happened in most of history. This puts a burden on leaders to behave democratically if they hope to make the ranks of great leaders. Failing to adopt democratic values is failure to understand the essence of leadership. Leaders are meant to serve others and as such they are expected to respect their constituencies' wishes and to listen to their voice. In today's world, leaders are supposed to serve at the pleasure of the led and not the other way around, even if this rule is often violated even in some sophisticated democracies. Regrettably the Economist Intelligence Unit report on democracy makes for bleak reading on the score of democratic polity around

the world. Here are two examples: a) the Democratic Republic of Congo scored a pitiful 0.88 on civil liberties and Guinea-Bissau scored a depressing 0.00 on the functioning of government index. (Eiu.com, 2019)

11. Means are means and ends are ends. The temptation to turn means into ends is there to tempt every leader; as such leaders should take care. Leaders that confuse the two in effect lose sight of their objective. A leader that loses his objective is basically good for nothing. Means can be turned into ends very easily in the minds of leaders that lose their way and lose focus. Just because the use of violence in war is permissible as a means to an end does not give carte blanche to twisted minds to exterminate whole societies and to persecute them relentlessly. The problem is that means and ends are easy to confuse. For example, was the wholesale extermination by the Turks of the Armenian population in Asia Minor at the beginning of the twentieth century a means to an end or was it an end in itself? How about the persecution and killing of Greeks and Jews by the Turks in the same period? How about the extermination of Jews in the holocaust? Try separating means from ends in some of the vicious civil wars that are now raging around the world.

12. Sense of [philosophical] humour. Great leaders are known to use philosophical rather than caustic or mordant humour. This distinction on its own would not give credit to Churchill considering his [sometimes] wicked humour. It was said that when a female MP told Churchill, "Winston, you are drunk, and what's more you are disgustingly drunk" he fired back, "you are ugly, and what's more, you are disgustingly ugly. But tomorrow I shall be sober and you will still be disgustingly ugly". But Mahatma Ghandi's more philosophical humour would give

him credit: His "An eye for an eye will make the whole world blind" is a good example.

13. Creativity. Great leaders have deep reserves of creativity and are able to generate new ideas. This we saw many times in peace as well as in war. The legendary Aleksei Brusilov and his Brusilov Offensive during WWI gives us a good example of a leader full of ingenuity and creativity. The Brusilov Offensive was devised by a great strategist who demonstrated how a small number of fighters can turn the tables on a much larger army through swift and well-drilled action.

14. Resist conformity. A great part of leadership has to do with change and the initiation of change. As such great leaders do not stay stuck in stereotypes and long-held beliefs; instead they challenge conformity. Interestingly some great leaders proved to be conformists and anti-conformists at the same time. Take some of the Chinese leaders of the last century who refused to stick to the norms of the accepted culture and managed to bring about significant changes without tearing up the system. We already talked about dynamic homeostasis and the need for programmed and managed change. There is a place for conformity as there is a place for change. Unquestioned conformity to culture will not solve problems, particularly in the world we live in now that frequently calls for managed change. Too much resistance to conformity may be unhealthy but too much conformity can be a recipe for stagnation and even regression. (Maslow, 1998)

15. Holism. No attempt to understand leadership can succeed unless one takes a holistic approach to the study of leadership. For better understanding of leadership one ought to take into account all important factors and parameters that relate to the behaviour of leaders.

Studying individual parts separately will not help, considering the factor of interdependency. Holism considers that behaviour is, "...understandable only in context, so that the total, functioning person together with the significant portions of his environment must be given simultaneous consideration if there is to be a fruitful outcome." (Lindzey and Hall, 1970: 23). In other words behaviour cannot be understood if studied in isolation and outside the whole person, including maybe his biological and physical make-up. Thus, "ten things leaders do" in no way answers the question of "what is leadership"?

Decision-making and decisiveness

"He believed in the straight line; a respectable optical illusion which ruins many a man" Victor Hugo, Les Miserables.

The willingness of the leader to make a decision at the time a decision ought to be taken, and the quality of this decision are critical to good leadership. Good leaders strive first for consensus and if that fails they take the difficult decisions on their own after weighing up all relevant matters. Leaders ought to show decisiveness when decisiveness is called for. Decision-making must be free of illusions if disaster is to be avoided. Consensus decisions are generally preferable over one-man decisions because these have the advantage of empowering the group, getting more cooperation and understanding out of the led and all that are affected by the decision. More often than not, consensus decision-making yields better results considering the positive effect of this approach on implementation. But consensus decisions are not necessarily sound, considering the effect of group pressure and group-think that usually creeps into the process.

Decisions are taken within context and within time frames that sometimes are very narrow, forcing the decision-maker to make mistakes under pressure. For example, under pressure leaders might be tempted to take the first available option or to decide on impulse rather than rational thinking. Impulsive decisions are known to be risky and dangerous and certainly bereft of deep thinking and objectivity. But the reality is that people are creatures of emotion because that is part of their human nature. Worse still, we sometimes fall prey to passions that are often destructive. Needless to say that decisions based on logic and rationality are superior even if at times these are constrained by conservatism. But this approach has limitations as well, considering that complete and perfect information is impossible to have. Plus, human logic is bounded, making it impossible for the human brain to make optimal decisions. As such decisions can only be satisfactory rather than optimal, meaning that they are the best under the circumstances and on available information. In other words decision makers examine available options and alternatives until they feel comfortable that one meets minimum criteria. The ideal of course would be to take rational decisions that are principle-based but I am afraid this is not the case in the majority of cases because realpolitik encourages some to think selfishly and to take decisions based on interest. Though morality ought to take centre stage in decision-making, in practice it often does not because of human frailty. Had morality and idealism been applied constantly in practice, the world we live in would be a far superior world.

Solving the one central problem

We have seen in our analysis in this treatise of America and the Eastern Mediterranean countries how the leadership in each of these countries failed to solve the one fundamental and glaring problem of the country. The leadership of each country knows the country's most serious problem and recognizes its importance, yet something intervenes in the mind of the leader to keep the problem alive. Leaders fail to address their one single major problem either because the central problem is intractable or worse, leader disorientation gives the decision maker the impression that not solving the problem is more profitable than solving it. Successive Turkish leaderships understood that aggression against their neighbours is not best practice and that peace is preferable. Yet they continue with aggression because they believe that this practice pays dividends in that it forces weaker, threatened countries to concede benefits to Turkey. This of course pushes Turkey into a pariah status, at least with her neighbours. To go into the pantheon leaders must be able to solve that one single problem that keeps the country back, and in most cases even threatens its future. Lincoln went into the pantheon for his management of the American Civil War (that was the central problem then), Churchill kept the country in WWII and never surrendered, Mandela saved the country from civil war, and Pausanias saved Greece and stopped the ongoing threat coming from the Persians, thus giving the Greeks security. Each of these great leaders managed to solve what was the country's central problem at the time.

Leaving a legacy

Leaving a positive legacy is, in my view, the hallmark of good leadership considering that legacies can be copied, emulated and applied ad infinitum and as such multiplying what is good. We know that the lives of the saints and wise men have become models for people to emulate; and this has been going on for years, centuries, and even millennia. Sound leader behaviour automatically registers and is quickly passed from one generation to another. Despite his inexcusable failure to fight corruption and his tolerance of some of the excesses of the ANC Mandela left the world the quality of forgiveness that is so rare and difficult to practice. Mandela was unlike former president Kennedy in character but he too left a legacy despite his many personal weaknesses, though Lincoln's legacy is the bench mark. On the other side would anyone in his right mind wish to be the nutty and ruthless Idi Amin of Uganda who exterminated hundreds of his own people during the 1970s?

Lincoln was an example of fortitude, which is a rare quality but which brings the best and finest out of people when under pressure. Tenacity and fortitude are also hallmarks of great leaders because adversity is never far away from leaders, and as such needs to be handled well. Lincoln had to face war and the highly alarming, for Lincoln in particular, prospect of secession. Lincoln was firm and uncompromising on this subject, "no state can leave the Federal Union". That's it. He stood by his edict. This combined with his great magnanimity, tolerance and compassion, particularly when the war was coming to an end, made him exceptional and left a timeless legacy for the world. But as we said earlier luck can play havoc with leaders' lives. Lincoln was assassinated and as such the Confederates lost more than what the union lost. They lost a friend who could have navigated excellently the path that led to healing, and maybe the southerners would have avoided the many hardships and vengefulness from certain northern quarters they had to endure as losers. President Andrew Johnson, who replaced Lincoln after the latter's assassination, was totally unprepared to run the country and lacked Lincoln's goodwill towards the Confederates. With Lincoln gone the travails of the beaten Confederate states began anew. "In all the annals of history I know of no man in a civil war who showed the generosity towards the enemy that Abraham Lincoln showed. In that he was unique.", wrote Brian Walden. (Walden, 1998: 15)

Harold Holzer, a Lincoln scholar, wrote on October 7, 2016 "Ever since the 16th president died, nine hours after Booth fired his fatal shot, American presidents have been judged against the myth that replaced the man. The saviour of the union, great emancipator and martyr of liberty has proven an all but impossible act to follow." (Holzer, 2016)

Now, our age does not produce leaders such as Lincoln and Mandela. One reason is that expectations have changed. People now demand other things from their leaders and are not willing to press for things to get done right. Here are some examples of the major issues current leaders fail to solve: a) stop the destruction of the environment, b) tame the excesses of globalisation, big business and big military, c) the spread of nuclear weapons, d) the clobbering of the weak by the strong, e) the worsening Gini coefficient, and f) the shortages the poor have to endure, including shortage of clean water and poor medical and education standards.

The three pillars of leadership

Having come to the end of this treatise I now need to provide a model which I believe provides the minimum requirements for leadership. Models can be as complicated as the model-developer wishes them to be. But even complicated models can miss the point through undulation and jargon load. From the start of this book I had decided to keep things simple and easy to understand. Equally I was careful to be objective as I was writing real cases whose aim was to help highlight the intellectual and to some extent spiritual underpinnings of leadership. In this regard I put forward the view that in its most basic but substantive form leadership is a function of the following three factors:

1. Will to assume a position of leadership. Not all people, no matter how gifted and capable they may be, are willing to move into leadership. Some find the exercise of leadership unattractive considering that not everyone is fascinated by power. Others believe that even if they assume a leadership position this will lead nowhere because the system in place precludes the possibility of change for the better. Entering into political leadership in many less-than-advanced democracies is fraught with problems and great risks, making some people unwilling to venture forward. Climbing up the leadership ladder may at times entail engagement in humbling experiences, particularly in the case of political leadership where stooping low to gain favour may be unavoidable. Not everyone is willing to go through the humbling and debilitating experience of having to heap hypocritical praise on the party leadership team to gain favour. If an outsider were to try and enter the Lebanese political system, for example, he would have an almost impossible task considering the hermetically sealed hierarchical party system there. So, what can an aspiring politician do if he wishes to move up the leadership ladder? Not very much is the answer, unless he is willing to make great sacrifices; but not everyone is willing to do this. All of the above reasons and many more exclude the majority from wishing to assume political

leadership. Plus of course that some are afraid of the burdens of leadership.

2. Efficiency and delivery of results. Peter Drucker's memorable quote, "efficiency is doing things right; effectiveness is doing the right things" says it all. Effective leaders are not just efficient and results oriented. Above all they know where they should be going. This last point, in my view, is difficult to internalise and easy to miss. Leaders often do projects excellently only to discover that they were working on the wrong project. It is like negotiating brilliantly around the wrong problem. Negotiations on the Cyprus problem have been going on for the last forty years but hardly ever touched the central problem, which is the occupation of the Island by the Turkish army and the importation of hundreds of thousands of colonisers. In these negotiations all peripheral issues have been discussed over and over in earnest. But the lifting of the occupation and return of the colonisers to Turkey to bring back the old population parity has hardly been discussed. "Having lost sight of our objectives, we redoubled our efforts" Walt Kelly once said. Wars are often fought successfully only for the leaders to find out that they were waging the wrong war for the wrong cause. G.W. Bush invaded Iraq with his generals fighting the war efficiently and professionally except that this was the wrong war. Iraq never had weapons of mass destruction to justify an attack on the country. The weapons issue was made up in the mind of Blair to serve as justification to attack Iraq. But when America got mired in the deserts of Iraq the penny dropped. So it did not matter how efficient the American generals proved to be, seeing the end result was catastrophic with hundreds of thousands killed or injured for nothing. The first thing a

leader ought to ensure is the rightness of the project, concentrating afterwards on doing the project efficiently One of the most indelible images in my mind was created when I first read about Alexander's victory in India. Instead of this being the height of his success as strategist this victory sowed the seeds of doubt in the troops who simply wanted to go back to Macedonia-Greece. At the tail end of Alexander's campaigns the troops realised that they did not know why they were asked to fight on. Their precious dream at that time was to go back to where they had started the campaign.

3. Morality. We covered morality adequately when we discussed Lincoln and Mandela. Not only should activity be in the right direction and done efficiently but it should also follow the rules of morality. Once the Confederates were beaten in war by a much larger and richer army that had massive resources and military reserves behind it, Lincoln had the world at his feet and could have dictated all the rules for the Confederates. He could have crushed anyone that submitted or surrendered and could have unleashed the passions of vengefulness that would have allowed the Northerners to go on the rampage in the South. Yet he chose the moral road and extended the loving hand of reconciliation and forgiveness. Having won the war, he never forgot to act morally, leaving a legacy as sixteenth president of the USA for all twenty nine presidents that succeeded him. The unsavoury, nasty and cruel behaviour of Sherman's army in the Carolinas and Georgia tarnished the effort for reconciliation. But this was the exception to the rule. Mandela won the struggle and could have basically used heavy-handed tactics against his former adversaries. Instead he chose the route of kindness and forgiveness. Jefferson left the legacy of democracy as an

incalculable gift to humanity that is second to none in modern history. Once the rules of democracy are applied properly morality is bound to be served to a great degree. Jefferson's insistence on, "all men are created equal" says it all and provides the beacon and guide for all leaders.

References

Adler, A. (1935). "The fundamental views of Individual Psychology". International Journal of Individual Psychology, Vol. 1. Chicago, pp. 5–8.

Allport, G. (1960). Becoming: Basic Considerations for a Psychology of Personality. New Haven: Yale Univ. Pr.

Aristotle. (n.d.). Aristotle's Nicomachean ethics. Chicago: University of Chicago Press.

Bonhoeffer, D. (2012). "Overcoming Fear," A Sermon by Dietrich Bonhoeffer | Political Theology Network. [online] Political Theology Network. Available at: https://politicaltheology.com/overcoming-fear-sermon-dietrich-bonhoeffer/ [Accessed 3 Apr. 2019].

Coleman, D. (2006). Emotional Intelligence. 10th ed. New York: Bantam.

Eiu.com. (2019). Country analysis, industry analysis — Market risk assessment. [online] Available at: https://www.eiu.com/topic/democracy-index retrieved 03.04.2019 [Accessed 3 Apr. 2019].

Hernandez, V. (2012). The world's poorest president. [online] BBC News. Available at: https://www.bbc.com/news/magazine-20243493 [Accessed 3 Apr. 2019].

Holzer, H. (2016). What if Abraham Lincoln had lived? [online] CNN. Available at: https://edition.cnn.com/2016/10/06/politics/had-abraham-lincoln-lived-counterfactual/index.html [Accessed 2 Apr. 2019].

Hutchings, L. (2013). Margaret Thacher's Most Famous Quotes. [online] Available at:

https://www.vogue.co.uk/gallery/margaret-thatcher-most-famous-quotes [Accessed 11 Aug. 2019]

Huntington, S. (2003). The clash of civilizations and the remaking of world order. New York: Simon & Schuster.

Independent. (2013). Nelson Mandela: 11 inspirational quotes to live your life by.

[online] Available at:

https://www.independent.co.uk/news/world/nelson-mandela-10-inspirational-quotes-to-live-your-life-by-8988290.html?action=gallery [Accessed 21.08.2019]

Lindzey, G. and Hall, C. (1970). Theories of personality. New York: Wiley & Sons.

Mauboussin, M. (2011). Untangling Skill and Luck. [online] Harvard Business Review. Available at: https://hbr.org/2011/02/untangling-skill-and-luck?referral=03759&cm_vc=rr_item_page.bottom [Accessed 31 Mar. 2019].

McGreal, S. (2015). Personality Profiles of Great American Presidents. [online] Psychology Today. Available at: https://www.psychologytoday.com/us/blog/unique-everybody-else/201512/personality-profiles-great-american-presidents [Accessed 4 Apr. 2019].

Marston, W. M. (1989). Emotions of normal people. Edited by Ian Lyster. With a new introduction by S. H. Irvine. Ormskirk, Lancashire: Thomas Lyster Ltd.

Maslow, A. (1998). Towards a psychology of being. New York: John Wiley and Sons.

Murray, H. (1938). Explorations in personality. New York: Oxford University Press.

Paravicini, G. (2018). Millions flow from Gaddafi's 'frozen funds' to unknown beneficiaries. [online] POLITICO. Available at: https://www.politico.eu/article/muammar-gaddafi-frozen-funds-belgium-unknown-beneficiaries/ [Accessed 3 Apr. 2019].

Petasis A. & Kyprianou T. (2016). "Fundamentals of a Holistic Approach to Critical Situations". In: A. Petasis, ed., Intractable

Dilemmas in the Energy-Rich Eastern Mediterranean. Newcastle upon Tyne: Cambridge Scholars Publishing, p.206–245.

Smith, G. (2014). The Lust for Power. [online]. Available at; https://www.libertarianism.org/columns/lust-power [Accessed 11 Aug. 2019].

Stephenson, C. (2011). Leaders of Good Character. [online] Ivey Business Journal. Available at: https://iveybusinessjournal.com/publication/leaders-of-good-character/ [Accessed 13 Mar. 2019].

Walden B. (1998). Walden on Heroes. London: BBC.

Image Credits

Index

www.ingramcontent.com/pod-product-compliance
Lightning Source LLC
Chambersburg PA
CBHW031437160726
47994CB00005B/1770